A FURY IN THE WORDS

94512

A Fury in the Words

LOVE AND EMBARRASSMENT IN
SHAKESPEARE'S VENICE

Harry Berger, Jr.

Fordham University Press

NEW YORK ‡ 2013

Library of Congress Cataloging-in-Publication Data

Berger, Harry.
    A fury in the words : love and embarrassment in Shakespeare's
Venice/Harry Berger Jr. — 1st ed.
        p. cm.
    ISBN 978-0-8232-4194-1 (cloth : alk. paper) — ISBN 978-0-8232-
4195-8 (pbk. : alk. paper)
        1. Embarrassment in literature.   2. Love in literature.
3. Shakespeare, William, 1564–1616. Merchant of Venice.
4. Shakespeare, William, 1564–1616. Othello.   I. Title.
    PR3069.E375B47 2012
    822.3'3—dc23

                                                        2012029531

Printed in the United States of America
15 14 13   5 4 3 2 1
First edition

To

Judith Anderson
    Leeds Barroll,
        Stephen Orgel,
     Lena Cowen Orlin,
  Susan Zimmerman

              with thanks and love
              for all you've given me
              throughout the years
             whether you know it or not

CONTENTS

———————•———————

Acknowledgments ix

Prologue: Language as Gesture 1

PART ONE. *Mercifixion in* The Merchant of Venice: *The Riches of Embarrassment*

Introduction *19*

1. Negotiating the Bond *21*

2. Antonio's Blues *23*

3. *Curiositas*: The Two Sallies *26*

4. Negative Usury and the Arts of Embarrassment *28*

5. Negative Usury: Portia's Ring Trick *30*

6. Portia the Embarrasser *32*

7. The Archery of Embarrassment *36*

8. The First Jason *41*

9. A Note on Verse and Prose in Act 1 *44*

10. Another Jason *50*

11. Portia Cheating *51*

12. Portia's Hair *55*

13. The Siege of Belmont *56*

14. Covinous Casketeers *59*

15. Moonlit Maundering *62*

16. Coigns of Vantage *67*

17. Standing for Judgment *69*

18. Standing for Sacrifice *73*

19. "Here is the money": Bassanio in the Bond Market *76*

20. Twilight in Belmont: Portia's Ring Cycle *77*

21. Death in Venice *79*

PART TWO. *Three's Company: Contaminated Intimacy in* Othello

22. Prehistory in *Othello* 87
23. Othello's Embarrassment in 1.2 and 1.3 100
24. Desdemona on Cyprus: Act 2 Scene 1 109
25. The Proclamation Scenes: Act 2 Scenes 2 and 3 119
26. Dark Triangles in 3.3 129
27. Desdemona's Greedy Ear 141
28. Impertinent Trifling: Desdemona's Handkerchief 149
29. On the Emilian Trail 169
30. Iago's Soliloquies 183
31. Othello's Infidelity 201
32. The Fury in Their Words 212

ACKNOWLEDGMENTS

THIS STUDY has been brewing for a long time. I began to warm it up in the late 1960s, turned it off for a decade or two, and then decided to reheat it. But it wasn't until the last two years that I actually put it back on the burner and let it finish percolating, partly in response to the encouragement of my friend and editor Helen Tartar. The trouble with the metaphorics of these sentences is that they make the book sound like stale coffee. I don't think *A Fury in the Words* has any more to do with coffee than taxation has to do with teabags. But in its own way it's just as political as the teabags of 2009–10. It unpacks an interpretation of the politics of discourse in Shakespeare's two Venetian plays.

I dedicate the book to five dear friends and mentors with whom I've walked side by side through the green Renaissance years of the late twentieth century and after. Their work has been a beacon and model to me, as it has to so many others. Their commitment to our profession and their contributions to it have not only lightened my labors but also brightened my life. Their generosity as my friends and neighbors in Shakespeare for so long has taught me the meaning of love.

And there are others. I'm deeply indebted to Graham Bradshaw, Jody Greene, and Will West not only because they had to put up with some of my more nuisancy demands but also because they did so with such grace and good will and, above all, with unfailingly helpful criticism. The insights of Zvi Jagendorf have contributed much to my understanding of the Venetian plays. I've also greatly profited from comments and suggestions by Lawrence Rhu of the University of South Carolina and by Michael Warren, my colleague at University of California, Santa Cruz, for more than four decades. Professor Warren's critique of a first draft of my Preface was invaluable. More generally, in my several visits to the University of South Carolina, Professor Rhu, his colleagues, and their students have been wonderfully responsive in their reactions to my work on *Othello*. I think with great affection and lingering enlightenment of conversations with Nina Levine, David Miller, Jill Frank, Ed Gieskes, Holly Crocker, and William Rivers.

Special thanks go to my friend, neighbor, colleague, and chief coffee-mate, Forrest Robinson. For the past few years, teaching and talking with Forrest have been and continue to be my most important source of enlightenment about the things that matter in life. Whether we talk about Shakespeare, Melville, Twain, family, literature, the university, our joys, our disappointments, or merely our current writing projects, I come away from my meetings with Forrest refreshed, reinvigorated, and ready and eager to go back to work and try again.

Much of my understanding of the Venetian plays derives from studies by Janet Adelman, Kenneth Gross, and Lawrence Danson, and from discussions with Richard Gabri. I was very much looking forward to the moment when, after finishing this study, I would call Janet and thank her for all she gave me—as she gave so many others—for so many years. But now it's too late.

Special thanks go to Helen Hill, of Cowell College Academic Services, not only for her technical expertise and the outstanding quality of her work but also for her supportive and encouraging attitude and the modesty with which she treats the most difficult assignments as if they were ten-minute trifles.

For their help in difficult times, I thank my daughters Cynthia and Caroline and my grandson, Ezra. Thanks also to Tilly, Pam, Colleen, Dion, and Marsh for their devotion and support.

But most of all, thanks to my best friend and critic and wife, Beth Pittenger. For twenty-five years I've been sustained by her love and courage and companionship, and by her deep insight into language, literature, and the human spirit.

Language as Gesture

"I UNDERSTAND a fury in your words,/But not the words." So a perplexed Desdemona stubbornly resists acknowledging the obvious cause of her husband's sarcasm in Act 4 Scene 2 of *Othello*. One of the critic-heroes of my youth, Richard P. Blackmur, borrows her words in the titular essay of his 1952 collection *Language as Gesture*. They introduce the anecdote with which he opens his account and I, in turn, open mine.

Blackmur tells how, as a small boy in Cambridge, passing by little dead-end streets and looking up at the street-name signs, he was struck by an inscription mounted on a placard beneath the signs. It read "Private Way Dangerous Passing." This was how the city warned passers-by that it was responsible neither for the state of the roadbed nor for any injury "sustained through its use."

But the placard "meant something else" to young Blackmur. It turned the dead-end street into a monstrous maw. "It meant," he writes, "that there was in passing across its mouth a clear and present danger which might, and especially if it was dusk, suddenly leap out and overcome me. Thus . . . whenever I passed one of these signs, I had the regular experience of that heightened, that excited, sense of being . . . we find in poetry. I understood the fury in its words, but not the words. . . . There was a steady over-arching gesture in those words . . . that . . . meant more and touched me more deeply than any merely communicative words, deprived of their native gesture, can ever do." "Gesture in language," Blackmur concludes, "is the outward and dramatic play of inward . . . meaning," and it "so animates . . . [meaning] as to make it independent of speaker or writer."[1]

---

1. R. P. Blackmur, *Language as Gesture* (1952; rpt. New York: Columbia University Press, 1981), 4–6.

Blackmur stops short of claiming that Desdemona's utterance is itself a gesture. For him her words only describe or characterize "the situation in which language gains the force of gesture."[2] But for me the utterance is very much a gesture in his sense of the term, and I'll return to it later. The gesture dormant in the words "Dangerous Passing" remained a sleeping monster until Blackmur woke it up with his misreading. The gesture of fury in Desdemona's words can only be awakened by a similar if monstrously more complex process of misreading.

The name of this process is close interpretation. But uttering that name is like uttering a curse. Close reading interrupts the rhythm and flow of theatrical performance in order to create problems where no problems exist. It makes every scene a problem scene and every play a problem play. The standard complaint is that in the course of doing this it succeeds only in leaching out the theater's "large effects." I borrow that last phrase from a 1983 review of Jane Adamson's *'Othello' as Tragedy*. The reviewer, Patrick Grant, criticized the book because its focus on "fine-tuned, intimate social and psychological interchange" led Adamson to ignore the fury in the words—"things in the play that are . . . larger than life"—"the extravagant, melodramatic depiction of an extreme situation, the punishing boldness of an old-fashioned morality of heaven and hell."[3]

Grant posed the central problem of what's come to be known as the stage-versus-page conflict, which I subsequently described as a conflict between the wide-eyed playgoer and the slit-eyed armchair interpreter (for example, me). Your garden-variety slit-eyed reader takes the play out of the theater by inching over its text like a snail and leaving nasty little tracks of interpretive scurf all over the gorgeous language.

A more wholesome, or stage-centered, model of interpretive interruption is the genre of performance criticism exemplified at its best by the wonderful studies of Barbara Hodgdon and Miriam Gilbert.[4] In

2. Ibid., 4.

3. Patrick Grant, "Victims and Victimizers in *Othello*," *Shakespeare Quarterly* 34 (1983): 363.

4. Barbara Hodgdon, *The End Crowns All: Closure and Contradiction in Shakespeare's History* (Princeton: Princeton University Press, 1991); Miriam Gilbert, *Shakespeare at Stratford: The Merchant of Venice* (London: Thomson Learning, 2002).

rich comparative analyses of episodes and scenes, they illuminate the possibilities of the text by attending with great critical sensitivity to the interpretations worked out by actors. Their concern is with the products of specific prior rehearsals. My concern is with a general fiction of rehearsal—with what I imagine actors, directors, and dramaturges do when they prepare their performances. I imagine that in order to prepare for the delivery of a play's large effects, actors enlarge theater's small effects. By this I mean two things.

First, actors distinguish what goes on between characters from what goes on within the language the characters speak. That is, they distinguish between the *interlocutory* and *intralocutory* properties of dialogue. Interlocutory action between characters is social, dramatic, and theatrical; intralocutory action within language is semantic and lexical. In Blackmur's terms, language as gesture is the interlocutory—"outward and dramatic"—play of intralocutory or "inward" meaning. Actors understand that even as their characters engage in *inter*locutory action with each other, their characters' words engage in *intra*locutory acts on their own. They also understand that the text's intralocutory properties may divert or even confound the interlocutory flow of dialogue and action.

Second, the actors explore these properties in order to parse the competitive and performative worries of their characters. In this slit-eyed perusal every scene becomes a problem scene when actors discover that Shakespeare's language insists on doing its own thing, apart from the things its speakers intend it to do. Two examples will suggest what slit-eyed perusal might turn up.

The first example, from *Macbeth*, is Banquo's advice to his fellow thanes after they have been roused from their beds by Duncan's murder. This is how he tells them to get dressed and convene: "when we have our naked frailties hid, / That suffer in exposure, let us meet" (2.3.126–27). At the interlocutory level he issues a simple directive or summons. But at the intralocutory level, there is a fury in his words. "When we have our naked frailties hid" is a gesture of fear, bad conscience, and moral weakness. It is a parodic gesture of mutual distrust: "when we have protected ourselves from each other."

It is also a gesture of embarrassment: "when we have protected ourselves from ourselves." The whole of *Macbeth* is about the anxiety of characters who try to hide the "naked frailties" of their murderous lust for power and who worry about exposure. Among the "frailties" Banquo hides is his motivated failure to tell Duncan about the witches' prophecy, thus insuring the old king's ignorance of and "exposure" to the murder he "suffers."

The second example, from Part Two of *Henry IV*, is the last line of the king's insomnia soliloquy in 3.1: "uneasy lies the head that wears the crown" (3.1.33). Throughout this long meditation, the guilt-ridden king tries to sedate his conscience by blaming his insomnia on the cares of state. He represents himself as the victim of his office, the unappreciated donor who gives his subjects all and sacrifices his peace of mind for theirs. But when you slow down and peruse his speech, it conveys the embarrassment of the regicide and usurper who can't escape the suspicion that he is lying to himself. What he tries not to say and not to hear is, "uneasy lies the head that *stole* the crown." This gesture of self-distrust leaps out and overcomes the effort to which the soliloquy as a whole is dedicated: the effort to hide the naked frailty of his conscience.

The corpus of Shakespearean drama is riddled with such uneasy lies, such embarrassments, such "outward and dramatic" betrayals of "inward meaning." But trying not to say is one thing. Trying not to hear is another. The representation of selective and interpretive listening is a well-established theatrical practice that didn't originate with Shakespeare.

———————

In the opening scene of *Gorboduc* (1561), the queen warns her older son Ferrex that the king plans to divide the realm between his two sons, so that Ferrex will get only half. She's afraid Gorboduc will succeed in persuading his counselors to flatter his "present fancy" and support the plan. But what happens is even worse. The king ignores the cogent objections of two of the three counselors. And he insists that by handing over the kingdom while he still lives he'll be able not only to enjoy his well-earned retirement but also to give his boys the on-the-job training guaranteed to make them good rulers.

In particular, Gorboduc belittles the fears expressed by his secretary, Eubulus, who worries that Ferrex and Porrex will succumb to flattery (1.2.291–96). The king well understands the problem. He rattles off an impressive list of the damages flattery could lead his boys to inflict (1.2.351–59). But he has already figured out how to prevent this—or at least how to shut his wordy counselors up with his own brand of preemptive flattery. It will be enough, he says, to assign a sage advisor to each son,

> Some one of those whose long approved faith
> And wisdom tried may well assure my heart
> That mining fraud shall find no way to creep
> Into their fencéd ears with grave advice—
>
> (1.2.361–64)

no way, he means, to creep into ears that have been protectively fencéd about with grave advice.

Gorboduc's proposal seems intended to silence his reverend inter-locutors, but when put into practice it produces atrocious results. In Act 2 Ferrex and Porrex heed their parasites but fob off the grave advi-sors their dad assigns them. This is predictable, because the corrective Gorboduc recommends is the very one that currently has no effect on him. Eubulus, whose name means Good Counsel, had just given him the good counsel that could have reined in his folly. The king sets the example his sons will soon follow: he gives advisors of "long approved faith" the brush-off. His royal ears fence out any grave advice that dif-fers from his own.

Gorboduc, the play, drowns in waves of wholesome advice that bil-low endlessly from longwinded counselors to whom nobody pays any attention. An embarrassment of wise counsel is set off and balanced, and perhaps mocked, by comparable excesses of rash or stupid behav-ior. As a result, Gorboduc's project, the division of the kingdom, spins out of control.

Critical commentary makes much of the idea that the same project and consequence reappear in *King Lear*. But my interest centers on an-other theme: the way Shakespeare develops the dramatic possibilities inherent in the notion of fencéd ears—the notion of ears that protect themselves against "naked frailties" and "mining fraud." Shakespear-ean characters fence their own ears, not only from what they hear oth-ers say but also from what they hear themselves say (and may prefer not to know they say).

In *Henry IV, Part Two*, when Falstaff chivies the Lord Chief Justice with his claim to be troubled by the disease of not listening, the malady of not marking, he parodies his own ear-fencing practice (1.2.110–21). But he also targets the Lord Chief Justice as part of the barricade of law and order behind which a shaky regime and embarrassed ruler seek to persuade themselves of their dubious legitimacy. In Gorboduc's words, Falstaff accuses them of fencing their ears with grave advice. In Stanley Cavell's version of the Gorbuduc formula, he accuses them of "disowning knowledge." [5]

What we hear characters saying is never limited to what they seem to hear themselves saying. Shakespeare makes their focus on the rhetorical effects of their language preoccupy them in ways that fence off their ears, ways that divert them from important intralocutory gestures the language performs on its own. His text invites actors to explore what language as gesture does to and for their characters, apart from what the characters are doing with it. This invitation offers the actor who plays Cordelia in *King Lear* a rich field of possibilities.

Her first two utterances are both asides, and in both she speaks of herself in the third person. To Goneril's slimy declaration of her love for Lear, she responds with, "What shall Cordelia speak? Love, and be silent." And after Regan's equally slimy speech, she says "Then poor Cordelia! / And yet not so; since I am sure my love's / More ponderous than my tongue." She is embarrassed not only for and by her sisters but also for (as well as by) her father.

The use of the third person indicates that she self-consciously observes herself—that she possesses a strong theatrical sense of her image and role. The first aside, "What shall Cordelia speak? Love and be silent," is like a stage direction: "Given this tasteless overblown rhetoric of Goneril's, how shall I respond? I'll have Cordelia do the opposite of Goneril. Cordelia will hide her love and say nothing." "Nothing, my lord" is the interlocutory gesture of challenge she throws down both to her sisters and to her father. She refuses his offer of "a third more opulent than your sisters." In exposing the extravagance of her sisters' declarations, she exposes Lear to ridicule.

---

5. Stanley Cavell, *Disowning Knowledge in Six Plays of Shakespeare* (Cambridge: Cambridge University Press, 1988).

When she addresses her sisters at the end of the scene, Cordelia again third-persons herself:

> The jewels of our father, with washed eyes
> Cordelia leaves you. I know you what you are,
> And, like a sister, am most loath to call
> Your faults as they are named. Use well our father:
> To your professed bosoms I commit him,
> But yet, alas, stood I within his Grace,
> I would prefer him to a better place.
> So farewell to you both.   (1.1.257–64)

After their snippy rejoinders, she exits with a dark prediction:

> Time shall unfold what plighted cunning hides;
> Who covers faults, at last shame them derides:
> Well may you prosper.   (1.1.269–71)

Let's touch down on the verbal gesture that does the damage: "To your professed bosoms I commit him." Cordelia's message is that, although she doesn't expect her sisters to tend and care for their father as she would, were she in the position to do so, she hopes they'll love and tend him as well as they can. This may be what the speech means to *say*. But what it *does* is to confer on her sisters the power to punish Lear. Her gesture of conferral is a classic example of the speech act J. L. Austin calls a performative utterance.

There is a fury in her words that doesn't penetrate Cordelia's fencéd ears. She knows her sisters for what they are. She knows they'll give Lear what he deserves for having cast her away. He has foolishly deprived himself of "a better place." For that, he will suffer. But what about "Time shall unfold what plighted cunning hides,/Who covers faults, at last shame them derides"? This couplet bites; it sings with anger. It momentarily Cassandrifies her, unfences her ears so that she hears the future. Her augury slithers out beyond the sisters toward Lear. Whoever covers his own faults, refuses to acknowledge his complicity, must be exposed and embarrassed—not only to and by others but also to and by himself. When he finally acknowledges his own guilt, he will deride and hate himself, and be ashamed.

Cordelia predicts that shame will deride those who cover their faults. But she herself will disprove the truth of her own prediction, or at least escape its force. For she won't be shamed by what she has done. She will ultimately be vindicated by the effect of her sisters' punishment of Lear without herself having had any hand in it.

Few traces of this "darker purpose" embarrass her language when she returns in the fourth act. She appears to join others in perceiving herself as a merciful redeemer who was more sinned against than sinning but who has forgiven her father and now returns to restore him from his crimes and woes. She joins Lear in harping on the violent wrongs her two sisters did when they threw him out of doors into the terrible storm.

The reunion scene is poignant, partly because of Cordelia's moving concern for Lear. When he says "I know you do not love me. . . . You have some cause," she protests, "No cause, no cause" (4.7.73–75). But she did have a share in the cause he gave her. Her language in the reunion scene forgets, or fences out, her gesture of rejection, "To your professed bosoms I commit him." For her to dismiss now what *he* did then is to dismiss what *she* did then—to discount her complicity in what was done to him.

This may be the only way their reunion can take place. This is its condition, its cost. But at the end of the day, she can't fully prevent a darker thought from mining under her fencéd ears:

> We are not the first
> Who, with best meaning, have incurred the worst.
> For thee, oppressed king, I am cast down;
> Myself could else out-frown false Fortune's frown.
> Shall we not see these daughters and these sisters?
> (5.3.3–7)

She moves into rhymed couplets with the old consolation (we are more sinned against than sinning). And yet, although the sing-song of the verse makes it sound as if she's rehearsing bromides, something sharper intrudes in the active shading of the word "incurred." "We aren't the first who have made the worst happen—brought it on ourselves and others—while intending the best."

Cordelia consoles, she commiserates, she's dejected for them both, and especially for Lear. Or so she tries to say. But a wild ambiguity breaks loose from her tightly controlled rhetoric: "For thee, oppressed king, I am cast down." "Oppressed king" has the force of a tactful oxymoron: it balances his dignity against his plight. The sentence could mean "I'm sorrier for you than for myself," but it incurs worse meanings. One is the clear-eyed acknowledgment of a difficult choice, "I have returned to save you and sacrificed my safety in your behalf," a choice that puts him in her debt. Another sense gives the fury in her words a keener edge: "because of you I have been disempowered and imprisoned." The point of accusation is sharpened by the suggestion of self-sacrifice. For she gave him all. And of course she's right. And those are her last words in the play.[6]

This is an example of intralocutory characterization. It illustrates the level at which language suggests the motives, desires, and anxieties speakers hide from others, those they try to hide from themselves, and also those that hide from them. The interpretive problem for actors as readers is to acknowledge the gestural slippage between inter- and intralocutory action—to acknowledge that while characters engage in *inter*locutory action with each other, their words engage in *intra*locutory acts on their own.

Intralocutory effects reveal the "inwardness" of language as gesture. There is inwardness not only in the senses Katharine Maus details in her instructive study of inwardness in the Renaissance—inwardness inside the body, behind doors, hidden in an unobservable and inaudible faculty of soul or mind.[7] There is also inwardness in discourse.

By "inwardness in discourse" I mean the goings-on that irrupt within speech, the things language does *for* its speakers, or *with* them, or *to* them, the things it says about them, regardless of their express intentions and interlocutory strategies. Language as gesture flares up when words arrange themselves to expose what characters feel, not what they ought to say. In my fiction of interpretation as rehearsal—and of rehearsal as an interpretive practice—there is tension between the interlocutory force of dialogue and the intralocutory pressure of

6. For a more detailed account of Cordelia's language and motives, see my *Making Trifles of Terrors: Redistributing Complicities in Shakespeare*, introd. Peter Erickson (Stanford: Stanford University Press, 1997), 41–47.

7. Katharine Eisaman Maus, *Inwardness and Theater in the English Renaissance* (Chicago: University of Chicago Press, 1995).

language. This tension challenges the actors of Shakespeare's plays no less than it challenges their characters and their readers, and it expresses itself in the medium of community *discourses*.

———————

> A discourse is a domain of language-use, a particular way of talking (and writing and thinking). A discourse involves certain shared assumptions which appear in the formulations that characterize it. . . . Ideology is inscribed in discourse in the sense that it is literally written or spoken in it; it is not a separate element which exists independently in some free-floating realm of "ideas" and is subsequently embodied in words, but a way of thinking, speaking, experiencing.[8]

Discourses are part of the cultural capital of speech communities. They are "language-games," that is, readymade community arguments or rationales informed by socially constructed patterns. These language-games may be performed by individuals, but they preexist performance. They are intrinsically "ideological" in Kenneth Burke's playful sense of that term: ideology "is like a god coming down to earth, where it will inhabit a place pervaded by its presence. An 'ideology' is like a spirit taking up its abode in a body: it makes that body hop about in certain ways; and that same body would have hopped about in different ways had a different ideology happened to inhabit it."[9] "Bodies hopping about in certain ways" is a possible definition of "gestures" and is synonymous with "the outward and dramatic play of inward meaning."

The liveliness of Burke's definition veils a deterministic spin: ideology is a seizure; it takes over the body like an attack of epilepsy. To protect against this spin while retaining Burke's insight, I turn for help to Anthony Giddens, whose accounts of institutions apply as well to discourses and their ideologies. Giddens insists that institutions "do not just work 'behind the backs' [or within the bodies] of the social actors who produce and reproduce them. . . . If actors are regarded as cultural dopes . . . with no worthwhile understanding of . . . their ac-

---

8. Catherine Belsey, *Critical Practice* (London: Methuen, 1980), 5.

9. Kenneth Burke, *Language as Symbolic Action: Essays on Life, Literature, and Method* (Berkeley: University of California Press, 1968), 6.

tion," then "their own views can be disregarded."[10] He therefore sets out to analyze the forms of consciousness involved in "the reflexive monitoring of conduct."[11]

Giddens distinguishes between *discursive* and *practical* consciousness. Discursive consciousness is what actors "are able to say . . . about social situations." Practical consciousness is what they know or believe "but cannot express discursively."[12] If competent actors can, when asked, "nearly always report discursively about their intentions . . . they cannot necessarily do so of [i.e., about] their own motives."[13]

To make these distinctions more flexible, I add two alternatives to Giddens's account of practical consciousness: it is what actors know or believe but cannot, or *do not*, or *may not want to*, express discursively. Shakespeare's texts dramatize situations in which characters may not want to, may try not to, confront and report on "their motives." On the contrary, they may "wish" or "try" *not* to become aware of their motives. They may wish or try to disown knowledge. Shakespeare equips them with the ability to occlude, ignore, or forget—to disown or "disremember"—whatever interferes with their belief in a chosen discourse.

Let's improvise on the Giddens lexicon and call this ability *practical unconsciousness*. Practical unconsciousness is a storehouse of disowned knowledge. But it is also a discourse function. Practical unconsciousness disowns knowledge by activating a set of specific gestural discourses, or language-games, which I discuss in the next section.

In the preface to the second edition of *The Critique of Pure Reason* (1787), Kant famously concedes that he found it necessary to curtail knowledge in order to make room for faith. My study of Shakespeare's two Venetian plays explores the intralocutory gestures by which characters curtail knowledge or self-knowledge. But I give Kant's dictum

10. Anthony Giddens, *Central Problems in Social Theory: Action, Structure and Contradiction in Social Analysis* (Berkeley: University of California Press, 1979), 71–72.

11. Anthony Giddens, *The Constitution of Society* (Berkeley: University of California Press, 1984), 49. Giddens obviously uses the term *actor* to refer to human agents, not theatrical agents.

12. Ibid., 374–75. See also 5–14.

13. Ibid., 6. For a brief account of the relation of these modes to the unconscious, see ibid., 45–51.

a Sartrean skew: it may be necessary to curtail knowledge in order to make room for *bad faith*. In their efforts to redistribute complicities from themselves to others, the characters in *The Merchant of Venice* and *Othello* curtail or disown knowledge by switching on the gestural power of the discourses stored in practical unconsciousness.[14]

———

Several kinds or families of discourses are housed in practical unconsciousness. Those that concern me are institutional, ideological, positional, affective, and ethical discourses. Institutional discourses include discourses of theater, social hierarchy, and political order. Ideological discourses include discourses of absolutism, republicanism, "liberal humanism," misanthropy, utopianism, and disenchantment. Positional discourses include discourses of ruler/subject, woman/man, parent/child, elder/junior, lover/beloved, and various combinations of these positions. Affective discourses are discourses of shame, love, desire, despair, guilt, embarrassment, and the like. They tend to be cultural readymades. The so-called seven deadly sins are not merely dispositions of the "soul." Each has its own discursive history and profile. Lust, greed, gluttony, sloth, wrath, envy, and pride are affective discourses.

As the foregoing discussion indicates, most of my attention will be devoted to the ethical discourses and to the affective discourse of embarrassment. *The Merchant of Venice* is a comedy of embarrassment, and *Othello* is a tragedy of embarrassment. This nomenclature is admittedly anachronistic, since the term *embarrassment* didn't enter the language until the late seventeenth century.[15]

Although its meanings may overlap with those of *shame*, I put *embarrassment* into play in this study to mark a phenomenon that differs from both shame and guilt in its restrictively social or public character:

14. These paragraphs have been lifted and heavily revised from a similar discussion in *Making Trifles of Terrors*, 222–28.

15. Before that, as Theresa Krier has shown in an excellent discussion, its work was chiefly performed by the word *abashedness*: Theresa M. Krier, *Gazing on Secret Sights: Spenser, Classical Imitation, and the Decorums of Vision* (Ithaca: Cornell University Press, 1990), 155–60. I was directed to Krier's study by Judith Anderson, whose critique of and suggestions about an earlier draft of this chapter were exceptionally helpful.

"shame does not necessarily involve public humiliation while embarrassment does, that is, one can feel shame for an act known only to oneself but in order to be embarrassed one's actions must be revealed to others." Furthermore, shame responds "to something that is morally wrong" while embarrassment responds to something that may be "morally neutral but [is] socially unacceptable."[16]

To embarrass is to make someone feel awkward or uncomfortable, humiliated or ashamed. Such feelings may respond to specific acts of criticism, blame, and accusation. They may get triggered by actions like those listed in the Larousse Dictionary under the French verb *embarrasser*: "to obstruct or block or hamper; to clutter up or weigh down." "To embarrass" is literally "to embar": to put up a barrier or deny access.[17] The *bar* of *embarrassment* may be raised by unpleasant experiences. It may also be raised when people are denied access to things, persons, and states of being they desire or feel entitled to.

Returning now to the notion of ethical discourse, in previous studies I've detailed the operations of six ethical discourses: those of the donor, the victim, the villain, the victim/revenger, the sinner, and the hero.[18] But why do I call these discourses "ethical"? The word *ethical* is normally used to mean something like "moral," "virtuous," "principled," and so on. But *ethical* and *ethics* ultimately derive from the Greek word "*ēthos*," which had a range of meanings that includes "custom, usage, character, disposition, bearing, manner." Aristotle uses *ēthos* in

16. Wikipedia article on shame. My brief comments on shame and embarrassment are informed by the following studies: Erving Goffman, "Embarrassment and Social Organization," *American Journal of Sociology* 62, no. 3 (November 1956): 264–71; Christopher Ricks, *Keats and Embarrassment* (Oxford: Oxford University Press, 1984); Bernard Williams, *Shame and Necessity* (Berkeley: University of California Press, 1993).

17. Of the five occurrences of "bar" in the play, four appear in connection with the courting of Portia. Speaking first to Morocco and later to Bassanio, Portia mentions the barrier put up by her father's lottery (2.1.16 and 3.2.19). Morocco crows that ocean swells are no bar to heroes questing from afar for Portia (2.7.45). In the oddest and most embarrassing usage, Bassanio turns Portia's mouth into candy: he salutes the "sweet . . . bar" of "sugared breath" that parts the "severed lips" in her "fair . . . counterfeit" (3.2.119).

18. For more on the ethical discourses, see *Making Trifles of Terrors*, xix–xx, 228–36, 300–301. See also my "The Ethics of Posing: Visual Epideixis in Some Seventeenth-Century Dutch Group Portraits," in *Reading Renaissance Ethics*, ed. Marshall Grossman (New York: Routledge, 2007), 38–84.

the *Poetics* to designate characters in drama and their moral quality as inferred or constructed by audiences. When a playwright (Aeschylus, Sophocles, Euripides) borrows a character from epic or other sources and remodels it, in Aristotelian parlance he "imitates" that character, as does the actor who plays the role.

Aristotle uses the term *ēthos* again in the *Art of Rhetoric* to designate the "character" a speaker assumes—performs or imitates—in order to persuade his audience of his moral authority. Both the *Poetics* and the *Art of Rhetoric* treat moral character as an effect of discourse rather than as its cause: *ēthos* is the product of art, not of nature. And in both cases the performance or *mimēsis* of a convincing "character" is treated as an effect of interpretation and rehearsal, an effect of the "reflexive monitoring of conduct" that transpires largely in the shadowy defiles of practical unconsciousness.

Donor, victim, sinner, villain, hero, victim/revenger: ethical discourses have the value of stock characters, which—like the Vice and other figures from medieval drama—can be assumed and modified by the dramatis personae of any play. *Persona*, from *per-sonando* ("sounding or speaking through"), denotes a mask. A mask is a frozen gesture, and William West reminds me that "in very early illustrated manuscripts of Terence . . . the masks sit on a rack before the play" and thus prepare incoming theater-goers by offering them "a kind of typing or stock characterization" that the verbal and behavioral gestures of the performance will complicate.[19]

In the foyer leading to my imaginary productions of *The Merchant of Venice* and *Othello*, I would hang six discursive masks. The first five are those mentioned above: victim, villain, donor, sinner, and victim/revenger. The sixth is the mask of embarrassment. The dramatic energy of the Venetian plays is generated by the interplay among these gestural discourses. The victim's gesture is plaintive: "I am more sinned against than sinning," The villain's gesture threatens: "I am more sinning than sinned against." Expressions of the donor's discourse can range from generosity and openhandedness to such complex and demanding ges-

19. Personal communication.

tures as Lear's "I gave you all" (*King Lear*, 3.4.47), whose inner lining combines threat with complaint.[20] The discourse of embarrassment will be further discussed below.[21]

"I am a man/More sinned against than sinning" (3.2.59–60). The fury in Lear's words is understandable because his invocation of the victim's discourse is imperiled from two directions. On the one hand, the comparative construction gives it a defensive edge: "what they did to me is worse than what I did to them." This acknowledges that "I" did something to them. A suspicion of bad faith therefore endangers his claim of victimization. The suspicion opens like a wound on its lurking obverse, "I am more sinning than sinned against," which is the confessional gesture of the sinner's discourse.

On the other hand, there *is* a fury in Lear's words. The strong accent and terminal position of "I am a man . . ." gestures toward his ability to victimize his victimizers: "I am a man, and will have my revenges." This hint or threat of retaliation converts his statement into an expression of the victim/revenger's discourse.

These examples illustrate what can go on in the intralocutory underground of practical unconsciousness. Shakespeare's protagonists often shelter behind the victim's discourse while they get the resident villains to do their dirty work for them. Lear depends on Goneril and Regan just as Edgar depends on Edmund. Victims are complicit with their villains. The chapters that follow will explore the complicity of Portia and Antonio with Shylock and of Othello, Desdemona, Cassio, and Emilia with Iago.

20. The importance of *giving* in *Merchant* is the subject of an excellent discussion by Lawrence Danson—a discussion on which I rely even as I deploy it in a reading that differs from his: Lawrence Danson, *The Harmonies of* The Merchant of Venice (New Haven: Yale University Press, 1978), 50–55.

21. See Chapters 6, 7, and 23, below.

PART ONE

Mercifixion in The Merchant of Venice: The Riches of Embarrassment

INTRODUCTION

The Merchant of Venice must be classed among
Shakespeare's "Unpleasant Plays."[1]

In *The Merchant of Venice*, Shakespeare spotlights shiny displays of self-sacrifice and gift giving. At the same time he lets the shadows of darker motives encroach on the glitter of those displays. The merchant Antonio borrows money from Shylock so that his young friend Bassanio can use it to visit and court the heiress Portia. Portia will be Antonio's gift to Bassanio. In performing this service, Antonio ostentatiously reins in his own desire for Bassanio. But no one in the Shakespeare canon deploys the art of donation with more theatrical verve than Portia when she conquers Bassanio by giving him herself and everything she owns.

She quickly discerns that Antonio poses as much of an obstacle as Shylock does to this conquest, and she decides to outman them all. Cross-dressed as "the young and learned doctor" Balthasar, she uses the courtroom scene in Act 4 Scene 1 to embarrass not only Shylock but also Antonio—*and* Bassanio. Although the performance of Shylock the Jew in 1.3 marks him as the villain of the piece, complicity gets redistributed throughout the play. By the end of the courtroom scene, the villain could well complain that he has been victimized and that he shares the discourse of villainy with the Christians who conspired to bring him down.

---

1. W. H. Auden, "Brothers and Others," in *The Dyer's Hand* (New York: Random House, 1989), 221.

Christian villainy in *Merchant* takes a deceptively mild form. In ancient times Jews were tied or nailed to a cross and left to hang until dead. In Shakespeare's Venice, strict justice is mitigated by an act of mercy: the Jew is denied his living but granted his life (4.1.365–94). Instead of being crucified, he is mercified. Mercifixion may be more humane than crucifixion: you mercify rather than punish. Nevertheless, it inflicts its own kind of pain: you punish by mercifying. Mercy "presents a problem," Lisa Freinkel writes, because it is the grace "that imputes righteousness where none has been deserved."[2] The pain mercifixion inflicts is the pain of embarrassment.

The Venetian plays represent embarrassment not merely as a condition but as a weapon and as the wound the weapon inflicts. Characters in *Merchant* and *Othello* devote their energies to embarrassing each other. Portia's mastery of the art of embarrassment is hilariously on display during the encounters in which she denies the Princes of Morocco and Aragon access to herself (2.1, 7, 9).[3]

One of the colloquial senses of *embarrassé* cuts close to the bone of *Merchant*: "short of money." Bassanio's problem is that he has first too little access to money and then too much. He is embarrassed when he has too little but becomes embarrassing when he gets too much.

Antonio's relations to money and to love, to purse and to person, are deeply embarrassed. He is embarrassed by desire for Bassanio and by a grating tendency to "stand for [self]-sacrifice" that blocks his access to our respect. As Shylock sees it, Antonio's behavior on the Rialto is oriented toward embarrassing Shylock (a claim Antonio doesn't deny). But as Shylock describes it, Antonio's behavior is itself embarrassing (1.3.101–13). The loan scene (1.3) as a whole features Antonio's embarrassment. He is embarrassed both by the need to beg a loan from the Jew he despises and by Bassanio's uneasiness during the transaction. The text itself presents his embarrassment with embarrassed reserve.

---

2. Lisa Freinkel, *Reading Shakespeare's Will: The Theology of Figure from Augustine to the Sonnets* (New York: Columbia University Press, 2002), 288.

3. In this book all passages from *The Merchant of Venice* will be cited from Lawrence Danson's excellent Longman's edition: William Shakespeare, *The Merchant of Venice*, ed. Lawrence Danson (New York: Pearson Longman, 2005). Passages from *Othello* will be cited from E. J. A. Honigmann's edition in The Arden Shakespeare, Third Series (Walton-on-Thames, Surrey: Thomas Nelson & Sons, 1997).

It hints at but never fully reveals the extent and character of his investment in his embarrassed and embarrassing protégé.

These embarrassments suffer inflammation when Antonio's access
to Bassanio is obstructed by Bassanio's access to Portia. Portia may or
may not be embarrassed by her inability to attract better suitors than
Bassanio and his predecessors. Nevertheless, her relationship to Bassanio, as it unfolds through the play, is itself an embarrassment. Consider, for example, the ringing phrase with which she assigns poor little
Bassanio the role of Herculean savior: "I stand for sacrifice" (3.2.57).
The words slither from one gesture to another: from "I stand here as
my father's sacrificial victim" through "I represent sacrifice, I stand
for the principle of self-giving," to "I advocate sacrifice and demand it
from you: I expect you to give and hazard all you have." This is said to
someone whose predatory smarminess assimilates him more closely to
the monster than to the hero.

I. NEGOTIATING THE BOND

No discussion of the play can proceed without taking into account the
darker implications of Shylock's bond discussed and impressively doc-
umented by James Shapiro in *Shakespeare and the Jews*. He shows that
it was more than possible for Elizabethan audiences, who "were en-
tertained with catalogues of Jewish villainy," to feel that "an occluded
threat of circumcision informs Shylock's desire to cut a pound of Antonio's flesh." Furthermore, they might have associated circumcision
with "ritualistic and surreptitious murder."[1] But if it's important not
to forget what may lie behind Shylock's proposal of a "merry bond," it's
equally important to factor in the situation that led him to propose it.

Shylock hates Antonio because "he is a Christian," but also for more
specific reasons. Antonio not only "lends out money gratis and brings
down / The rate of usance here with us in Venice." He also "hates our

1. James Shapiro, *Shakespeare and the Jews* (New York: Columbia University Press,
1996), 92, 114, 117. As Shapiro points out (121), the darker implications of the bond may
linger through the play because we don't learn until the trial scene "that Shylock intends
to cut from Antonio's 'breast' near his heart." W. H. Auden speculates that Shakespeare
was aware of the association of usury with sodomy that Dante depicted ("Brothers and
Others," 231).

sacred nation" and he despises Shylock. On the Rialto, "where merchants most do congregate," he "rails . . ./On me, my bargains, and
my well-won thrift/Which he calls interest" (1.3.36–45). When Shylock asks him whether he takes interest, Antonio answers with tightlipped pride and a tiny pun, "I do never use it" (1.3.65). And when
Shylock later berates him for his anti-Semitism and general hostility,
Antonio snaps back that he is likely to continue behaving the same
way (1.3.101–26). All the more reason for Shylock to want to turn the
tables on Antonio by Judifying him. And what better way to Judify
than to circumcise?

In "lending money without interest to defaulters," Lars Engle points
out, Antonio "is generous to the point of being unbusinesslike" and
puts "himself at risk."[2] But his motive is not restrictively philanthropic.
It has an antagonistic edge. He himself admits that Shylock hates him
not merely because he lends gratis in principle but because he has specifically aimed this practice at Shylock: "I oft delivered from his forfei-
tures/Many that have at times made moan to me" (3.3.22–23).

From Antonio's standpoint, the immediate risk in signing on to the
bond—what it will cost him to get his money back—is not the loss
of a pound of flesh to Shylock but the loss of Bassanio to Portia. His
objective appears to be to keep Bassanio permanently in his debt. In
order to accomplish this he chooses to put himself in jeopardy. He
knows the Jew hates him, and, during their discussion in 1.3, he provokes Shylock into exacting a harsh penalty: "I am as like . . . / To spit
on thee again, to spurn thee too./If thou wilt lend this money," lend it
as if "to thine enemy" (1.3.125–30). And Shylock does.

To state it colloquially, Antonio tries to goad Shylock into sticking
it to him. Shylock perceives and frustrates that effort: he will charge
no interest if Antonio will agree to the "merry bond." The merchant
responds to Shylock's outlandish terms of forfeit not with shock or
surprise but with weird alacrity: "Content, in faith. I'll seal to such a
bond/And say there is much kindness in the Jew" (1.3.147–48). Either

2. Lars Engle, *Shakespearean Pragmatism: Market of His Time* (Chicago: University of
Chicago Press, 1993), 80–81. Engle's chapter on *Merchant of Venice* should be required
reading for anyone who studies or writes about the play.

he wasn't paying close attention or else he didn't think Shylock's terms were objectionable—or else something like this, some threat to his personal being, was what he wanted to elicit and put on display. He goes on to assure Bassanio that the surgical outcome is unlikely. Yet he seems happy enough to find it on the table.

Bassanio of course protests. But he protests in such a jingly couplet that his words rhetorically mock his melodramatic offer of self-sacrifice: "You shall not seal to such a bond for me! / I'll rather dwell in my necessity" (1.3.149–50). Bouncy though it is, this appreciation of Antonio's charitable risk taking is no doubt just what the merchant wants to hear. It must only confirm him in his folly.

Shylock is well aware that Antonio has been "prodigal" (3.1.37). Early in his discussion with Bassanio, he itemizes the many ventures Antonio has "squandered" abroad. If in Shakespeare's time "squandered" chiefly meant "widely scattered," Shylock pushes it toward its later connotation of prodigality by prefacing his list of Antonio's ventures with "his means are in supposition" (1.3.13–18).

For his part, Antonio must know as much about his own ventures as Shylock does. Therefore he knows what he is getting into when he accepts Shylock's terms. Sparks may fly between Shylock and Antonio in this scene, but its focus is on the embarrassing spectacle of Antonio showing off before Bassanio. While Bassanio remains suspicious, Antonio all but slaps Shylock on the back: "The Hebrew will turn Christian; he grows kind" (1.3.173). Auditors and readers may cringe at Antonio's heartiness, but the same sentiment will be repeated in seriously altered form at 4.1.384: let Shylock "presently become a Christian." Antonio is a problem.

2. ANTONIO'S BLUES

Let's approach this problem by homing in on the play's first speech, in which Antonio responds to the busybodies Salerio and Solanio. They have obviously just commented on his dejection:

> In sooth, I know not why I am so sad,
> It wearies me; you say it wearies you;
> But how I caught it, found it, or came by it,

> What stuff 'tis made of, whereof it is born,
> I am to learn;
> And such a want-wit sadness makes of me,
> That I have much ado to know myself.
>
> (1.1.1–7)

The short line visually opens up a space, dramatizes a blankness, that pleads to be filled in. "I am to learn" at first registers as "I don't know yet, I still have to find out." We soon discover that it is anticipatory. If Antonio is sad, uneasy, apprehensive, it must be because he's waiting to hear about the courtship venture Bassanio had "promis'd to tell me of" (1.1.119–21)—waiting to hear about the "lady" who is Antonio's next rival. And we learn more, as Thomas Cartelli notes, "from the successive disclosures of . . . Antonio's love for Bassanio, Bassanio's love for Portia, and Antonio's hatred of Shylock."[1] But already in his stagey and head-scratching doldrums we begin to sense Antonio's fondness for the pleasures of victimization.

His encounter with Bassanio retrospectively redefines the tone of his responses to Salerio and Solanio—or, to use Dover Wilson's nickname for them, the two Sallies.[2] It becomes clear that he wishes they would just go away. He listens impatiently and puts them off with replies that are either uninformative or misleading.[3] Solanio's farewell conveys tart awareness of Antonio's impatience while hinting at a reason for it:

> Here comes Bassanio your most noble kinsman.
> Gratiano, and Lorenzo. Fare ye well,
> We leave you now with better company.
>
> (1.1.57–59)

Salerio chimes in with echoing pique: "I would have stay'd . . . / If worthier friends had not prevented me" (59–61).

"Your most noble kinsman": some editors note that this relationship is not mentioned elsewhere in the play. Solanio's epithet may only sig-

1. Thomas Cartelli, "Shakespeare's *Merchant*, Marlowe's *Jew*: The Problem of Cultural Difference," *Shakespeare Studies* 20 (1988): 257.

2. Sir Arthur Quiller-Couch and John Dover Wilson, *The Merchant of Venice*, New Shakespeare (Cambridge: Cambridge University Press, 1953), 100–104.

3. See 1.1.1–7 and 41–45.

nify a touch of rancor directed toward an insider by an outsider. But "only" understates its significance. If the epithet is meant ironically, it suggests something about the way social competitiveness and contention structure the normal patterns of talk in "Venice." And the irony would be sharper if we construed "most noble kinsman" as an over-polite synonym for "lover."

This dialogue conveys more than generic social friction. All the speakers seem exercised by something going on under the surface, something conspicuously unstated, something they seem to assume but don't, or won't, or aren't expected to, talk about. This is sustained in Bassanio's first lines to the Sallies: "Good signiors both, when shall we laugh? Say, when? / You grow exceeding strange. Must it be so?" To which Salerio responds guardedly, even defensively, "We'll make our leisures to attend on yours" (1.1.66–68), that is, "that's entirely up to you." It's hard to dismiss these interchanges as conventional instances of phatic communion. They're charged with aggressive coolness, and Bassanio's "grow" suggests his sense that the coolness predates this moment. Our first impression of Shakespeare's Venice is of a community of speakers who don't particularly like or trust each other.

The Sallies pretend to know their place. Their chief function, apart from giving voice to the citizenry of Venice, is to convey the kind of plot information that reduces the number of scenes necessary to dramatize the story. But they are by no means neutral reporters of news. They suck, truckle, and smarm as they follow the major characters about. And they relieve themselves of fat speeches.

Shakespeare's Venice is a performative society. Its citizens like to hear each other talk almost as much as they like to hear themselves talk. They often subordinate the matter of their speech to its manner. Salerio in particular tends to truckle in time-consuming tropes:

> Your mind is tossing on the ocean,
> There, where your argosies with portly sail,
> Like signors and rich burghers on the flood,
> Or, as it were the pageants of the sea,
> Do overpeer the petty traffickers
> That curtsy to them, do them reverence,
> As they fly by them with their woven wings.
>
> (1.1.8–14)

My wind cooling my broth
Would blow me to an ague, when I thought
What harm a wind too great might do at sea.
I should not see the sandy hourglass run
But I should think of shallows and of flats,
And see my wealthy *Andrew* docked in sand,
Vailing her high-top lower than her ribs
To kiss her burial. (1.1.23–29)

Antonio tries to speed the Sallies on their way with a brusque fare-well: "I take it your own business calls on you,/And you embrace th'occasion to depart" (63–64). But their intrusiveness has its effect: it makes his talk of melancholy appear to be his way of protecting his privacy in a nosy world where everyone gazes and squints at everyone else and entertains theories about them. The Sallies are at least sensitive to the problem. They carefully avoid asking about the real source of Antonio's blues except in passing, as when Solanio exclaims, "Why then you are in love" (1.1.46).

Salerio's mercatorial rhetoric establishes a context for thinking about Antonio's relation to Bassanio. If ships interact like burghers, then burghers must interact like their ships. Bassanio is potentially Antonio's "wealthy *Andrew* ['man'] docked in sand" (1.1.27). The merchant dredges him up and fits him out so that Bassanio can sail to Belmont and win the wife who will replace Antonio in his affections. Another way to look at it is that he trades Bassanio to Portia for a return on his latest investment of three thousand ducats.

3. *CURIOSITAS*: THE TWO SALLIES

Solanio and Salerio are "the small fry of the Rialto," as Lars Engle engagingly calls them.[1] They appear together in four scenes (1.1, 2.4, 2.8, and 3.1).[2] In Lawrence Danson's fine characterization, "they may

1. Engle, *Shakespearean Pragmatism*, 79. Lorna Hutson calls them "the gossips of the Rialto": *The Usurer's Daughter: Male Friendship and Fictions of Women in Sixteenth-Century England* (London: Routledge, 1997), 234.

2. For a concise and annotated statement dealing with questions concerning the numbers and names of the Sallies, see Jay Halio's textual introduction to his Oxford Shakespeare edition of the play: *The Merchant of Venice* (Oxford: Oxford University Press,

be lightweights but they are well-spoken." Their descriptions of Antonio's "argosies" express a "pastoral mode of entrepreneurial anxiety," one that "calls attention to itself as comfortable poetry as much as to the unhappy state it describes."[3] Their *curiositas*, which Scholastic writers defined as "the passion for knowing unnecessary things," is infectious.[4]

In 2.8, the one scene they have to themselves, the Sallies are well behaved. They serve up the news with admirable economy but also with the affect appropriate to partisans of the distressed Antonio. We learn that Bassanio is under sail to Belmont, Lorenzo and Jessica were seen in a gondola, Shylock threw a fit upon hearing of Jessica's theft and affair, and Antonio—who may have lost a ship—was moved to tears by Bassanio's departure. It is Solanio who reports Shylock's outcry about his daughter and his ducats, and, as John Gross notes, the report "shows every sign of being a highly colored comic turn" intended to disparage Shylock.[5]

In their final moments alone together, before they encounter Shylock in 3.1, the Sallies are at their liveliest, but also at their silliest. They fancy themselves wit-crackers. They divulge critical information about Antonio, but their news doesn't run smoothly before the wind. It capsizes on the shoals of rhetorical self-consciousness:

SOLANIO   Now, what news on the Rialto?

SALERIO   Why, yet it lives there unchecked that Antonio hath a ship
          of rich lading wrecked on the narrow seas—the Goodwins, I

1993), 87. I've passively adopted the versions ("Salerio" and "Solanio") in Danson's Longman edition. *Sale* and *sole* play important roles in the Venetian climate. *Salerio* reminds me of *salire* and thus makes me think of a climber or someone who scrambles to get on board.

Near the end of the casket scene in 3.2, Lorenzo and Jessica enter with "Salerio, a messenger from Venice." Some editors speculate this is a different Salerio. But he is welcomed as an old friend and echoes the other Salerio when he briefly laments Antonio's losses and vilifies Shylock.

3. Lawrence Danson, *The Harmonies of* The Merchant of Venice (New Haven: Yale University Press, 1978) 41–42.

4. "*Libido sciendi non necessaria*": see William of Auvergne, *De universo*, 2.3.22.

5. John Gross, *Shylock: A Legend and Its Legacy* (New York: Simon and Schuster, 1992), 73.

think they call the place, a very dangerous flat, and fatal, where the carcasses of many a tall ship lie buried, as they say, if my gossip Report be an honest woman of her word.

SOLANIO   I would she were as lying a gossip in that as ever knapped ginger or made her neighbors believe she wept for the death of a third husband. But it is true, without any slips of prolixity or crossing the plain highway of talk, that the good Antonio, the honest Antonio,— oh, that I had a title good enough to keep his name company!—

SALERIO   Come, the full stop.

SOLANIO   Ha! what sayest thou? Why, the end is, he hath lost a ship.

SALERIO   I would it might prove the end of his losses.

SOLANIO   Let me say "amen" betimes, lest the devil cross my prayer, for here he comes in the likeness of a Jew.   (3.1.1–18)

Their predictable fleers punctuate the subsequent dialogue with Shylock and elicit some of his most powerful and moving assertions of ethnic identity. That interchange turns the tide of feeling from Venetian Christians to the Jew.

4. NEGATIVE USURY AND THE ARTS OF EMBARRASSMENT

Since Shylock is the play's only usurer and moneylender, usury is marked as a Jewish practice. The Christians in the play "do never use it." Antonio showily flouts the standard practice of usury: he gives more than he takes by taking no more than he gives. But he and the other Christians practice a metaphoric version of it, a form I call *negative usury* and will now characterize.

Portia's deeding herself to Bassanio, her deliverance of Antonio, and his willingness to lend gratis, have been praised by C. L. Barber in *Shakespeare's Festive Comedy*. Barber cites these acts and behaviors as examples of the benign "something-for-nothing" economy by which the Venetian Christians distinguish themselves from the Jew.[1] He sympathetically describes the way Antonio and Portia and the Duke,

1. C. L. Barber, *Shakespeare's Festive Comedy* (Cleveland: The World Publishing Company, 1963), 167.

who speaks for the city, express their sense of themselves as members of a gracious and humane society.

It's true that the generosity of Antonio and Portia appears to be a positive value in the play.[2] But it's also true, as Bassanio learns from Portia's casket chorus at 3.2.63–107, that appearances are deceiving. Barber's sympathy for Antonio is misplaced because he ignores the kicker in the merchant's practice of donation: I'll give you something for nothing. Don't try to pay me back. Remain in my debt.

So assertive a display of "generosity" is always in danger of edging toward the more insidious form of donation identified by Marcel Mauss in his classic account of the gift as a kind of moral usury.[3] If usury boils down to taking more than you give, the donor's discourse is a form of negative or deferred usury: it consists of giving more than you take in a manner that makes it possible for you to end up getting more than you gave.[4] Negative usury as a strategy aims to embarrass the victims of donation by placing them under a moral debt they can't easily pay off, much less shake off.

This is the burden Lear tries to impose on his daughters ("I gave you all") and Prospero on Miranda ("I have done nothing but in care of thee"). It is the game Othello plays with the handkerchief he gave Desdemona. In *Merchant* it is not only Antonio's game but also Portia's. Finally, it's a game played with special clumsiness by Bassanio. Joan Holmer comments on the way Shakespeare indicates "Bassanio's nature as a bringer of gifts" in order "to reassure his audience that Bassanio's attitude toward Portia's wealth is kept in its proper perspective."[5] The problem with this comment is that whatever gifts Bassanio brought must have been paid for with Antonio's and Shylock's money. The proper perspective on his attitude toward Portia's wealth is to assume that he wants all of it.

2. See Danson, *Harmonies*, 50–55, for helpful comments on the role of gifts and giving in the play.

3. Marcel Mauss, *The Gift: Forms and Functions of Exchange in Archaic Societies*, trans. Ian Cunnison (New York: Norton, 1967).

4. "Usury" in this context is metaphoric: a specific economic practice is extended to a general ethical practice.

5. Joan Ozark Holmer, *The Merchant of Venice: Choice, Hazard and Consequence* (New York: St. Martin's Press, 1995), 107.

5. NEGATIVE USURY: PORTIA'S
RING TRICK

Poised with studied if anxious irony between the donor's power and the victim's plight, Portia mines the donor's discourse of the gift more effectively than, say, Lear does in the self-pitying variations on "I gave you all" he aims at his thankless daughter Regan. Regan easily parries the blow: you took your sweet time giving it. "In good time you gave it." She knows what he's up to. He wants to get more than he gave by dealing her the wound of unrepayable obligation we associate with such sacrificial acts as those performed once for all time by the Christian Father and repeatedly about once a day by my Jewish mother (as in "don't thank me, it was nothing").

Portia is initially disadvantaged by desire: "I pray you, tarry. Pause a day or two/Before you hazard, for in choosing wrong/I lose your company" (3.2.1–3). After Bassanio hazards correctly (her use of the word "hazard" doesn't exactly stand in his way) she vows that "Myself and what is mine to you and yours/Is now converted."[1] In this exposed position she tries to regain her autonomy and authority with a menacing act of donation:

> But now I was the lord
> Of this fair mansion, master of my servants,
> Queen o'er myself: and even now, but now,
> This house, these servants and this same myself
> Are yours, my lord's. I give them with this ring;
> Which when you part from, lose, or give away,
> Let it presage the ruin of your love
> And be my vantage to exclaim on you.
>
> (3.2.167–74)

"The ruin of your love" is a harsh phrase, but Bassanio tunes it out. "Madam," he replies, "you have bereft me of all words," after which he lights up Belmont's sky with a blazing six-line epic simile followed

---

1. "Hazard" is, of course, a clue to the correct casket because the word is part of the inscription. But Portia also uses the word when speaking with Morocco at 2.1.45 and with Aragon in 2.9. Before Aragon chooses she says, "To these injunctions everyone doth swear/That comes to hazard for my worthless self." Aragon then reads the lead inscription aloud and responds disdainfully: "You shall look fairer ere I give or hazard" (2.9.17–22).

by a pledge of undying allegiance: "when this ring/Parts from this finger, then parts life from hence./Oh, then be bold to say Bassanio's dead" (3.2.175–85).

Portia's ring giving recalls a similar moment near the end of the preceding scene: Shylock gets deeply upset when he hears Jessica has traded his ring for a monkey (3.1.98–102). He treasures the ring because it was a gift from his wife.[2] But unlike Portia he performs no ring tricks. The simplicity and directness of his sentiment stand in sharp contrast to the devious power play Portia enacts in its shadow.

Her practice of donation consists in setting up a premonitory "vantage to exclaim": she gives gifts that can be transformed to debts. The gift betrays the anxiety engendered by her vulnerable position in the "something-for-nothing" economy. It shows that "something-for-nothing" is a type of usury in a society whose members protect themselves and savage others through displays of generosity, kindness, benevolence, and self-sacrifice.

Portia protects herself against her own ardent desire by performing an act of negative or deferred usury: she gives Bassanio more than he can give back so that at last she'll have him perpetually in her debt. "I stand for sacrifice" (3.2.57): she stands first for her sacrifice and then for his. Her use of "when" in line 172 ("Which, when you part from") wobbles dangerously between threat and prophecy, between the counterfactual force of "if ever you lose or give away the ring" and the predictive force of "whenever it happens (as it's bound to) that you lose it or give it away." What we've seen of Bassanio so far suggests that her precaution is as sensible as her ardor is questionable.

Her aggressive strategy of donation gets wryly illuminated by Lorna Hutson in *The Usurer's Daughter*:

> The code of "faithful friendship" which pre-dated the advent of humanism in England had a very precise regulatory function. It was, essentially, a system of credit articulated through the exchange of

2. Stephen Orgel remarks that the "model of marriage" in the play "is Shylock's: he had a ring from Leah when he was a bachelor, he would not have given it up for a wilderness of monkeys": "Shylock's Tribe," in *Shakespeare and the Mediterranean: The Selected Proceedings of the International Shakespeare Association World Congress, Valencia 2001*, ed. Tom Clayton, Susan Brock, and Vicente Fores (Newark: University of Delaware Press, 2004), 49.

gifts and services between a lord and his "fee'd man." By responding to his servant's needs, overlooking his debts, offering him gifts
beyond what he could claim as annuity or by letters patent, a lord en-
sured that his servant would be faithful to him . . . while the servant
could trust to the future of the relationship.[3]

A few modifications make the core of this analysis applicable to *Merchant*: "The code of 'faithful friendship' . . . was, essentially, a system of
credit articulated through the exchange of gifts and services" between
Portia and her husband or "fee'd man," Bassanio. "By responding to
his . . . needs, overlooking his debts, offering him gifts," Portia en-
sured that he would be faithful to her. Her gift of the ring represents
a one-sided version of the exchange of rings characterized by Hutson
as "the 'pledge' or 'wager' of the good faith and honour" that "defers
into the future the obligation to reciprocate. . . . There is danger as
well as credit in the pledge, for both giver and recipient are bound
through it to fulfill an obligation to one another."[4] Hutson's account
doesn't reflect the extent to which all the conditions she enumerates
provide incentives for embarrassment.[5]

6. PORTIA THE EMBARRASSER

Among the resources of embarrassment is the one we call, metaphorically and colloquially, castration. The play directly alludes to it three
times, and commentaries tend to focus more on the ritual of circumcision than on the metaphorics of castration.[1] But Portia's deploy-

3. Lorna Hutson, *The Usurer's Daughter*, 3.

4. Ibid., 5.

5. Hutson concludes *The Usurer's Daughter* with a discussion of *The Merchant of Venice*
in which she is too easy on Bassanio and Antonio. In spite of the fact that she characterizes the symbolic figure of the usurer's daughter as "the ultimate fantasy of the creditless
adventurer, the hero of fiction, the younger brother, the man-on-the-make" (224), her
portrayal of Bassanio is unwarrantedly benign. She commends his "economic prudence"
and describes his relation to Antonio as an example of "humanist *amicitia*" and "pru-
dential consultation," which she opposes to Shylock's "anxious mistrust" and "paranoid
thrift" (235–37).

1. Antonio calls himself "a tainted wether of the flock" at 4.1.111, and Gratiano twice
jokes about gelding "the judge's clerk" and marring his "pen" (5.1.144, 237). See Shapiro,
Shakespeare and the Jews, 113–30.

ment of this resource is masterly. She practices a kind of motherly boa-constriction. When she learns Antonio is in trouble because of his loan to Bassanio she all but cradles her lover in her arms even as she's careful to note that he's at fault: no one, she proclaims, "Shall lose a hair through Bassanio's fault" (3.2.300).[2]

Her next sentence makes sure Bassanio has his priorities right: "First go with me to church and call me wife, / And then away to Venice to your friend" (3.2.301–2). "Since you are dear bought," she tells him a few lines later, "I will love you dear." Even an offer of love and assistance sounds like a threat: "It's costing me. It will cost you."

This is the first move in Portia's war against Antonio. It anticipates the opening gambit inscribed in the letter from Antonio that Bassanio proceeds to read at her request: "it is impossible I should live, all debts are cleared between you and I if I might but see you at my death. Notwithstanding, use your pleasure. If your love do not persuade you to come, let not my letter" (3.2.317–19). As Portia might say, he seems ready at a moment's notice to make "a swanlike end, / Fading in music" (3.2.44–45).

Here, as elsewhere in the play, "notwithstanding" empties both barrels. It is a gesture with passive-aggressive force: "in spite of everything I've done for you."[3] But Portia sees what Antonio is up to and spoils his game by capitalizing on the ambiguity of "If *your love* do not persuade you." She, Bassanio's love, duly persuades him: "O love, dispatch all business and begone!" (3.2.320). She meets Antonio's plaintive demand with an act of generosity: a visit from Bassanio will be her gift, or at least her loan, to Antonio. In this skirmish, the gesture of donation trounces that of self-sacrificial victimization.

Portia's quiet but persistent warfare continues in 3.4. After Lorenzo commends her for putting up with Bassanio's absence, he slathers praise on Antonio:

> You have a noble and a true conceit
> Of godlike amity, which appears most strongly
> In bearing thus the absence of your lord.

2. Michael Ferber ignores the competitive context when he characterizes this response as "prompt and bounteous": "The Ideology of *The Merchant of Venice*," *English Literary Renaissance* 20 (1990): 436.

3. See 5.1.239.

> But if you knew to whom you show this honor,
> How true a gentleman you send relief,
> How dear a lover of my lord your husband,
> I know you would be prouder of the work
> Than customary bounty can enforce you.
>
> (3.4.2–9)

Portia modestly but happily acknowledges the justice of Lorenzo's praise of herself, but she ventures a more cautious response to his praise of Antonio:

> I never did repent for doing good,
> Nor shall not now; for in companions
> That do converse and waste the time together,
> Whose souls do bear an equal yoke of love,
> There must be needs a like proportion
> Of lineaments, of manners and of spirit;
> Which makes me think that this Antonio,
> Being the bosom lover of my lord,
> Must needs be like my lord. If it be so,
> How little is the cost I have bestowed
> In purchasing the semblance of my soul
> From out the state of hellish misery!
>
> (3.4.10–21)

Editors are quick to Platonize these sentiments by glossing "lover" in line 7 and "bosom lover" in line 17 as "friend," and they are also careful to remind readers that "waste" in line 12 means "spend" rather than, say, "squander" or "fritter away." I think their eagerness to sidestep a blurry and mischievous sense of "lover" isn't warranted by anything the text shows about Portia's attitude toward Antonio. Nor is it entirely clear to me that she would agree with them about the more benign implication of "waste." Finally, what "cost" has she "bestowed"? Does she mean she's "paying" in the sense of giving up Bassanio for a few days? Or is she announcing that she has sent him off to Venice loaded down with moneybags?

The gestural force of "this Antonio" would be that of a neutral demonstrative if he were present. But since he isn't, and since—as we just saw—Portia is at war with Antonio, the phrase sounds more invidious: "*this* Antonio" ("whoever *he* is"). She then conspicuously minimizes her latest good deed ("How little is the cost . . .") and concludes with a self-conscious gesture of embarrassment uttered as a reflex to her auto-laudatory outburst: "This comes too near the praising of myself;/Therefore no more of it" (3.4.22–23).

Let's recall that before this scene began she had already made her plans to participate in the hearing in Venice. There, as Stephen Orgel trenchantly observes, her "behavior toward Antonio is in fact as cruel as anything Shylock does. The scene is drawn out excruciatingly, and its theatrical power has much less to do with the quality of mercy than with the pleasures of sadism on the one hand and revenge on the other."[4] Shylock's bond threatens Antonio with bodily harm and possible death but Portia quickly neutralizes that threat because Shylock isn't her real target. Her problem is to overgo Antonio, her competitor in noble deeds, by proving that she can save someone for Bassanio. If she can put Antonio in her debt, she will loosen his powerful hold over Bassanio.

She thus eases into her prosecution of the Jew by throwing a scare at Antonio. Since the bond is forfeit she commands him to bare his bosom to the knife, much to Shylock's excitement, which she encourages by quibbling over the more gruesome details of the surgery:

PORTIA [*to Antonio*]
    Therefore lay bare your bosom.
SHYLOCK   Ay, his breast.
    So says the bond, doth it not, noble judge?
    "Nearest his heart," those are the very words.
PORTIA
    It is so. Are there balance here
    To weigh the flesh?
SHYLOCK   I have them ready.
PORTIA
    Have by some surgeon, Shylock, on your charge,
    To stop his wounds, lest he do bleed to death.
SHYLOCK
    Is it so nominated in the bond?

4. Orgel, "Shylock's Tribe," 51.

PORTIA

> It is not so expressed, but what of that?
> 'Twere good you do so much for charity.

SHYLOCK

> I cannot find it, 'Tis not in the bond.

$$(4.1.249-59)$$

Portia then invites Antonio to comment. He obliges by sacrificing himself at some length to the tune of "Don't worry about me," whereupon Bassanio jumps in with his competing offer to sacrifice not himself but his wife (4.1.261–84). From the moment Portia enters and takes over the inquiry, any observer who views the courtroom event through her eyes must share her embarrassment—an embarrassment caused not by Shylock, whom she quickly disables, but by the husband with whom she has contracted to share life after Happy Ending, and by the professional scapegoat he is attached to.

7. THE ARCHERY OF EMBARRASSMENT

When Gratiano first addresses Antonio after the Sallies leave, his reaction echoes theirs: "You look unwell. You must worry too much about your business." "No, no," Antonio replies, "it's just that my role on the world's stage is to be sad" (1.1.73–79). Gratiano doesn't buy that. He performs his own role as the resident Venetian motormouth with a long speech encouraging Antonio to make more long speeches: "stop trying to use 'your melancholy silence as the bait to fool people' into thinking you're a wise man and a deep thinker."[1]

Antonio promises to be more talkative ("I'll grow a talker for this gear"). But after Gratiano leaves, he asks Bassanio what that was all about, and Bassanio tells him to ignore Gratiano because he talks too much and says nothing. Antonio then asks to hear the story Bassanio had promised to tell him about his "secret pilgrimage" to a "lady" (1.1.119–21). Bassanio responds by talking too much. He obliges Antonio with a "long-winded request for a loan."[2]

---

1. 1.1.79–104. The phrase in single quotation marks is Lawrence Danson's gloss. See Danson, *Harmonies*, 111–13, for a persuasive analysis of the play's critique of Gratiano.

2. Ibid., 110.

Bassanio's comment on Gratiano is significant chiefly for its form: "Gratiano speaks an infinite deal of nothing, more than any man in all Venice. His reasons are as two grains of wheat hid in two bushels of chaff; you shall seek all day ere you find them, and when you have them they are not worth the search" (1.1.114–18). This is the first and only prose passage in 1.1. Its very prosiness as a comment on an interlocutor's verse accentuates its critical tone. But it also has a subsidiary function.

Short as it is, the comment makes us freshly aware of the iambic pentameter that carries the speakers through the remainder of the scene, and it cues us to attend to its effects: the shamefaced roguishness of one speaker and the haplessness of the other.[3] The verse rhythms enliven the declamatory contest in which Bassanio leans on Antonio for help to get free of him and Antonio tries to delay this outcome while appearing to advance it. My paraphrases are interspersed in italics between the speeches.

BASSANIO

> 'Tis not unknown to you, Antonio,
> How much I have disabled mine estate
> By something showing a more swelling port
> Than my faint means would grant continuance.
> Nor do I now make moan to be abridged
> From such a noble rate; but my chief care
> Is to come fairly off from the great debts
> Wherein my time, something too prodigal,
> Hath left me gaged. To you, Antonio,
> I owe the most, in money and in love,
> And from your love I have a warranty
> To unburden all my plots and purposes
> How to get clear of all the debts I owe.

3. For a brilliant account of Bassanio's dodgy behavior in this exchange, see Zvi Jagendorf, "Innocent Arrows and Sexy Sticks: The Rival Economies of Male Friendship and Heterosexual Love in *The Merchant of Venice*," in *Strands Afar Remote: Israeli Perspectives on Shakespeare*, ed. Avraham Oz (Newark: University of Delaware Press, 1998), 17–37. See also Miriam Gilbert, *Shakespeare at Stratford: The Merchant of Venice* (London: Thomson Learning, 2002), 51–53.

I am awash in debt because I've been a wee bit lavish in my lifestyle, which I have no plans to scale back. "'Tis not unknown to you": you may be vaguely aware of my embarrassment since you're my best friend and chief loan officer. But I think I have a solution which I'd like to share with you. If I can count on just a little more of your love for just a little more of your cash, I may be able to keep my head above water.

ANTONIO

> I pray you, good Bassanio, let me know it;
> And if it stand, as you yourself still do,
> Within the eye of honor, be assured
> My purse, my person, my extremest means
> Lie all unlocked to your occasions.

I'm an open casket and everything I have is yours—as long as what you propose is as honorable as you still are. [The qualifier, "as you yourself still do," puts moral term limits on the offer.]

BASSANIO

> In my schooldays, when I had lost one shaft,
> I shot his fellow by the selfsame flight
> The selfsame way with more advised watch
> To find the other forth, and by adventuring both
> I oft found both. I urge this childhood proof
> Because what follows is pure innocence.
> I owe you much, and, like a wilful youth,
> That which I owe is lost; but if you please
> To shoot another arrow that self way
> Which you did shoot the first, I do not doubt,
> As I will watch the aim, or to find both
> Or bring your latter hazard back again
> And thankfully rest debtor for the first.

[Not so fast. He's all but asking me to name a sum. That would be indelicate. Let's first beat around the bush:]

When I was a child practicing archery in school, this is how I found a lost arrow. I shot a second arrow in the same direction and that helped me find the first. By adventuring both and risking their loss I often found both.

I use this childhood example to dramatize the childlike sincerity with which I make the request you're about to hear. The only difference is that

*shooting my arrows will be replaced by borrowing your money. Let my lost
arrows represent the still unpaid loans you shot in my direction. If you shoot
me another loan, you're sure to find the one you shot before and lost, since
I'll then be able to pay you everything I owe. Or if I can't, I'll not only repay
what you're now lending me. I'll remain your grateful debtor for the rest!*

ANTONIO

  You know me well, and herein spend but time
  To wind about my love with circumstance;
  And out of doubt you do me now more wrong
  In making question of my uttermost
  Than if you had made waste of all I have.
  Then do but say to me what I should do
  That in your knowledge may by me be done,
  And I am prest unto it. Therefore speak.

*Why don't you stop beating around the bush? I find it insulting that
you won't ask me what you want straight out instead of wasting time with
silly ambages about archery. I've already said that everything I have is
yours. Speak up. Or, in Lars Engle's "tendentious paraphrase in the Emp-
sonian manner," "you should acknowledge that you are making emotional
use of me, and not hide behind fictions of practicality which insult my
intelligence."*[4]

BASSANIO

  In Belmont is a lady richly left;
  And she is fair and, fairer than that word,
  Of wondrous virtues. Sometimes from her eyes
  I did receive fair speechless messages.
  Her name is Portia, nothing undervalued
  To Cato's daughter, Brutus' Portia.
  Nor is the wide world ignorant of her worth,
  For the four winds blow in from every coast
  Renownèd suitors, and her sunny locks
  Hang on her temples like a golden fleece,
  Which makes her seat of Belmont Colchis' strand,
  And many Jasons come in quest of her.
  O my Antonio, had I but the means

4. Engle, *Shakespearean Pragmatism*, 81.

> To hold a rival place with one of them,
> I have a mind presages me such thrift
> That I should questionless be fortunate.

Well, then, my plan is to compete with the many suitors who, like Jason questing for Medea and the golden fleece, pursue a rich young heiress in Belmont named Portia. We've seen each other and she clearly finds me attractive, so I think I stand a good chance of unlocking her golden fleece, if you know what I mean.

ANTONIO

> Thou know'st that all my fortunes are at sea;
> Neither have I money nor commodity
> To raise a present sum. Therefore go forth.
> Try what my credit can in Venice do;
> That shall be racked even to the uttermost
> To furnish thee to Belmont, to fair Portia.
> Go presently inquire, and so will I,
> Where money is, and I no question make
> To have it of my trust or for my sake.

[Not so fast. You'll have to hang out with me in Venice a little longer because, although everything I have is yours,] you well know that everything I have is currently tied up with my ships at sea. So I'm strapped for cash right now. But if we can borrow some money in town, I'll make great sacrifices and stretch my credit "even to the uttermost / To furnish thee to Belmont, to fair Portia" (1.1.122–85).

Objections have been raised to the view "that Bassanio is no more than a fortune-hunter," but this exchange supports that view.[5] My comments on the exchange are deeply indebted to stunning analyses by Zvi Jagendorf and Lars Engle. To Jagendorf, "Bassanio sounds like a mealy mouthed lawyer," who treats his prodigality as if it were "a minor carelessness, a gentlemanly oversight, like not paying one's tailor." Yet the message he conveys is that "he needs more of Antonio's money in order to be free of Antonio's love." The merchant's "declaration of availability," his tender of "My purse, my person," is "darkly

---

5. Catherine Belsey, "Love in Venice," in *The Merchant of Venice*, ed. Martin Coyle, New Casebooks (New York: St. Martin's Press, 1998), 159.

dangerous in its blurring of the borders between the offering of gold and the offering of self." The "openness of the unlocked . . . purse is embarrassingly linked with a defenselessness of person."[6]

In *Shakespeare's Pragmatism*. Engle shows how Bassanio, by "infantilizing himself . . . , metaphorically shifts responsibility for the previous money lost to Antonio."[7] In addition, Bassanio is a notorious poormouth. At 2.2.132–34 he wonders about Launcelot's decision to leave Shylock's service and "become/The follower of so poor a gentleman."

Some time between the dialogue quoted above and his nuptial exchange with Portia in 3.2, Bassanio apparently told *her* he was indigent. He reminds her of this before announcing the bad news about Antonio that Salerio had just delivered:

> Gentle Lady,
> When I did first impart my love to you,
> I freely told you all the wealth I had
> Ran in my veins, I was a gentleman;
> And then I told you true.   (3.2.250–54)

He now admits that even in "rating myself at nothing," he was "a braggart"—or, in normal English, a liar—because he had "engaged" himself to Antonio and thereby forced Antonio to "engage" himself to Shylock (3.2.258–61). As Marc Shell puts it, "Portia learns that Bassanio did not give and hazard all he has. . . . He hazarded only the purse of Shylock and the person of Antonio."[8]

8. THE FIRST JASON

The trouble with Bassanio has been soft-pedaled by calling him "a soldier of fortune"[1] and "a kind of merchant-adventurer."[2] Part of what

6. Jagendorf, "Innocent Arrows and Sexy Sticks," 22–23.

7. Engle, *Shakespearean Pragmatism*, 83.

8. Marc Shell, *Money, Language, and Thought: Literary and Philosophical Economies from the Medieval to the Modern Era* (Berkeley: University of California Press, 1982), 60.

1. Shell, *Money, Language, and Thought*, 60.

2. Ferber, "The Ideology of *The Merchant of Venice*," 447.

makes *The Merchant of Venice* a richly embarrassing play is that one
of Shakespeare's most accomplished heroines engages herself to one
of his sleaziest protagonists. Their relation is complicated by the fact
that this engagement is acted out against a backdrop stitched together
from allusions to the play's central mythologeme.

Although the most frequently cited source is a tale in Giovanni
Fiorentino's collection, "Il pecorone" ('The Dunce"), *Merchant* reaches
out several times to Ovid's *Metamorphoses*. Medea's speech at *Metamorphoses* 7.197–209, for example, is familiar as the source of Prospero's
incantation at *Tempest* 5.1.33–50. Parts of the same text, Englished
in the rhymed fourteeners of Arthur Golding's 1567 translation, also
haunt several lines and images in *Merchant*, 5.1:

> Before the moon should circlewise close both her horns in one
> Three nights were yet as then to come. As soon as that she
>   shone
> Most full of light, and did behold the earth with fulsome face,
> Medea with her hair not trussed so much as in a lace,
> But flaring on her shoulders twain, and barefoot, with her
>   gown
> Ungirded, got her out of doors and wandered up and down
> Alone the dead time of the night . . .
>   . . . . [she said,] "O golden stars whose light
> Doth jointly with the moon succeed the beams that blaze by
>   day. . . .
> By charms I raise and lay the winds and burst the viper's jaw,
> And from the bowels of the earth both stones and trees do
>   draw.
> Whole woods and forests I remove; I make the mountains
>   shake,
> And even the earth itself to groan and fearfully to quake.
> I call up dead men from their graves, and thee, O lightsome
>   moon,
> I darken oft."[3]

---

3. From *The xv. Bookes of P. Ovidius Naso, entytuled Metamorphosis, translated oute of Latin into English meter, by Arthur Golding Gentleman* . . . (1567), in William Shakespeare, *The Tempest*, ed. Stephen Orgel, The Oxford Shakespeare (Oxford: Oxford University Press, 1987), 240–41.

Thus when editors gloss Lorenzo's reference at 5.1.79–82 to "the poet" who feigned "that Orpheus drew trees, stones, and floods" with his music, they invariably supply the name "Ovid." But these words also echo a passage at the beginning of an earlier tale of nautical venture and adventure, one familiar to both Ovid and Virgil.

When Apollonius Rhodius introduces the members of Jason's crew early in the *Argonautica*, the first Argonaut he profiles is Orpheus. The magic of Orpheus's songs, he writes, "enchanted stubborn mountain rocks" and "rushing streams" and trees.[4] Lorenzo's is but one of several references and allusions to the tale of Jason, Medea, and the golden fleece.

1. Bassanio's description of Portia's "sunny locks" early in the play first strikes the Apollonian gong: they "Hang on her temples like a golden fleece,/Which makes her seat of Belmont Colchis' strand,/And many Jasons come in quest of her" (1.1.169–72). Bassanio here displays the breadth of reference that leads some to call him "a scholar" (Nerissa at 1.2.98) and others a gold-digger.

2. Gratiano brays at 3.2.239 that "we are the Jasons, we have won the fleece."[5]

3. Once the *Argonautica* allusion machine has been switched on, it lights up at the several occurrences of the word "argosy" (or "argosies").[6]

4. After Lorenzo and Jessica kick off their moonlit colloquy in 5.1 with mentions of the unhappy lovers Troilus, Thisbe, and Dido, Jessica adds another candidate: "In such a night/Medea gathered the enchanted herbs/That did renew old Aeson," Jason's father (5.1.12–14). This glances back at Golding's Ovidian Medea: "Now have I need of herbs that can by virtue of their juice/To flowering prime of lusty youth old withered age reduce."

4. Apollonius Rhodius, *Argonautica*, trans. R. C. Seaton (Cambridge: Harvard University Press, 1980), 1.26–28.

5. Since Gratiano was not present when Bassanio mentioned Jason in 1.1, he isn't recalling or repeating that reference but independently citing the same allusion.

6. Four of the nine incidences of the word recorded in *The Shakespeare Concordance* are in *Merchant*: 1.1.9, 1.3.15, 3.1.85, and 5.1.276. An argosy is a very large merchant ship. According to the *OED*, which derives the word from the name of the Sicilian city Ragusa: "No reference to the ship Argo is traceable in the early use of the word." This is true only if the four instances uttered in a play that indexes *Argonautica* are discounted.

5. Finally, in the same scene, soon after Lorenzo exclaims, "How sweet the moonlight sleeps upon this bank," Portia enters and expressly articulates the myth of sleeping moonlight that lurks in Lorenzo's statement: "Peace ho! The moon sleeps with Endymion / And would not be awaked!" (5.1.109–10). The reference to Endymion specifically picks up on a passage at *Argonautica* 4.57–58: the goddess of the moon saw the love-crazed Medea wandering about and said to herself "in wicked glee: So I am not the only one to go astray for love, I that burn for beautiful Endymion."

What effect does Shakespeare produce by encircling Portia in the dark halo of Medea and casting the shadow of Jason across Bassanio? Bassanio well fits E. V. Rieu's characterization of Jason as less an action hero than "a man who gets things done for him."[7] And although Portia is not a witch, she stands in Medea's shadow as the loving agent chiefly responsible for getting those things done. If Bassanio initially reduces Portia to the golden fleece, her father validated that reduction when he imitated Aeetes (Medea's father) by imposing a task as the price of winning the fleece.

9. A NOTE ON VERSE AND PROSE IN ACT I

Portia's opening complaint in 1.2 ("my little body is aweary of this great world") threatens to echo Antonio's blues but is immediately cut off by Nerissa's "don't complain, you're doing fine." Nerissa voices this in eloquent prose, but when Portia commends it, she protests that the praise ignores her point. Portia responds a little defensively—and a little wordily (1.2.11–23)—that it's easier to say than to do what should be done, given the fact that her choice of husband must be determined by the casket lottery:

O me, the word "choose!" I may neither choose who I would nor refuse who I dislike; so is the will of a living daughter curbed by the

---

7. Apollonius of Rhodes, *The Voyage of the Argo*, trans. E. V. Rieu, 2nd edition (London: Penguin Books, 1971), 16.

will of a dead father. Is it not hard, Nerissa, that I cannot choose one
nor refuse none? (1.2.19–23)

Nerissa, however, is a tad starry-eyed about the idea: "the lottery that
he hath devised in these three chests of gold, silver, and lead, whereof
who chooses his meaning chooses you, will no doubt never be chosen
by any rightly but one who you shall rightly love" (1.2.25–29).

Nerissa's is one of only two utterances of the word, "chest" (the
other is by Aragon at 2.9.23). "Casket," which occurs seventeen times,
four of them in stage directions, denotes a "small cask," probably the
size of a jewelry chest and small enough for Jessica to throw from a
window or balcony. Contrary to what Freud and others have written,
the contexts of these mentions don't encourage the symbolization of
the caskets as figures of woman or of death.[1]

During the remainder of the scene, Portia and Nerissa discuss the
shortcomings of the string of ridiculous suitors they've been blessed
with so far. Nerissa then mentions the one visitor to the house they
liked—Bassanio, who came not as a suitor but (ironically) as a guest of
Portia's father (1.2.97–99). Finally, the next suitor, the Prince of Morocco, is announced, much to Portia's irritation.

Comparison between the verse exchanges of 1.1 and the prose of
1.2 retroactively shows that Portia's conversation with Nerissa is less
guarded and more open than Antonio's with Bassanio.[2] The women
are more comfortable with each other. The echoing exchanges of 1.1
become by contrast more theatrical, more defensively toned, more fo-
cused on getting a particular message across, and more expressive of
the speakers' lack of confidence that they *are* getting it across.

Looking back at 1.1 from the perspective of 1.2, Bassanio seems
to have been gaming an interlocutor who was willing if not eager to
be gamed. The iambic pentameters of 1.1 sustain the barrier to inter-

1. See Sigmund Freud, "The Theme of the Three Caskets," *Collected Papers*, translation supervised by Joan Riviere (London: The Hogarth Press, 1953), 4:244–56. For a
compelling development of Freud's argument, see Julia Reinhard Lupton and Kenneth
Reinhard, "The Motif of the Three Caskets," in their *After Oedipus: Shakespeare in Psycho-
analysis* (Ithaca: Cornell University Press, 1993), 145–62.

2. See Danson, *Harmonies*, 44–45, for an excellent account of the way 1.2 relates
to 1.1.

locutory openness. The potentiality for embarrassment is correspondingly greater in the performative medium of verse, which encourages posturing, than in the easy waves of opinion that flow back and forth through the prose of Nerissa and Portia.

Tension rises again when Shylock enters the play in 1.3.[3] He begins by mischievously teasing Bassanio in prose with terse repetitions of the latter's statements about the terms of the bond :

SHYLOCK   Three thousand ducats, well.

BASSANIO   Ay, sir, for three months.

SHYLOCK   For three months, well.

BASSANIO   For the which, as I told you, Antonio shall be bound.

SHYLOCK   Antonio shall become bound, well.

BASSANIO   May you stead me? Will you pleasure me? Shall I know your answer?

SHYLOCK   Three thousand ducats for three months and Antonio bound.   (1.3.1–9)

Even though this cross-talk is primarily an exchange of information, its stichomythic rhythm sharpens the tone. Bassanio is eager to close the deal. Shylock accordingly stalls.

How does the "well" that punctuates his first three statements alter them? Does it mean "O.K., that's fine"? "I'm thinking about it"? "I still need more persuading"?[4] Whatever he intends, Shylock's repetitions of "well" qualify statements that would otherwise express agreement. He keeps Bassanio squirming on the hook. So also do the variations on the figure of Antonio bound. Bassanio's "Antonio shall be bound" is obviously promissory: "Antonio is willing to be bound." But Shylock's shift to "shall *become* bound" implies something else: it will be done to him. A moment later it has already been done to him: "Antonio bound." These repetitions are charged with dark humor: "Ah, so! Antonio bonded, bound, tied up—willy-nilly. That would be worth thinking about, well."

3. See ibid., 150–57, for a superb analysis of this scene.

4. Joan Holmer, who reminds us that Shylock's first words in the play are "words about money," reads the repetitions of "well" as Shylock's way of emphasizing "how much he needs to think about this loan" (*The Merchant of Venice*, 145).

Shylock goes on to remind Bassanio that although Antonio "is sufficient"—he can be trusted to pay his bills—he has many bills to pay. His far-flung operations include argosies headed for Tripolis, the Indies, Mexico, and England, and these are not the only "ventures he hath squandered abroad. . . . The man is, notwithstanding, sufficient. Three thousand ducats; I think I may take his bond" (1.3.13–23). "Notwithstanding" smirks: it conspicuously dismisses so many potential squanders that it inflates both Antonio's peril and Shylock's magnanimity.

One of the more embarrassing aspects of this scene is that Shylock doesn't show his interlocutor much respect. Until Bassanio invites him to dinner, Shylock cuffs him about in a relatively relaxed prose. He saves the full force of his pentametrical animus for Antonio. But Bassanio's buttery invitation to socialize ("If it please you to dine with us") lights Shylock's fuse. He defines his boundaries in a staccato of repetitive phrases and then gruffly pretends not to recognize Antonio, whom he recognizes:

> I will buy with you, sell with you, talk with you, walk with you, and so following, but I will not eat with you, drink with you, nor pray with you. What news on the Rialto? Who is he comes here?
> (1.3.29–33)

The mere sight of Antonio drives Shylock into verse. Withdrawing from dialogue to a vituperative aside, he drops prose for the pentameters that pulse through the remainder of the scene. But what does it mean to converse with others in prose and speechify to oneself in verse?

> [aside]
> How like a fawning publican he looks!
> I hate him for he is a Christian,
> But more for that in low simplicity
> He lends out money gratis and brings down
> The rate of usance here with us in Venice.
> If I can catch him once upon the hip,
> I will feed fat the ancient grudge I bear him.
> He hates our sacred nation, and he rails,

> Even there where merchants most do congregate,
> On me, my bargains, and my well-won thrift,
> Which he calls interest. Cursed be my tribe
> If I forgive him!   (1.3.35–46)

Because lines of verse potentially offer themselves as units of itemization, and Shylock's first two lines promise to follow that pattern, the effect of the subsequent runover sequences is intensified. As he enumerates their mutual grievances and works himself up, as he not only sets but also motivates the agenda for his future behavior, the three periods driving through the pentameters express both agitation and anticipation. They shove the commas aside. Those that terminate lines 36, 40, 42, and 43 are uselessly obstructive. They should be expunged from the next edition of the play.

When Bassanio tugs at his sleeve, Shylock responds by advertising the trouble it will cost him to float Antonio the loan.

> BASSANIO   Shylock, do you hear?
> SHYLOCK [*to Bassanio*]
>   I am debating of my present store,
>   And, by the near guess of my memory,
>   I cannot instantly raise up the gross
>   Of full three thousand ducats. What of that?
>   Tubal, a wealthy Hebrew of my tribe,
>   Will furnish me. But soft! how many months
>   Do you desire? [*to Antonio*] Rest you fair, good signior!
>   Your Worship was the last man in our mouths.
>
>   (1.3.47–54)

Since Shylock had twice confirmed the three-month period in the preceding discussion, this repetition puts forgetfulness on parade and, as Danson argues, rubs the persona of "fussy, slow-witted old man" in his interlocutors' faces even as he turns to chew on Antonio.[5]

Antonio pushes past the unsavory image and gets right to the point. He emphasizes the extent to which he'll jeopardize his own probity to help a friend:

---

5. Danson, *Harmonies*, 150.

> Shylock, albeit I neither lend nor borrow
> By taking nor by giving of excess,
> Yet, to supply the ripe wants of my friend,
> I'll break a custom. [to Bassanio] Is he yet possessed
> How much ye would?

SHYLOCK   Ay, ay, three thousand ducats.

(1.3.55–59)

Shylock's is a quietly aggressive intervention. He completes a line begun by Antonio and answers the question Antonio directed at Bassanio. He then goes on to tease Bassanio by "forgetting" the term limit he had twice enunciated earlier.

ANTONIO

> And for three months.

SHYLOCK

> I had forgot—three months, you told me so.
> Well then, your bond. And let me see—but hear you;
> Methought you said you neither lend nor borrow
> Upon advantage.

ANTONIO   I do never use it.

(1.3.55–65)

Shylock reacts to the Christian merchant's puckered Tartuffery by drawing the sword of Jewishness and poking at Antonio with a pun-powered Old Testament anecdote about sheep-grazing rights. The anecdote seems at first maddeningly off the subject (1.3.66–85).[6] He praises the patriarch Jacob's "thrift," which is his redefinition of "taking interest," and which, by the end of the anecdote, means "skill in cheating." "Thrift" is Jacob's ability to take more than his fair share without actually stealing. Shylock's message to Antonio: if you don't cheat like Jacob did, you won't thrive. Antonio justifies Jacob by attributing his "venture" to the trickery of his God but wonders testily about the relevance of this pastoral tale to the subject under discussion: "Was this inserted to make interest good? / Or is your gold and silver

---

6. See the now classic discussion of Shylock's punning play on "ewes," "use," and "Iewes," in Shell, *Money, Language, and Thought*, 48–55.

ewes and rams?" A blank-eyed Shylock shares his wonder: "I cannot tell. I make it breed as fast" (1.3.89–91).

10. ANOTHER JASON

Portia and Bassanio had seen and appraised each other before the play began. In 1.2, when Nerissa recalls the visit by "a Venetian, a scholar and soldier," Portia excitedly responds, "Yes, yes, it was Bassanio," but then catches herself, "—as I think, so was he called." Nerissa encourages her: "He, of all the men that ever my foolish eyes looked upon was the best deserving a fair lady." Portia remembers "him well, and . . . remember[s] him worthy of thy praise" (1.2.97–102).

Bassanio lives up to his scholarly reputation by framing Portia in classical analogies, the most bizarre of which turns her into the world's eighth wonder—"her sunny locks / Hang on her temples like a golden fleece" (1.1.169–70). This is a fancy way to improvise on the major attraction he had already mentioned, "a lady richly left" (1.1.161). Thoughts of Jason are sustained throughout the play by the repeated occurrences of "argosy," which painfully affect such pitiful latter-day Argonauts as Bassanio—and Gratiano, who excitedly announces at 3.2.239 that "we are the Jasons, we have won the fleece." Thoughts of Jason also bring thoughts of Medea.

The scholarly endeavors of Bassanio and Portia continue unabated in the casket scene (3.2). Before he chooses the casket, she melodramatically compares this action to the deed accomplished by Jason's fellow Argonaut, Hercules, when he rescued a Trojan maiden whose father had offered her as a sacrifice to a sea monster. "Go, Hercules!," she then exhorts poor Bassanio (3.2.54–60). This analogy to the conquering hero must be flattering to him unless he knows the full story— which is that Hercules comes to the father's assistance in order to win not his daughter but his horses. If we assume that Portia knows the story, her allusion to it throws an early shadow over our sense of her sense of Bassanio.

It's as if she guesses that he had earlier described himself to Antonio as one of the many Jasons questing for her golden locks. The keys that will open those locks are in her father's gift, like those to the caskets in one of which her future lurks. The paternal lock is a shy lock—an emblem of wariness and apprehensiveness, of the father's refusal to trust to his daughter's discretion in handling his property, which includes herself.[1]

Even though Portia affects Bassanio and distinguishes him from the other suitors, she seems aware that suitors as such tend to identify daughters with ducats and person with purse. Her desire for the latest Jason may expose her to Medea's doom. Like Medea, who also betrayed her father's secret and helped her lover to the fleece, she may betray herself. She knows fathers are in league with monsters that venture on the deep in search of prey, and she may even suspect that monster and hero are one. Caught in the male conspiracy, she may feel she can win her freedom from her father only by accepting captivity to a husband. Thus she uses the act of donation and sets up the ring trick to limit their power over her.

II. PORTIA CHEATING

By the time Bassanio makes his first visit to Belmont, Portia knows which casket is the money casket because the other two have been chosen and thereby identified. In earlier scenes, however, she made statements that suggest she may have had this knowledge prior to the wrong choices. At 2.7.11–12 she told Morocco that one of the caskets contains her picture. Since she knows that much—and how she learned it isn't specified—it's tempting to assume she also knows which casket will deprive her of her independence.

Even earlier, Nerissa warns Portia that if the German suitor she dislikes "should offer to choose, and choose the right casket, you should refuse to perform your father's will, if you should refuse to accept him." "Therefore," Portia replies, "for fear of the worst, I pray thee, set a deep glass of rhenish wine on the contrary casket, for if the devil

---

1. Corinne S. Abate makes the important point that "Laomedon's own missteps are responsible for endangering the life of his daughter": "'Nerissa Teaches Me What to Believe': Portia's Wifely Empowerment in *The Merchant of Venice*," in *The Merchant of Venice: New Critical Essays*, ed. John W. Mahon and Ellen MacLeod Mahon (New York: Routledge, 2002), 299. This excellent essay persuasively details the sources and effects of Portia's wifely power and develops a strong profile of what can only be called Bassanio's sleaziness.

be within and that temptation without, I know he will choose it. I will do any thing, Nerissa, ere I'll be married to a sponge" (1.2.88–95). Nerissa then assures her that they needn't go this far because the discouraged suitors are planning to return home unless they can vie for her by some method other than her "father's imposition." Portia expresses relief but reiterates her commitment to that "imposition": "I will die as chaste as Diana, unless I be obtained by the manner of my father's will" (1.2.102–4).

This interchange nevertheless shows that Portia knows which casket is the right one, and it establishes the possibility that she is willing to cheat. It reinforces the probability that (like Jessica) she does cheat when the right man comes along.[1] Furthermore, her mischievous ring play in 3.2, 4.1, and 5.1 displays a strong propensity for self-protective connivance—for "coigns of vantage" as well as "vantage to exclaim."[2]

The evidence of Portia's cheating in 3.2 is manifold and so obvious that I find it hard to understand why critics resist it.[3] First, she gives Bassanio verbal clues to the inscription on the lead casket, "Who chooseth me must give and *hazard* all he hath." At the beginning of the scene she begs him to "tarry . . . /Before you hazard," and later her "I stand for sacrifice" virtually translates the inscription (3.2.1–2, 3.2.57).

Second, the song she calls for contains a clue that Bassanio clearly picks up: fancy is "engendered in the eyes,/With gazing fed" (3.2.67–68). He fully agrees: "So may the outward shows be least themselves;/The world is still deceived with ornament" (3.2.73–74). Therefore the beautiful surfaces of gold and silver must conceal evil

---

1. That (and how) she cheats is the subject of my "Marriage and Mercifixion in *The Merchant of Venice*: The Casket Scene Revisited," in *Making Trifles of Terrors*, 1–9. Originally published in *Shakespeare Quarterly* 32 (1981): 156–62.

2. For "coign of vantage" see *Macbeth*, 1.6.7.

3. For examples of resistance to the idea that Portia cheats, see Danson, *Harmonies*, 117–18, and Barber, *Shakespeare's Festive Comedy*, 174. Danson admits that "there is no immediate way to disprove" the idea that Portia cheats "except by appealing to our sense of the play as a whole" (ibid.). And this is true: his sense of the play centers on harmony, while mine centers on embarrassment. For a compact and illuminating assessment of the range of opinions on this topic, see the comments and glosses in Jay Halio's Oxford edition of the play, 34–36 and 164–68.

and should be rejected. After continuing in this worldly wise vein for thirty lines, he chooses the "meager lead" casket.

Third, the fact that the first three song lines end in words that rhyme with "lead" has been both cited and rejected as evidence of cheating. In the context of the practices just described, we are entitled to read the "lead" rhymes as an additional clue. It's notable that no lyrics were provided Morocco or Aragon while they were choosing. According to Michael Ferber, Bassanio differs from Morocco and Aragon in that he "chooses 'not by the view' of the casket but by an inner eloquence in it." It would be more correct to say that he chooses not by the view but by the clue.[4]

Fourth, Portia's address toward Morocco and Aragon is marked not only by impatience and occasional rudeness but also by actions that bespeak a desire for revenge. She begins by blaming the lottery on her father and then creamily murmurs that were it not for his rules Morocco would be her choice (2.1.17–22). After he thanks her and spends a few lines boasting, she goes on to impose another condition: "swear, before you choose, if you choose wrong / Never to speak to lady afterward / In way of marriage" (2.1.40–42).

She doesn't attribute this gag rule to her father. It must therefore be her idea to keep him from pestering half the human race. It reveals a desire not merely to get rid of him but literally to embarrass him for life—*to embar* him from future access to marriage. As he hurries off he mutters, "Thus losers part." She sighs in relief and discharges a short burst of xenophobic bile: "A gentle riddance. Draw the curtains, go. / Let all of his complexion choose me so" (2.7.77–79).

Portia imposes the same restraint on Aragon in 2.9 but festoons it with two new ones: he is not to reveal to anyone which casket he chose and, more importantly, "if you fail, without more speech, my lord, / You must be gone from hence immediately" (2.9.7–8). After having wasted two scenes and a supper on Morocco, she isn't about to tolerate another talkative tarrier. When Aragon agrees to the three conditions, she lies that "To these injunctions everyone doth swear / That comes to hazard for my worthless self" (2.9.17–18).[5]

4. Ferber, "The Ideology of *The Merchant of Venice*," 455.

5. Her statement is false because those conditions were not imposed on Morocco, the only other suitor to appear in the play so far.

He obligingly delivers an oration fourteen lines shorter than Morocco's major opus, makes his wrong choice, reads the scroll, and limps off in embarrassed tetrameters.

ARAGON   What is here?
            [*he reads*]
                        The fire seven times tried this;
                        Seven times tried that judgment is
                        That did never choose amiss.
                        Some there be that shadows kiss;
                        Such have but a shadow's bliss.
                        There be fools alive, iwis,
                        Silver'd o'er, and so was this.
                        Take what wife you will to bed;
                        I will ever be your head.
                        So be gone; you are sped.
            Still more fool I shall appear
            By the time I linger here.
            With one fool's head I came to woo,
            But I go away with two.
            Sweet, adieu. I'll keep my oath,
            Patiently to bear my wroth.
                        [*Exeunt Aragon and train*]
                              (2.9.62–78)

After they recite their respective verses, both Morocco and Aragon shift from the pentameter they had been using and utter their hurried farewells in rhymed tetrametrical couplets. This reduces them to extensions of the death's head and fool to which the verses are attributed.

The scroll verses are basically in trochaic tetrameter, with occasional variant lines. In Morocco's case they are confined to a single-rhyme pattern (2.7.65–73), but in Aragon's verses the rhyme changes at line 8 to emphasize the critical statement that distinguishes Aragon's fate from Morocco's: "Take what wife you will to bed." According to Marc Shell, this distinction is evidence of Portia's xenophobia. Unlike the black Muslim suitor, "the white Christian is allowed to try to generate kin in wedlock."[6] But Shell obscures a more interesting point: the

---

6. Shell, *Money, Language, and Thought*, 57.

schedule was presumably prepared by her father, and Portia's ban on Aragon's marrying directly contradicts it. We're left with the impression that dealing with the two suitors has made her progressively more twitchy.

12. PORTIA'S HAIR

When Bassanio first mentions Portia to Antonio, he mythologizes her "sunny locks" (1.1.169–72). But during the commonplace arguments that lead him to reject the gold casket, he says harsh things about wigs:

> Look on beauty,
> And you shall see 'tis purchased by the weight,
> Which therein works a miracle in nature,
> Making them lightest that wear most of it.
> So are those crispèd, snaky, golden locks
> Which make such wanton gambols with the wind
> Upon supposèd fairness, often known
> To be the dowry of a second head,
> The skull that bred them in the sepulcher.
> Thus ornament is but . . .
> The seeming truth which cunning times put on
> To entrap the wisest.   (3.2.88–101)

This comment makes his subsequent reaction to the image in the lead casket all the more puzzling:

> Fair Portia's counterfeit! What demi-god
> Hath come so near creation? Move these eyes?
> Or whether, riding on the balls of mine,
> Seem they in motion? Here are severed lips,
> Parted with sugar breath; so sweet a bar
> Should sunder such sweet friends. Here in her hairs
> The painter plays the spider, and hath woven
> A golden mesh t'entrap the hearts of men
> Faster than gnats in cobwebs. But her eyes—
> How could he see to do them? Having made one,
> Methinks it should have power to steal both his
> And leave itself unfurnished.   (3.2.115–26)

Apart from the strangely oppressive figure of her eyes "riding on the balls" of his, several terms and notions play havoc with his effort to emblazon the portrait: "severed," "sunder," "spider," "t'entrap," "gnats in cobwebs," the blinded painter, the apparition of a Cyclopean Portia.

Richard Halpern's incisive analysis of lines 120–26 addresses this problem:

> At the very moment when Bassanio thinks to have discovered the hidden truth, he is confronted with another representation, another mediation. His words, moreover, suggest a second meaning: Fair Portia is counterfeit, empty, a sham, the sum of nothing, just as she claims. Bassanio's description of the portrait reinforces this suspicion . . . [and] verges on idolatry or fetishism. Moreover, his fantasy of an eyeless [one-eyed] portrait surely evokes the skull with the "empty eye" (2.7.63) contained in the golden casket, just as the "golden meshes" of the portrait's hair evokes the golden casket itself and its false allure. Thus Portia's picture somehow doubles or reproduces the vacant death's head which symbolized the void. . . . Choosing the lead casket produces identical results to choosing the gold or silver ones, for the chooser's reward is a counterfeit Portia, at once empty death's head and mocking fool's head.[1]

Halpern doesn't elaborate on the difference between what Bassanio's words suggest and what he means to say. He means to praise, but bolts of terror flash through his speech.

13. THE SIEGE OF BELMONT

Janet Adelman devotes a chapter of her remarkable study of *Merchant* to the representation in 2.2 of Shylock's truant servant, Launcelot Gobbo. She asks why his "decision to leave Shylock" should be "so much more difficult, and so much more fraught with guilt, than Jessica's." Her answer is that Launcelot's leaving Shylock's service enacts "a kind of mock conversion from Jew to Christian, as though he were

---

1. Richard Halpern, "The Jewish Question: Shakespeare and Anti-Semitism," in *Shakespeare Among the Moderns* (Ithaca: Cornell University Press, 1997), 199–200.

parodying Jessica's conversion before the fact."[1] Just as Jessica deceives and abandons her father, so Launcelot tries to escape from Shylock and deceive his own father. These "turnings," Adelman concludes, remind us that Christianity "represents a kind of originary turning away from Judaism . . . that can never be wholly complete. Anxiety about this incompletion . . . shapes almost every element in 2.2."[2]

It says something about the culture of "Venice" that *Merchant's* only instance of conscience-driven inner conflict is consigned to a clown named Launcelot Gobbo and staged as something to be laughed at.[3] However laughable, Launcelot's account of the struggle between his conscience and the fiend (2.2.1–27) features what is significantly absent from the major event on which 2.2 centers: the onset of Bassanio's siege of Belmont.[4]

We first hear about the siege when Launcelot tells his father to offer his doves "to one Master Bassanio, who indeed gives rare new liveries." No sooner has that hallowed name dropped from his lips than, *mirabile dictu*, "Oh, rare fortune! Here comes the man"! "[*Enter Bassanio with (Leonardo and) a follower or two]*"—or three, or four (2.2.98–103). Enter Bassanio with a retinue, putting on airs. He has obviously been dunking the ducats Antonio borrowed from Shylock, and as he walks onstage he barks out orders about dinner, mail, and liveries.

As he will remind Portia at 3.2.253–54, Bassanio—unlike the merchant Antonio—is an aristocrat. But here, well before that reminder, he luxuriates in his lordliness. When old Gobbo salutes him—"God bless your worship!"—he graciously replies with the tetrametrical hauteur of a prince astride his pony: "Gramercy. Wouldst thou aught with me?" (2.2.108–9).

---

1. Janet Adelman, *Blood Relations: Christian and Jew in The Merchant of Venice* (Chicago: University of Chicago Press, 2008), 38. I'm deeply indebted to this great book for many of the ideas and formulations in the present chapter.

2. Ibid., 65.

3. "Gobbo," hunchback, punctures the romance of "Launcelot," who was a kind of medieval Jason. Launcelot Gobbo: The Hunchback of the Table Round.

4. Although Adelman's chapter on Launcelot is a powerful study of the bad-faith dynamics of conversion, it doesn't discuss this event.

After the clown volunteers for service, Lord Bassanio embosses the good news by shifting from Gobbo's homey prose to upscale iambics:

> I know thee well; thou hast obtain'd thy suit.
> Shylock thy master spoke with me this day,
> And hath preferred thee, if it be preferment
> To leave a rich Jew's service, to become
> The follower of so poor a gentleman.
>
> (2.2.130–34)

Even as he all but slips from the saddle, Bassanio begins by executing a smart pun and concludes by referring with mischievous mock modesty to the downscale condition from which he is now working hard to escape. Lawrence Danson sees in this performance a sign of Bassanio's "increased awareness of generosity's ungarrulous spontaneity."[5] But if he is being generous, it is, characteristically, with someone else's money, and when he begins spouting iambics, his speech seems less spontaneous than labored.

His interactions with both Gobbo and Gratiano show that he has been busy transforming himself into Lord Bassanio, the granter of suits. He graciously orders a servant to give Gobbo a fancy outfit—"a livery/More guarded than his fellows" (2.2.140–41). After the Gobbos leave, he continues to harangue his servant about dinner, this time in verse. Gratiano then rushes in with a request ("I have a suit to you"), which Lord Bassanio graciously grants ("You have obtained it").[6] But when Gratiano begs to accompany him to Belmont, Bassanio lectures him on his lack of grace. His lecture betrays continuing nervousness:

> Pray thee, take pain
> To allay with some cold drops of modesty
> Thy skipping spirit, lest through thy wild behavior
> I be misconstered in the place I go to
> And lose my hopes.   (2.2.167–71)

---

5. Danson, *Harmonies*, 111.

6. Michael Ferber interprets Bassanio's response as "the instant generosity of a noble friend." This misses the silliness of the moment. Ferber should have put the statement in scare quotes to mark it as part of Bassanio's performative effort rather than as an expression of his sincerity: "The Ideology of *The Merchant of Venice*," 436.

The shift in this scene from Gobboesque prose (1–152) to Bassanian verse (153–88) accentuates both the pretentiousness and the edginess of our hero's siege of Belmont.[7]

14. COVINOUS CASKETEERS

In the 2004 film by Michael Radford, the homosexual bond between Bassanio and Antonio gets expeditiously sealed with a kiss well before the plot begins to heat up. That crude giveaway shows exactly what the play refuses to do. It reminds us that the question of whether Bassanio and Antonio "have sex" is similar to the same question about Othello and Desdemona. It is both central and unanswerable.[1] Do Bassanio and Antonio appear to want to have sex with each other? Does Antonio appear to want to have sex with Bassanio?

Danson rejects outright "the psychosocial [sexual] explanation for Antonio's sadness," because it presupposes "a competition between Antonio and Portia" that he finds untenable: "The love of Antonio and Bassanio (whether or not it dares to speak its name) is a textual fact; but a sexual competition between Antonio and Portia is not."[2] This rejection prevents him from exploring such obviously homoerotic or "parasexual" issues as the one identified by Lawrence Hyman: whether or not Antonio harbors "some unconscious sexual feeling for Bassanio," he "feels rejected when he sees that his friend is determined to marry."[3]

Adelman takes this further when she emphasizes the embarrassing blockage produced by the fusion of erotic with economic affect:

7. Actually, Bassanio begins raising the tone of discourse by modulating into genteel iambics at lines 130–34 and 138–41.

1. On this topic, see the interesting comments by Simon Palfrey, *Doing Shakespeare* (London: Thomson Learning, 2005), 253–58.

2. Danson, *Harmonies*, 38–40.

3. Lawrence Hyman, "The Rival Lovers in *The Merchant of Venice*," *Shakespeare Quarterly* 21 (1970): 110. Even more persuasive is Alan Sinfield's argument that *Merchant*'s "traffic in boys is casual, ubiquitous, and hardly remarkable. It becomes significant in its resonances for the relationship between Antonio and Bassanio because Portia, subject to her father's will, has reason to feel insecure about the affections of her stranger-husband": "How to Read *The Merchant* Without Being Heterosexist," in *Shakespeare, Authority, Sexuality: Unfinished Business in Cultural Materialism* (London: Routledge, 2006), 62.

Antonio registers his longing to be opened up to—or by—Bassanio in the only terms available to him:

> Be assured
> My purse, my person, my extremest means
> Lie all unlocked to your occasions.   (1.1.137–39)

My purse, my person: the equivalence simultaneously under-scores Antonio's erotic fantasy and marks its limits: spending his wealth appears to be the only form of spending himself that he can articulate, and unlocking his purse the only form of unlocking his person. No wonder the merchant and his ships tend to become indistinguishable.[4]

If the issue of gendered agency is melodramatically understated in Antonio's discussions with Bassanio, it pops up as a central strategy in the elopement of Lorenzo and Jessica. When Lorenzo shares with his friends the substance of Jessica's letter detailing her getaway plans, his paraphrase of her instructions indicates that she is more than half the wooer:

> I must needs tell thee all. She hath directed
> How I shall take her from her father's house,
> What gold and jewels she is furnished with,
> What page's suit she hath in readiness. . . .
> Come, go with me. Peruse this as thou goest.
> Fair Jessica shall be my torchbearer.
>   (2.4.29–39)

Even as he demotes Jessica to his torchbearer, reducing her to an amorous symbol and a servant, he acknowledges her initiative and direction.

The same confused sense of gendered agency surfaces at the begin-ning of the elopement scene (2.6). Gratiano and Salerio enter dressed as masquers and express surprise that Lorenzo isn't there on time, since "lovers ever run before the clock." After they agree that no one expects such lovers' larks to produce stable unions, Gratiano puts his worldly wise cynicism on parade: "All things that are / Are with more spirit chasèd than enjoyed" (2.6.12–13). He precedes and follows this

---

4. Adelman, *Blood Relations*, 118.

statement of the obvious with a trio of examples that progressively obfuscate it:

> Who riseth from a feast
> With that keen appetite that he sits down?
> Where is the horse that doth untread again
> His tedious measures with the unbated fire
> That he did pace them first? All things that are
> Are with more spirit chasèd than enjoyed.
> How like a younger or a prodigal
> The scarfèd bark puts from her native bay,
> Hugged and embracèd by the strumpet wind!
> How like the prodigal doth she return,
> With over-weathered ribs and ragged sails,
> Lean, rent and beggared by the strumpet wind!
>
> (2.6.9–20)

The diner and horse are at least appropriately male (since Lorenzo is the implied subject of the analogy), but the figure of a horse treading and untreading throws less light on the erotic appetite than on Gratiano's inclination to blather. He shoots off analogies like Roman candles, and the third and longest figure is the most perplexing. The comparison of a bedizened female ship to "a younger [younker] or a prodigal" emphasizes the foolishness of a cross-dressed prodigal who gets disempowered by his or her strumpet.

This analogy chiefly brings out Gratiano's rhetorical windiness. But as Adelman brilliantly suggests, it may also bring out both his impatience with and his uneasiness about Lorenzo's cross-racial adventure: the figure of "the rent ship . . . identifies Lorenzo with the ship and Jessica with the strumpet wind that would simultaneously embrace and rend the body of the younker who sets out so confidently."[5] Adelman further notes that Gratiano's speech

> perfectly anticipates the fate of Antonio's ships. . . . That "prodigal" ship, "lean, rent, and beggared," anticipates both Shylock's characterization of Antonio as "a bankrupt, a prodigal, . . . a beggar" . . . and the rending to which Antonio's bankruptcy would subject him. . . .

5. Ibid., 105.

The ship . . . is thus not only an anticipation of but also a metonymy for Antonio's rent body.[6]

When Lorenzo enters immediately after Gratiano's figure, its shadow falls across and troubles his flippant apology for being late: "When you shall please to play the thieves for wives/I'll watch as long as you." "To play the thieves for wives" means either (1) to steal wives or (2) to steal on behalf of wives. The first sense conflates daughters with ducats, but the second glances at the complicity, and even the bossiness, of daughters who would be wives. The prepositional pun thus assimilates Jessica to Portia, Lorenzo to Bassanio, and Shylock to Portia's father. This prepares the way for Jessica, who appears on the balcony and aims a snappy directive at Lorenzo: "Here catch this casket, it is worth the pains" (2.6.33). She worries less about having stolen her father's gold and jewels than about prancing through the streets disguised as a page (35–39).[7]

All the elements in these stretches of dialogue converge on one effect. They anticipate and indeed model Portia's negotiations with Bassanio in 3.2 and with Antonio in Acts 4 and 5. The elopement of Lorenzo and Jessica moves *scherzando* through a sequence of four short lively scenes (2.3–6) that expose the motives more competently masked or disowned by those who orchestrate the *andante* of the Belmont venture. The 325 lines of the single casket scene in 3.2 burrow under the 184 lines of the four elopement scenes. In retrospect, the overt knavery of Lorenzo and Jessica becomes a proleptic parody of what transpires more slowly and deviously at Belmont. They don't merely elope. They rob Jessica's father.[8] Lorenzo's thievery parodies Bassanio's, Jessica's casketry and cross-dressing parody Portia's, and Shylock's prissy paternal precaution parodies Portia's parent.

15. MOONLIT MAUNDERING

Jessica and Lorenzo first appear alone together near the end of 3.5. Given the problems inherent in her "would-be escape from her fa-

6. Ibid., 106–7.

7. Adelman argues that by eliding Jessica's "conversion with her marriage, Shakespeare occludes the paternal betrayal inherent in that conversion" (*Blood Relations*, 39). But "Here catch this casket" draws attention to her betrayal.

8. Thanks to Michael Warren for emphasizing this point.

ther's Jewishness," the tone of their conversation is surprisingly up-beat.[1] Nothing in 3.5 suggests that there is, has been, or will be any trouble between them. They exchange opinions and banter in playful intimacy. But the tone of their backchat in 5.1 is markedly different. There, the community that gathers together around the scapegoating of Shylock continues its forced, rhetorically edgy, and morally precarious efforts to turn duplicity into harmony.

Everything in the dialogue between Jessica and Lorenzo that opens Act 5 is slightly out of tune. Lorenzo plays the romantic tenor for three lines: "The moon shines bright. In such a night as this,/When the sweet wind did gently kiss the trees,/And they did make no noise, in such a night. . . ." From here he suddenly and sardonically veers toward a cameo of poor Troilus lamenting his betrayal by Cressida. Jessica retorts with two and a half lines about the plight of poor Thisbe, Lorenzo parries with three about poor Dido, and Jessica comes back with another two and a half about poor Medea (5.1.1–14).

These kickshaws from the classical cupboard of calamitous love serve up a single theme: Portia's "the ruin of your love" (3.2.173). And in a strange Cimmerian displacement, the trifles bandied back and forth between Lorenzo and Jessica are darkened by their shadowy evocation of Portia and Bassanio. It's been said that Jessica focuses on the plight of untrue lovers, but in what sense is Thisbe, whom Jessica mentions first, an untrue lover? The example seems anomalous. That Thisbe suffers for or fails to consummate her love may at most be attributed to her being "untrue" as a disobedient daughter. Yet this makes it less anomalous. It speaks to Jessica's scruple about her father. And it speaks more deeply to Portia's about hers.

Jessica swerves back to *Argonautica* and *Metamorphoses* with her next example, Medea, who also disobeyed her father (like Portia) but magically renewed her false lover's father. Here, the allusion to daughterly bad conscience makes the same moral claims on Lorenzo that Portia had made on Bassanio: "Look at all I've done for you and risked for you. See what you owe me. 'I stand for sacrifice.'" Lorenzo strikes

---

1. Janet Adelman, "Her Father's Blood: Race, Conversion, and Nation in *The Merchant of Venice*," *Representations* 81 (2003): 6. The whole essay (4–30) develops an original and striking interpretation of Jessica's dilemma. Especially valuable are Adelman's comments on Portia's aloofness toward Jessica (6 and 22). *Blood Relations* expands these topics with equal brilliance.

back in a Bassanian vein by reminding Jessica that she, like Medea, was foolish enough to "steal" from her wealthy father and run off with "an unthrift love" (5.1.1–17). Like Medea, and also like Portia. The Jason-Medea paradigm looms over *Merchant* like a tempest that has rolled in from the Black Sea and hangs darkly above Venice.[2]

"An unthrift love": the phrase evokes the economy of untrust this paradigm generates, and it fuses the improvident—or careless, or expensive—lovers Lorenzo and Bassanio with Jessica's and Portia's imprudent desire. In the repartée that follows, the lovers threaten, as Jessica then puts it, to "out-night" each other (5.1.23)—to waste the night exchanging parables of darkness. But they're interrupted by the messenger who announces Portia's imminent return from Venice. It is as if the spirit presiding over their talk suddenly materialized out of the shadows.

Why the strain in their pedantic palaver? Is it because they're trying to act out and fend off predictable strains within the relationship? They may be comically—or pathetically—"heroizing" themselves and their precarious situation by invoking the plight of famous literary lovers who are undone not merely by the faithlessness of their beloveds but also by the demands of policy and empire, and by the conflicting claims of passion and filial obedience or loyalty. Or they may be whistling in the dark.

Their preemptive wit-play acknowledges the morally dubious character of their elopement and glances at its potentially unhappy consequences. Adelman speculates that Jessica's "love song with Lorenzo alludes only to doomed and childless couples" because she "is never fully absorbed into Belmont"—Portia stubbornly ignores her, and her "children will always be Jews, no less Shylock's flesh and blood than she is."[3] But what gives this interchange its profoundly troubling reso-

---

2. "Even a cursory knowledge of the story of Medea would have enabled Elizabethan theatergoers to recognize that she had become an emblem of a daughter who abandoned her father and her culture in marrying her husband (whom she would soon betray and abandon, after his abandonment of her). . . . Having been reminded of Jessica's infidelity to her father, Shakespeare's audience may have wondered how long her own vows of faith, religious and marital, would remain firm" (Shapiro, *Shakespeare and the Jews*, 158–59).

3. Adelman, *Blood Relations*, 88–89.

nance is the obvious set of thematic analogies to the Portia/Bassanio plot. The "legendary disasters" they rehearse "are only the first of many shadows cast across the play's conventionally happy ending."[4]

Stephano, the messenger who interrupts them, brings pretty strange news about Portia.

> My mistress will before the break of day
> Be here at Belmont; she doth stray about
> By holy crosses, where she kneels and prays
> For happy wedlock hours.
>
> LORENZO   Who comes with her?
>
> STEPHANO
>   None but a holy hermit and her maid.
>
>   (5.1.29–33)

Why should she do that after her great coup in court has saved Antonio, her rival for Bassanio's attentions? The question partly answers itself, especially after we've seen Lorenzo and Jessica act out the problems Portia and Bassanio evade. But the report is strange because in the short preceding scene (4.2) Portia and Nerissa were in good spirits. Having received the ring Bassanio sent via Gratiano, they looked forward to making fools of their husbands:

> We shall have old swearing
> That they did give their rings away to men;
> But we'll outface them, and outswear them too.
>
>   (4.2.15–17)

The messenger's report of her straying and praying nevertheless glances at doubts Portia might be expected to have after getting the ring—questions about Bassanio's performance in 4.1, questions about his capacity for faith and trust and love. It also glances at Goulding's Ovidian Medea, who, before invoking the forces of night, "barefoot, with her gown/Ungirded, got her out of doors and wandered up and down/Alone the dead time of the night."

Questions about Bassanio are only reinforced when Launcelot Gobbo gallumps across the stage, blowing an imaginary post-horn to

---

4. A. R. Braunmuller, ed. *The Merchant of Venice*, The Pelican Shakespeare (New York: Penguin Books, 2000), xlix.

announce news of good news. He has learned from another messenger that his master is on the way (5.1.38–48). Lord Bassanio's complex courier service indicates that Portia's "unthrift love" continues to spruce up his equipage, though he has yet to buy Launcelot a real post-horn.

In the onstage quiet Launcelot leaves behind him, Lorenzo changes the tone: "How sweet the moonlight sleeps upon this bank." He all but converts Jessica with a description of the night sky that transforms it first into a galaxy of hosts—"the floor of heaven/inlaid with patens"— and then into an angelic choir. Since this music is inaudible, he calls in real musicians and commands them to "wake Diana with a hymn" so as to draw Portia "home with music" (5.1.54–66).

Portia herself enters with Nerissa soon after and expressly articulates the myth of sleeping moonlight lurking in Lorenzo's statement: "Peace!—how the moon sleeps with Endymion/And would not be awak'd!" (5.1.109)—another citation from and reminder of *Argonautica*.[5] After her dealings with "an unthrift love" during the courtroom scene, she must envy the moon. If she could have Bassanio put to sleep forever, and watch and enjoy him as he sleeps, and share his sleep, wouldn't she have what she wants?

In her waking life, this night holds none of the romance Lorenzo saw in it. Still busily engaged in planning the terminal embarrassment of Bassanio, she has Nerissa order the servants to "take/No note at all of our being absent hence;/Nor you, Lorenzo; Jessica, nor you." Lorenzo signals the approach of Bassanio and reassures her that her lie is safe with them: "We are no telltales, madam, fear you not" (5.1.119–23). But her next words indicate that something else disturbs her. She darkens what she describes with a troubled and troubling remark: "This night, methinks, is but the daylight sick,/It looks a little paler,—'tis a day,/Such as the day is when the sun is hid" (5.1.124–26). The sun began to hide when Bassanio gave her ring to Balthasar in Venice.

Portia welcomes Bassanio with an awkward joke about sexual disloyalty and his reply is equally clumsy: "This is the man, this is Antonio,/To whom I am so infinitely bound." This gives her an op-

5. *Argonautica* 4.57–61.

portunity for prepositional pinpricks she can't resist: "You should in all sense be much bound *to* him,/For, as I hear, he was much bound *for* you."

16. COIGNS OF VANTAGE

Portia's gift to Bassanio is an act of self-protection "in a naughty world" (5.1.91). The ring is a something for nothing that she can transform into a weapon, or into a debt, whenever she finds it useful to disadvantage the donee. This lays the groundwork for her interlocutory victories at the end of the play. First, she frees Antonio from Shylock in order to pry Bassanio loose from Antonio. Then, after the merchant speaks up for his Bassanio, she doubly seals her double triumph by forcing Antonio to be the ring-giver, in effect the minister, who returns Bassanio to the nuptial fold (5.1.254–56). Finally, she all but steams open Antonio's mail and mercifies him with the good news of his solvency (5.1.273–78).

Antonio's struggle with Portia over Bassanio becomes a battle of competitive donation. But poor Antonio! He loses, despite the fact that he actually stands for sacrifice several times—more often and more enthusiastically than Portia. When Shylock proposes in 1.3 to forego usury for a merry bond, he performs a bracingly sarcastic send-up of Antonio's Christlike generosity (1.3.138–72). And when he flaunts his commitment to usury, it's partly to show his impatience with Antonio's resort to the something for nothing that's never truly free—and that is in fact aggressively aimed at Shylock.

By the end of the trial scene, Antonio finds that he has placed himself and Bassanio in the very hands he feared. Before, Shylock had become a means to enable him to keep Portia from taking over his share of love. Now Shylock has become the means by which Portia imposes her bond on him as well as on Bassanio. She outclasses Antonio in the battle of donors and then humiliates him by saving him, after which she announces the good news about his ships in such a manner as to take at least stage credit for it.

Critics who view *The Merchant of Venice* as an anti-Semitic play fail to appreciate the parodic charges that flash like lightning between Shylock and the other principals, between his direct and their devious

negotiations with the modes of usury.[1] His usury inverts and carica-
tures the negative usury practiced by Portia and Antonio. His exple-
tory wrath inverts and parodies the lust Antonio quietly displaces to
his pious gestures of self-sacrificing friendship.

In the late sixteenth century, according to James Shapiro, "Jews were
increasingly identified not with usury per se, but with outrageous and
exploitative lending for profit." This enabled the English "to imagine a villainous moneylender whose fictional excesses overshadowed
their own very real acts of exploitation."[2] Shapiro's characterization of
Shylock fits this historical context, but it leaves other features out of
account. It ignores the possibility that Shakespeare's script encourages
the actor playing Shylock not merely to play him with histrionic flair
but to make Shylock play Shylock with histrionic flair. Lars Engle and
Kenneth Gross argue that he recognizes "the kind of emotional 'interest'" Antonio exacts "from his own loans" and responds by playing the
Jew as victim/revenger.[3]

In a finely nuanced analysis of Shylock's rhetoric in 1.3, Danson
portrays him as a witty thespian who controls his interlocutors' responses to him.[4] His raspy and theatrically expressive performance
of anti-Semitic stereotypes—stereotypes of Jewish greed, wrath,
and vengeance—works the same way. His portrayal of the victim/
revenger inverts and mocks the appeal to the melodramatic sacrificial pose in which Antonio dresses up his lending, his losses, and
his lust.[5] Antonio is asking for trouble. Shylock lets him have it.
Nor does he have any patience with Portia's talk of mercy. In the
history of *Merchant* interpretation, Shylock is the original critic of
mercifixion.

Gross thinks that even as Shylock "refuses to yield to the Christians'
persuasions" he shows himself to be "their creature, their cur, the em-

1. See, for example, Derek Cohen, *Shakespearean Motives* (London: Macmillan, 1988),
104–18.
2. Shapiro, *Shakespeare and the Jews*, 99.
3. Engle, *Shakespearean Pragmatism*, 240; Kenneth Gross, *Shylock Is Shakespeare* (Chicago: University of Chicago Press, 2006), 65–96 and passim.
4. Danson, *Harmonies*, 139–57.
5. On this, see the excellent commentary by Gross in *Shylock Is Shakespeare*, 75–77,
85–86, 153–57, and passim.

bodied form of their fears (including their hidden terror at their own rage as it is directed at this imaginary monster). . . . Shylock's hatred is a mirror of Christian hatred; he shows that hatred in its ferocity and its arbitrariness."[6] I'm not sure that or how the text of the play shows the Christians to be terrified by their own rage. What it does show is this: the ferocity of their hatred of Shylock measures their failure to acknowledge the cost of the embarrassment and distrust that dominates their relations with each other.

Shylock treats his daughter in a manner that stands in sharp contrast to the subterfuges of Portia and her father. He mistakenly trusts Jessica to lock up the house, stay out of trouble, and be responsible when he's gone. But at least he trusts her. By comparison, there is something deeply sick in the elaborate legal stratagem by which Portia's father tries to lock up his daughter within the confines of his dead and surviving will. Both daughters defy their fathers, but because Jessica's blithely straightforward "here, catch this casket" precedes the more surreptitious casketry of Belmont, it has the force (as I note above) of proleptic parody. Parody demystifies, but in doing so it brings out the obliquity, the furtiveness and underhandedness, the profound creepiness, of what has been demystified.

17. STANDING FOR JUDGMENT

Against any assertion or enactment of the stand for sacrifice, Shylock pits his Old Testament imperative. The Duke asks Shylock how he can "hope for mercy, rendering none," and Shylock brushes that hope aside: "What judgment shall I dread . . .? . . . I stand for judgment" (4.1.89, 103). Jewishness would triumph over Christianity if Shylock's call for judgment were to be repaid in kind, for then the Christians would be playing by Jewish rules and be untrue to themselves. But at the end he abandons the stand for judgment. His three whining demands are tests of Christian mercy: "Pay the bond thrice / And let the Christian go" (4.1.315–16); "Give me my principal and let me go" (4.1.333); give Antonio the principal and let me go—"Why, then, the devil give him good of it! / I'll stay no longer question" (4.1.342–43).

6. Ibid., 77.

Despite her paean to the gentle rain, Portia responds to Shylock's demands not with mercy but with strict justice. She respects his claim and treats the bond as seriously as it deserves. Since the forfeit in question would jeopardize Antonio's life, she changes the charge to attempted murder, for she has done her homework and found among "the laws of Venice" one that applies to an alien guilty of this charge: he is to forfeit one half of his estate to the injured party and the other half to the state. Let the villain therefore kneel down and "beg mercy of the Duke" (4.1.343–60).

At this point Gratiano shoots off another of his trademark insults which the Duke immediately counters with a good deed, as if to show that Venetians are more gracious and generous than Gratiano. He mercifies Shylock: "That thou shall see the difference of our spirit,/I pardon thee thy life before thou ask it" (4.1.365–66). He then goes on to impose the penalty Portia had just described.

Shylock protests that to keep him alive so he can suffer punishment is factitious mercy: "Nay, take my life and all, pardon not that" (4.1.370). This could be a demand that they commit themselves to strict Jewish justice and bypass Christian mercy. Or it could be a request for mercy: if you're going to spare me and show true mercy, you'll have to do better. Shylock may expect or even hope to be condemned to death to prove the Jewishness and hypocrisy of the Christians.

Asked what mercy he can render Shylock, Antonio offers to sprinkle some gentle rain along the path to lawful revenge: "I am content" to let Shylock keep "one half of his goods," provided that he invest the other half in a trust for "the gentleman/That lately stole his daughter" (4.1.377–87). The last line commands attention because its shortness—it is an iambic trimeter—intensifies the effect of "stole." "Stole" twists the knife: let Lorenzo's thievery be rewarded with a trust fund. Antonio then adds a gratuitous, humiliating, and not very merciful rider: let Shylock "presently [immediately] become a Christian" (4.1.384).

Portia drives this package home, "Art thou contented, Jew?" and insists on a response: "What dost thou say?" His "I am content" is an act of submission. Danson states that, although it "may be pronounced bitterly," the deeper feeling it expresses is "profound weariness."[1] But

---

1. Danson, *Harmonies*, 168. Danson's analysis of Shylock's deterioration is detailed, compelling, and persuasive. See *Harmonies*, 126–69, in general, but especially 157–69.

because Shylock echoes Antonio's words, it has the force of a riposte (4.1.390–91).[2] It may also be read as a conspicuous refusal to betray true feelings to the enemies who fill the courtroom. After Portia instructs the clerk to "draw a deed of gift," his final words are "I pray you, give me leave to go from hence;/I am not well." He asks to have the deed sent to him, promises to sign it, and hurriedly departs.

The feelings registered in Shylock's language have been well described by Kenneth Gross in the course of explaining a variant in 4.1. After the Duke opens the session by asking Shylock whether and why he intends to persist in his demand, Shylock curtly answers that "it is my humor." He goes on to cite other examples of irrational prejudice and concludes that "I can give no reason, nor I will not,/More than a lodged hate and certain loathing/I bear Antonio" (4.1.43, 59–61).

In one of these examples, a man can't contain his urine when he hears a bagpipe "but of force/Must yield to such inevitable shame/As *to offend himself being offended*" (4.1.56–58, my italics). This is the First Quarto and Folio reading. Subsequent editors often follow the Second Quarto text and place a comma after "offend": "to offend, himself being offended." Gross prefers the compressed-chiasmus effect of the unpointed Folio version ("to offend himself being offended") because it intensifies the "idea of self-offense": "Shylock . . . implicitly acknowledges something of his own shame, humiliation, and terror in this scene, his willful abandonment of human dignity and answerability in the process of making his revenge 'inevitable.'"[3]

In David Miller's words, Antonio "manipulates and entraps" Shylock, "maneuvering him into the role of latter-day Christ-killer and using him ruthlessly to underwrite a sanctimonious homoerotic martyrdom."[4] When the Duke and Antonio spare both his life and his means of living, he suffers the defeat of mercifixion. He loses the

---

For the idea that "I am content" expresses "weary acknowledgment" rather than "mean-spiritedness," see Barbara K. Lewalski, "Biblical Allusion and Allegory in *The Merchant of Venice*," *Shakespeare Quarterly* 13 (1962): 341.

2. "Art thou contented, Jew?": placing the accent on "thou" sharpens the challenge. It invites an echoing accent on the first word of Shylock's "I am content." Were an actor to accent Shylock's third word, the tone would shift from submission to anger. To accent "am" would produce too obliging a response.

3. Gross, *Shylock Is Shakespeare*, 69.

4. Personal communication.

game he could have won only if they had acted like Jews. Having been judged and mercified, he leaves. He doesn't explode. He doesn't go up in flames. As Gratiano continues to vilify him he slips out quickly, quietly, and forever, elbowed off stage not by embarrassment merely but, like Lear, by "a sovereign shame" (*King Lear* 4.3.42–43).[5] And the Duke's "Get thee gone" has the effect of a kick administered to the departing figure.

He leaves, but he doesn't vanish. After he leaves and Portia (as Balthasar) turns down a ducal invitation to dinner, the Duke urges Antonio to "gratify this gentleman,/For in my mind you are much bound to him" (4.1.402–3). Poor Antonio! No sooner has he been freed from Shylock's bond than he hears that he is "much bound" to someone else. Does "much bound" ring the same bell for him as for the reader? "For three months . . . Antonio shall become bound. . . . Three thousand ducats for three months and Antonio bound" (1.3.3–9). As he is about to find out, the bond to Shylock has just been replaced by a more embarrassing and bitter bond to Portia.

Shylock haunts the fifth act as a remnant or remainder, "a residual threat within the Christian scene," even after his exit.[6] When Portia and Nerissa at play's end present Lorenzo with the deed, he responds, "Fair ladies, you drop manna in the way/Of starved people" (5.1.294–95). Shylock's new heir glibly steps into the role of Wandering Jew headed for the promised land of property.[7] References to the bond, the forfeit, and the deed of gift throw Shylock's shadow over the closing conversations, even as the elimination of the scapegoat sharpens our awareness of another effect.[8]

His defeat doesn't pacify or placate the others. At the end of the play, his marked absence resonates in and as the hollowness of their reas-

---

5. Many thanks to Jody Greene for helping me sort out the distinction and interaction between embarrassment and shame.

6. Julia Reinhard Lupton, *Citizen-Saints: Shakespeare and Political Theory* (Chicago: University of Chicago Press, 2005), 92. See, more generally, 75–101. See also Lauren Silberman, "Shakespeare as Spenserian Allegorist," paper delivered at the 2003 Modern Language Association meeting, San Diego.

7. Adelman notes that "manna spoils when it is used with the kind of greed that Jessica and Lorenzo have already amply demonstrated" (*Blood Relations*, 62).

8. See 5.1.14–17, 134–35, 142ff., 249–53, and 291–93.

sembly. They try, without much success, to keep their repartée sportive. Uneasiness of tone characterizes all the interchanges of Act 5, from the troubled moonlit badinage of Lorenzo and Jessica to the chivying that vexes the final discussion.

For example, although Portia scolds the delinquents in mock outrage, she is having too much fun. She likes to win. She sets up Bassanio to look bad, and he, predictably, doesn't disappoint: the worm squirms as she enjoys not only her triumph but also her adventures in cross-dressing and lawyering. Her final words are salted by a legalism that suggests she plans to continue lawyering after the play ends: "Let us go in;/And charge us there upon inter'gatories,/And we will answer all things faithfully" (5.1.297–99). But who has any more questions to ask or news to give?

18. STANDING FOR SACRIFICE

Antonio spends most of Act 4 Scene 1 preparing to stand for sacrifice: the Jew is hard-hearted and will not relent; make no more offers. "Let me have judgment and the Jew his will" (4.1.80–83). Shylock's "I stand for judgment" oddly echoes Portia's "I stand for sacrifice," even as it pillories in advance Antonio's pathetic effort to overgo Portia by carrying out the sacrifice she merely stands for:

> I am a tainted wether of the flock,
> Meetest for death: the weakest kind of fruit
> Drops earliest to the ground; and so let me.
> You cannot better be employed, Bassanio,
> Than to live still and write mine epitaph.
>
> (4.1.114–18)

This follows and competes with one of Bassanio's loose-lipped proclamations of self-sacrifice:

> Good cheer, Antonio. What, man, courage yet!
> The Jew shall have my flesh, blood, bones and all,
> Ere thou shalt lose for me one drop of blood.
>
> (4.1.111–13)

To this the proper response is, "Yeah, sure."

The arrival of Nerissa onstage temporarily clears the air of sancti-monious bluster, and some forty lines later Portia appears, disguised as Balthasar. The courtroom scene sizzles with metatheatrical energy as the boy actors who play the two women shift into higher gear and lower voice when their women pretend to be men.

Portia's Balthasar is not only a "young and learned doctor." "He" is very wicked. His brashly direct question, "Which is the merchant here, and which the Jew" (4.1.171), is often taken to insinuate that there isn't much difference between them.[1] He delivers his famous "qual-ity of mercy" speech almost as soon as he enters the courtroom, and its message to Shylock is clear: "No one can be forced to be merciful. But if you don't show mercy to Antonio, he'll suffer the sentence pro-nounced by this strict Venetian court. You don't want that, do you?" Of course he does, and Portia knows it. Therefore he deserves no mercy himself. Her paean to mercy is the first step in her plan to deny Shy-lock mercy.

A. R. Braunmuller reads her speech as "the opening salvo of a bar-rage that steadily forces Shylock to a louder and louder insistence on the bond and a growing certainty that Portia unequivocally supports his demand."[2] He acknowledges that it is possible to see 4.1 as "some-thing far nastier" than a hearing and that Portia's treatment of Shylock may appear "vengeful" and "repugnant" to a modern audience. But he goes on to cite biblical precedents and generic conventions that would soften the effect—would persuade Shakespeare's contemporaries to view the treatment of Shylock as a form of comic come-uppance.[3]

My own view is a little different because it is based on darker read-ings of the play like those of René Girard and Stephen Orgel. Girard

---

1. See, for example, Leah Marcus's statement in William Shakespeare, *The Merchant of Venice*, ed. Marcus (New York: W.W. Norton, 2006), x. Both the tone and the intent of Portia's question themselves depend on more basic decisions at the level of production—the decision, for example, to racialize the conflict by physically accentuating Shylock's ethnicity. On this issue in general, the discussion I've found most illuminating is again Adelman's. See *Blood Relations*, 63–96 and passim.

2. Braunmuller, *The Merchant of Venice*, xliv.

3. Ibid., xlvi–xlvii. The specific comic conventions Braunmuller cites are those of "the Biter Bit" and "the heavy father." For a trenchant critique and revision of earlier defenses of the comic come-uppance view (by C. L. Barber and E. E. Stoll), see Gross, *Shylock Is Shakespeare*, 79–83.

argues that, although the Christians are eager to demonstrate their difference from the Jews, even the words they use to differentiate themselves are the same as those Shylock uses. "Everywhere the same senseless obsession with differences becomes exacerbated as it keeps defeating itself."[4] The assurance of the comic rhythm doesn't purge this nastiness but lets it safely run its course. Portia's performance as Balthasar is a case in point.

"He" is by turns brusque and disdainful toward both Shylock and Antonio. He addresses or refers to Antonio as "merchant" four times and doesn't name him until line 370. He calls Shylock "Jew" nine times (three in direct address) and "Shylock" only thrice. But "Which is the merchant here, and which the Jew" arrows toward Antonio: Portia pretends she can't distinguish her rival for Bassanio's affections from the Jew.

Girard finds this surprising "in view of the enormous difference, visible to all," which supposedly distinguishes Shylock from the Christians.[5] But the motive behind Portia's snide act of "undifferentiation" is clear. Her prosecution of Shylock both masks and expedites her pursuit of Antonio.

Antonio is Portia's Shylock. She proceeds in a manner calculated to let him sweat the outcome of a hearing that threatens him either with a painful loss of life or with a painful loss of Bassanio. After affirming Shylock's right, she warns Antonio to prepare his bosom for the knife. The merchant needs no encouragement:

> I am armed and well prepared.
> Give me your hand, Bassanio; fare you well!
> Grieve not that I am fall'n to this for you.
>
> (4.1.261–63)

This is the tainted wether's revenge on Bassanio and Portia. It will be his last—and therefore his winning—gift. He goes on reassuringly if irrelevantly to explain that the final forfeit will help him escape the horrors of old age (4.1.265–69). Even better, it will teach his rival Portia what it takes to be a true lover:

---

4. René Girard, *A Theater of Envy: William Shakespeare* (New York: Oxford University Press, 1991), 246.

5. Ibid., 247.

> Commend me to your honorable wife.
> Tell her the process of Antonio's end,
> Say how I loved you, speak me fair in death;
> And when the tale is told, bid her be judge
> Whether Bassanio had not once a love.
>
> (4.1.270–74)

Bassanio seems ready to fend off Antonio's claim when he replies, "I am married to a wife,/Which is as dear to me as life itself." But he then turns around and accedes to the claim when he offers up that very wife to save Antonio (4.1.280–91).[6] Gratiano follows suit, and the wives respond with light-hearted umbrage. They savor both the fruits of their disguise and the foretaste of their revenge:

> Your wife would give you little thanks for that,
> If she were by to hear you make the offer.
>
> (4.1.285–86)

> 'Tis well you offer it behind her back;
> The wish would make else an unquiet house.
>
> (4.1.290–91)

Only Shylock greets the husbands' tactless offers with appropriate disdain: "These be the Christian husbands" (4.1.292). He might well have added, "These be the Christian wives."

19. "HERE IS THE MONEY": BASSANIO IN THE BOND MARKET

During the courtroom scene, Bassanio offers five times to repay Antonio's debt. Before Portia enters he threatens to give Shylock twice what

---

6. In the excellent introduction to her edition of the play, Lindsay Kaplan observes that "Antonio seems to set up a competition here between himself and Portia, one he apparently wins, given Bassanio's response that he esteems his friend above his wife and his subsequent willingness to give up Portia's ring to thank the 'doctor of law' for saving his friend." At the conclusion, however, Portia "appears to win" when she shames "Antonio into insuring that her husband will remain true to her": M. Lindsay Kaplan, introduction to *The Merchant of Venice: Texts and Contexts* (New York: Palgrave, 2002), 16.

Antonio owes (4.1.84). He then restates and sweetens his offer four times in her presence, and each time she overrules him (4.1.206–19, 279–86, 316–19, 334–36). After his libertine generosity leads him to tender from two to ten times the sum and even more (his hands, his head, his heart), Portia shuts him down, asks to scrutinize the bond, and reminds Shylock that he has been offered thrice the sum he demanded (4.1.206–24).

Since 3.2 Portia has in effect been giving Bassanio his allowance. Therefore she fully understands the first principle of Bassanian finance: any cash he eagerly presses on Shylock will be hers. At 4.1.212–13 she watches as Bassanio offers to save Antonio's life with her money and then beseeches her to cut corners and cheat a little: "Wrest once the law to your authority./To do a great right, do a little wrong." She had already expressed her willingness to discharge the debt (3.2.297–306). But although she's prepared to rescue Antonio and help Bassanio, she refuses to pay and instead draws the process out as if to tweak them before she saves them.

At the end of the hearing, she turns down the payment of three thousand ducats tendered by Bassanio and Antonio: "I, delivering you, am satisfied,/And therein do account myself well paid" (4.1.413–14). Portia thus stays ahead in the game of imposing obligations. This is the charity that wounds.

"It wasn't my fault," Bassanio whimpers in the final scene, "Antonio made me do it" (5.1.216, 240). And as his glib if musically redundant disclaimer at 5.1.193–98 shows, his capacity for embarrassment protects him from shame. Portia can hardly be unaware of this. Yet that must be what she wants.

20. TWILIGHT IN BELMONT: PORTIA'S RING CYCLE

None of this seems to matter in the glow of happy ending. But the glow is garish. Its forced brightness is the flush of embarrassment, which makes the Belmont night seem "but the daylight sick." How else could the situation appear to Portia, who has to tolerate confessional treacle not only from Bassanio but also from Antonio? As she and the others try to initiate closure, the merchant listens silently to their accusations and protestations for almost a hundred lines. He knows he is the true subject of the reproach Portia aims at Bassanio in the form of a general rhetorical question:

> What man is there so much unreasonable,
> If you had pleased to have defended it
> With any terms of zeal, wanted the modesty
> To urge the thing held as a ceremony?
>
> (5.1.203–6)

Finally, Antonio breaks in to remind them that "I am th'unhappy subject of these quarrels" (5.1.238).

Portia's response is cunningly bland: "Sir, grieve not you; you are welcome notwithstanding" (5.1.239). But "notwithstanding" bites deep. It recalls Antonio's charged use of the term in his Last-Things letter to Bassanio (3.2.317). "Notwithstanding"—"in spite of everything you did"—includes a reference to the moment in which he specifically asked Bassanio "to choose between his promise to his wife and his debt to Antonio":[1]

> My Lord Bassanio, let him have the ring.
> Let his deservings and my love withal
> Be valued 'gainst your wife's commandement.
>
> (4.1.446–48)

And, as Gilbert adds, when Bassanio defends this act in the final scene, he "never directly mentions Antonio's request."[2]

In 5.1, Antonio documents his own deservings:

> I once did lend my body for his wealth,
> Which, but for him that had your husband's ring,
> Had quite miscarried. I dare be bound again,
> My soul upon the forfeit, that your lord
> Will nevermore break faith advisedly.
>
> (5.1.249–53)

He acknowledges his obligation to Portia by recalling the bond and forfeit from which she saved him. At the same time, he continues hap-

---

1. Miriam Gilbert, *Shakespeare at Stratford: The Merchant of Venice* (London: Thomson Learning, 2002), 53.
2. Ibid.

lessly to speak as if he still owned Bassanio and as if he, not Portia, were determining Bassanio's choices.

After Shylock has been taken down, the Venetians redirect their apprehensions toward each other. Portia berates Gratiano in words aimed at Antonio and Bassanio:

> You were to blame—I must be plain with you—
> To part so slightly with your wife's first gift,
> A thing stuck on with oaths upon your finger,
> And so riveted with faith unto your flesh.
> I gave my love a ring and made him swear
> Never to part with it; and here he stands.
> I dare be sworn for him he would not leave it,
> Nor pluck it from his finger for the wealth
> That the world masters.   (5.1.164–74)

There is a fury in these words, even as they clang with Portia's self-satisfaction at the success of the stratagem she herself had devised and put into play at 3.2.171: "I give . . . this ring/Which when you part from, lose, or give away,/Let it presage the ruin of your love." Portia would be the last to acknowledge the truth of the motivation behind the ring trick: "All the ruse does, all it is designed to do, is give the wives a grudge to hold over their husbands forever: this is what the primacy of marriage depends on, this is the reason that husbands should be faithful."[3] The fury in her words is the fury of embarrassment.

21. DEATH IN VENICE

The "stand for judgment" is a stand Shylock can't sustain, a battle he can't win, not because he is a villain or a clown but because he is caught in the deeper, more intense conflict between Portia and Antonio over the final disposition of Bassanio. He has let himself become the means by which, the target at which, they displace their aggression against each other.

At the end, his simple straightforward tightlipped concession of defeat—"I am content"—is like a breath of fresh air in the murky

---

3. Orgel, "Shylock's Tribe," 50.

moral perimeter of embarrassment Shakespeare calls Venice. It is a relief from the knavish arts of casketry practiced crudely by Jessica and Lorenzo, and more subtly or at least more cautiously by Portia and Bassanio. It's also a relief from Antonio's persistent tendency to show that whatever his words say, they always mean "I stand for crucifixion."

Adelman remarks that "the vulnerability of Antonio's body to the Jew's knife makes him briefly a type of Christ."[1] The trouble is that this is an opinion Antonio appears—at least briefly—to share and even to advertise. He takes his stand not against Shylock but against his real rival, Portia. She retaliates with an appropriate act of negative usury. She gives Antonio more than he asks for and takes from him more than he offers.

The good news that he is solvent first strikes him dumb—so he says (5.1.279)—and then triggers his last words in the play: "Sweet lady, you have given me life and living,/For here I read for certain that my ships/Are safely come to road" (5.1.286–88). Why this calorific exhalation of gratitude? Portia is only the messenger. What I imagine the merchant of Venice to have on his mind but avoid saying is that she has out-bartered him. She gives him news of "life and living" and in exchange prevents him from loving.

The important thing Portia notes about God's mercy is that it is "twice blest." It blesses not only givers—she describes mercy as the privilege of kings and God—but also takers (4.1.183–84). And she is a taker. During the casket scene she competes both with her late father and with Bassanio. In the courtroom she uses her attack on Shylock to embarrass Antonio, subjugate Bassanio, and tear him apart from Antonio. As the play ends, she inflicts God's mercy in the form of the Christlike wound of mercifixion. Her salvific mercy drops on Antonio less like the gentle rain than like a ton of bricks. He understands the fury in her words.

The Merchant of Venice represents "Venice" as the site of polyglot cultural activity, a trading center that brings together people of different origins. Insiders mingle with outsiders, Christians with Jews and Moors, merchants and moneylenders with soldiers, servants, aris-

---

1. Adelman, "Her Father's Blood," 23. "Briefly" is the important term in this formulation.

tocrats, and rulers.[2] Their relations with each other are intimately affected by the fortunes floating on their flotillas far from home and by
the news or gossip about these flotillas that travels through town. Consequently, as a system of inheritance, alliance, and exchange, Shakespeare's Venice is both ordered and embarrassed by overlapping racial,
social, religious, and economic boundaries that are permeable, that in-
vite transgression, and that are affected by remote events.

As W. H. Auden describes it, Venice is "inhabited by various communities with different loves . . . who do not regard each other personally as brothers, but must tolerate each other's existence." Like most
commentators, Auden emphasizes the incompatibility of "the romantic fairy story of Belmont" and "the historical reality of money-making
Venice," but he differs at one point when he insists the play compels
us "to acknowledge that the attraction which we naturally feel toward
Belmont is highly questionable." For this reason "*The Merchant of Venice* must be classed among Shakespeare's 'Unpleasant Plays.'"[3]

I don't think this standard distinction between Belmont and Venice
cuts very deep. The themes of property and inheritance affect both
Portia's story and Jessica's with equal force. If anything, Belmont is a
kind of marriage entrepôt, a place for the temporary deposit of suitors
who come to exchange their self-respect for "a lady richly left."

"Politically speaking," Auden writes of the level of society represented in *Merchant*, "the more advanced the social organization, the
greater the moral demands it makes upon its members and the greater
degree of guilt which they incur if they fail to meet these demands."[4]
In the light of the preceding account, Auden's statement can be im-
proved by replacing "guilt" with "embarrassment."

Michael Ferber identifies three "ideologies" in the play: "aristocratic
virtues," "mercantile interests," and "Christianity."[5] But "ideologies,"
as Ferber uses the term, is too neutral to apply to what we've seen so

2. On the "local color" of Shakespeare's Venice, see M. M. Mahood's introduction to
her New Cambridge Shakespeare edition of the play (Cambridge: Cambridge University
Press, 1987), 12–15.

3. Auden, "Brothers and Others," 220–21, 233.

4. Ibid., 235.

5. Ferber, "The Ideology of *The Merchant of Venice*," 435–41.

far: "systems of institutionalized bad faith" would be more accurate.[6] *The Merchant of Venice* features a conflict between two such systems. One claims to stand for justice and the other for sacrifice, but both legitimize the pursuit of avarice and revenge in ways that embarrass the agents of pursuit no less than their victims. The bad faith of the Jewish minority features the justice of the bond and the justified revenge of an eye for an eye. Christian bad faith derides Jewish bad faith and opposes to it the discourse of the gift, the sacrificial display of "something for nothing."[7] But "something for nothing" is the Christians' own weapon of revenge: revenge through the charity that embarrasses the donee; revenge through mercifixion.

"Venice" is the culture produced by this conflict. Its failure has been well described by Girard:

> [Shylock] alone speaks a truth that the Christians hypocritically deny. The truth of the play is retribution and revenge. The Christians manage to hide that truth even from themselves. They do not live by the law of charity, but this law is enough of a presence in their language to drive the law of revenge underground, to make this revenge almost invisible. As a result, this revenge becomes more subtle, skillful, and feline than the revenge of Shylock. The Christians will easily destroy Shylock, but they will go on living in a world that is sad without knowing why, a world in which even the difference between revenge and charity has been abolished.[8]

If *Merchant* is not a tragedy, it's because nobody manages to kill or to die before the play ends. But as Grace Tiffany has so effectively shown in her study of the characters' names, there *is* "death in Venice."

---

6. "An ideology is a set of related ideas, images, and values more or less distorted by the social or material interests of those who believe and propagate it. It gives 'the form of universality' to a particular bias, ignoring certain facts while privileging others, and defining certain unequal social relationships as natural and divinely ordained": Ferber, "The Ideology of *The Merchant of Venice*," 434.

7. "The Christians in this play . . . need Shylock in order to stage the possibility of mercy. And yet it is precisely this sense of staginess that engenders the concern of bad faith. The more Portia tries to compel mercy through demonstrating the failure of justice, the more the whole setup risks seeming rigged" (Freinkel, *Reading Shakespeare's Will*, 291).

8. Girard, *A Theater of Envy*, 247.

Death lurks not only in the caskets of Belmont and "the locked spaces of Shylock's house."[9] A quiet deadliness curls like a mist around the characters and wraps them in the sadness Girard describes—a mist in which the *curiositas* that fuels gossip mingles with distrust of others and sends xenophobia drifting inward from outsiders to fellow citizens.

The play concludes with a salvo of uneasy exchanges dominated by the "noise-maker," Gratiano, who can't stop cracking jokes about cuckolds and rings.[10] Portia rebukes him at one point in order to keep everyone on message: "Speak not so grossly. You are all amazed./Here is a letter; read it at your leisure" (5.1.266–67). But in her eagerness to shoot the final arrow she forestalls leisurely reading: "There you shall find that Portia was the doctor,/Nerissa there her clerk" (5.1.269–70). It is, tellingly, Gratiano who leaves the taste of Venice in our mouths by polishing off the play with three couplets full of silly snarks about sex with Nerissa (5.1.302–7). The taste of Venice is the taste of embarrassment.

I stand for sacrifice. I stand for judgment. Only the rhythm of comedy can impose on these dissonant claims the harmony of "a mutual stand" (5.1.77). And only, to borrow Lorenzo's qualifying words, "for the time" (5.1.82)—for the brief moment immured within the garden of the comic genre. Into the moral mistiness of *Merchant*'s Venice, *Othello* will send its more lethal characters with their more furious words. If *Merchant* is a comedy of embarrassment, *Othello* is a tragedy of embarrassment. With a sharpness of focus absent from the portrayal of Shylock, it mercilessly targets the protagonist's embarrassment at being a black outsider involved with and married to a young white Venetian aristocrat.

Tragedy breaks down the garden wall, undermines it with the seismic force of its peculiar complicity: the complicity between the victims and their villain, who is unable to ruin them without their help. Lynda Boose's classic essay on *Othello* has shown how, in Shakespeare's Ven-

9. Grace Tiffany, "Names in *The Merchant of Venice*," in *The Merchant of Venice: New Critical Essays*, ed. John W. Mahon and Ellen MacLeod Mahon (New York: Routledge, 2002), 360.

10. For Gratiano as "noise-maker," see Gilbert, *Shakespeare at Stratford*, 59.

ice, rage is embedded in wifely love and entwined with lurking contempt.[11] This is what Portia's language and behavior betray about her feeling for Bassanio. It is what finally pushes up through Desdemona's language (with Emilia's help) at the end of her life.

"I am more sinned against than sinning" is the formula for the victim's discourse. Its obverse is the villain's boast, "I am more sinning than sinned against." But villainy, despite its brassiness, thrives on contingency, on redundancy. For all his blather, Iago is embarrassed by redundancy. He is not the autogenetic source of evil he fancies himself to be. His victims started doing his work for him well before he started doing it. His agency gets progressively hollowed out by Othello, Cassio, Desdemona, and Emilia. In the remainder of this book, I'll try to develop aspects of Boose's great insight: the most compelling and unsettling feature of Shakespeare's Venetian tragedy is that Iago's basic plan to triangulate the lovers with Cassio was embarrassingly anticipated and put into play by the lovers themselves.

What seems truly bizarre in all this is that, during most of the play, the great thing of them forgot—them being Othello, Desdemona, and Cassio—is Cassio's role in the courtship. At least they don't bring it up until Act 3 Scene 3. Are we to suppose that it was never in their thoughts during the conversations and events preceding its revelation? And wouldn't actors who decelerate the play in rehearsal imagine and discuss the ways in which their characters' physical or verbal behavior might be affected by that knowledge?

11. Lynda E. Boose, "Let It Be Hid: The Pornographic Aesthetic of Shakespeare's *Othello*," in *'Othello': Contemporary Critical Essays*, ed. Lena Cowen Orlin (New York: Palgrave Macmillan, 2004), 22–48. Reprinted from *Women, Violence, and English Renaissance Literature*, ed. Linda Woodbridge and Sharon Beehler (Phoenix: Arizona State University Press, 2003), 34–58. See also Boose, "Scolding Brides and Bridling Scolds: Taming the Woman's Unruly Member," *Shakespeare Quarterly* 42 (1991): 179–213.

PART TWO

Three's Company: Contaminated Intimacy *in* Othello

22. PREHISTORY IN *OTHELLO*

A gentle riddance. Draw the curtains, go.
Let all of his complexion choose me so.
—*The Merchant of Venice*, 2.7.77–79

The Tragedie of Othello the Moore of Venice targets the embarrassment of the middle-aged Moorish commander of the Venetian army who elopes with a young white woman just before the play begins. Desdemona is the daughter of a Venetian aristocrat, Brabantio. The elopement follows a period of courtship during which Othello asked Michael Cassio, his ancient (ensign or standard-bearer), to serve as a go-between and help him woo her. We learn about the elopement at the start of the play. We also learn that, while Othello promoted Cassio from ancient to lieutenant, he failed to promote his other ancient, Iago. But Cassio's part in the elopement is revealed neither to us nor (more importantly) to Iago until later in the play—well after Iago has decided to "abuse Othello's ear" that Cassio "is too familiar with his wife" (1.3.391–98).[1]

What makes this dicey situation even more difficult and compromising is the comic backwash lengthening in the wake of *The Mer-*

---

1. As I noted in the Introduction, the text of Shakespeare's *Othello* cited in this study is E. J. A. Honigmann's in *The Arden Shakespeare*, Third Series (Walton-on-Thames, Surrey: Thomas Nelson & Sons, 1997). Honigmann's interpretive essay and glosses are among the very best in the Arden series. I've benefited greatly from them, even—or perhaps especially—when my uncertainty about his readings have forced me back into the text to reevaluate my own.

chant of Venice. We approach the Moor of Venice through the misty
spume of his positional predecessors. The embarrassing protagonist he
replaces is Bassanio, and the alien is Shylock. He fares no better in his
choice of friends: Iago and Cassio pick up where Antonio left off. The
shift from the comedy to the tragedy of embarrassment is especially
costly to the female protagonist. Portia is the Embarrasser, but Desdemona is the Embarrassee.

Finally, Othello's entrance into the play is festooned with the ridiculous memory of his kinsman, another man "of royal siege," the Prince
of Morocco:

> Mislike me not for my complexion,
> The shadowed livery of the burnish'd sun,
> To whom I am a neighbour and near bred.
> Bring me the fairest creature northward born,
> Where Phoebus' fire scarce thaws the icicles,
> And let us make incision for your love
> To prove whose blood is reddest, his or mine.
> *(Merchant of Venice* 2.1.1–7)

It isn't easy for the Moor of Venice to make his proper mark against
this backdrop of buffoonery, and matters aren't helped by the invidious epithets Roderigo and Iago spray at "his Moorship" in 1.1, well
before he appears on stage: "thicklips," "old black ram," "Barbary
horse," "beast," "the gross clasps of a lascivious Moor," "an extravagant
and wheeling stranger / Of here and everywhere."[2]

The first scene plunges viewers and readers so deeply in medias res as
to make them feel like outsiders intruding on a conversation whose wandering course is hard to follow but obviously clear to the participants:

RODERIGO

> Tush! never tell me; I take it much unkindly
> That thou, Iago, who hast had my purse
> As if the strings were thine, shouldst know of this.

IAGO

> 'Sblood, but you'll not hear me. If ever I did dream
> Of such a matter, abhor me.

2. 1.1.65, 87, 110, 115, 124, 134–35.

RODERIGO   Thou told'st me
    Thou didst hold him in thy hate.
IAGO   Despise me
    If I do not.   (1.1.1–7)

We can see that Roderigo has a grievance against Iago. But we have no idea what Roderigo's "this" and Iago's "such a matter" refer to. We take it for granted that they know what they're talking about, and eventually we catch up. Yet because Iago goes on to change the subject from Roderigo's grievance to his own, disclosure of the initial topic is conspicuously deferred.[3]

It isn't until line 66 that we begin to find out they opened the scene discussing the elopement. Only then do we understand the initial situation. Roderigo is a suitor whom Desdemona's father has rejected (1.1.95–97). He had been pressing—and paying—Iago to advance his cause. Just before 1.1.1 Iago must have broken the bad news to Roderigo and tried to commiserate him. Roderigo irritatedly cuts him off with "Tush! never tell me" and intimates that Iago knew about the elopement well before he mentioned it. Iago in effect responds: "You haven't been listening to me. I never dreamed it would happen. It's as surprising to me as it is to you."

The wordy protestation that follows (1.1.7–64) retroactively confers another sense on Roderigo's first speech: Iago seems to be defending against the suspicion that he not only knew about his commander's elopement but betrayed Roderigo by helping it happen. His defense consists in parading his sense of injured merit. He lashes out at "his Moorship," who astonishingly rejected his request for promotion and instead advanced

        a great arithmetician,
    One Michael Cassio, a Florentine,
    A fellow almost damned in a fair wife
    That never set a squadron in the field
    Nor the division of a battle knows
    More than a spinster.   (1.1.18–23)

---

3. The vagueness of exposition has often been noted. See, for example, Honigmann, 115, and M. R. Ridley, *Othello*, The Arden Shakespeare, Second Series, 7th ed. rev. (London: Methuen, 1958), xlix–l.

The status of these characterizations is unclear—line 20 is especially, and famously, mystifying—but their general import is very clear, and accentuated by the enjambment that binds the different attributions together into a singular portrait of effeminacy and unmanliness. Subsequent action interprets "almost damned in a fair wife" as meaning "almost damned in someone else's fair wife."

Iago assures Roderigo that, although he has been undervalued and victimized by Othello, he is very wicked, very dishonest, very dangerous:

> I follow him to serve my turn upon him. . . .
> In following him I follow but myself:
> Heaven is my judge, not I for love and duty
> But seeming so, for my peculiar end, . . .
>   . . . . I am not what I am.
>   (1.1.41–64)

Having thus cleared the air, he returns to Roderigo's problem and urges him to start making trouble for Othello by rousing Desdemona's father.

Throughout 1.1, the speakers demonstrate their familiarity with the topics under discussion (and inhibit ours) by relying on personal pronouns rather than proper nouns. Othello's name is not uttered until two scenes later (1.3.49). In 1.1 he is referred to only pronominally or by any of several invidious epithets. Desdemona is not mentioned until 1.1.66 and not named until 1.2.25.

The effect of conspicuous deferral combines with the stenographic quality of the conversational interchanges to reinforce our sense that the speakers are insiders and we are outsiders. This is especially frustrating because, since the play opens in medias res, it invites its viewers and readers to wonder what went on in the prehistory or back story it alludes to. Some details of that prehistory get filled in during 1.1 and many more in 1.3, when Othello tells his tale. But the most vital piece of information concerning the events that preceded 1.1—the role played by Cassio—is not disclosed until more than halfway through the play. This belated disclosure has uncanny force because it demands us to reinterpret everything that precedes it.

What happens in 3.3 is that Desdemona tries to arrange a meeting between Cassio and Othello with the aim of getting Cassio reinstated after his suspension in 2.3 for Dueling Under the Influence. Othello's reluctance to oblige irritates her and she reminds him how important Cassio was to their courtship:

> Tell me, Othello, I wonder in my soul
> What you would ask me that I should deny
> Or stand so mamm'ring on? What, Michael Cassio
> That came a-wooing with you? and so many a time
> When I have spoke of you dispraisingly
> Hathe ta'en your part, to have so much to do
> To bring him in? (3.3.68–74)

Cassio "came a-wooing with you." Snap! Just like that, we learn for the first time that the three principals have been choreographed in René Girard's dance of mimetic desire since before the play began.[4] Girard himself notes that, since Othello is an outsider who lacks confidence, he resorts to a go-between, and he sees in Cassio everything that he himself "is not: white, young, handsome, elegant, always at ease among the likes of Desdemona."[5]

Othello's jealousy, Girard concludes, "is rooted neither in what Desdemona does nor in what Iago says, but in the internal weakness that forces him to resort to a go-between in the first place."[6] Cassio has a daily beauty in his life that makes Othello ugly. Girard mistakenly calls Cassio "a true Venetian aristocrat." Cassio is a Florentine (1.1.19), an outsider like Othello. But the mistake is useful for two reasons: first, it picks out an impression Cassio would like to make, and second, it suggests that Othello may have chosen Cassio because he saw him as a successfully assimilated outsider.

Girard ignores the dramatic impact produced by deferring the information that Cassio had been the mediator who helped Othello win Desdemona. This means that Girard's triangular structure of fantasy,

---

4. A dance, incidentally, that gets performed in the shifting shadows of another triangle, the one in which Desdemona vies with her father for Othello's attention. On mimetic desire, see René Girard, *Deceit, Desire, and the Novel; Self and Other in Literary Structure*, trans. Yvonne Freccero (Baltimore: Johns Hopkins University Press, 1965).

5. René Girard, *A Theater of Envy: William Shakespeare* (New York: Oxford University Press, 1991), 290.

6. Ibid.

desire, and distrust was already in place and simmering beneath the surface before the play began. As Graham Bradshaw notes during his landmark study of *Othello* in *Misrepresentations*, all this is news to Iago, as well as to spectators and readers.[7] They are asked to reconsider, re-evaluate, reinterpret everything that has occurred since the beginning of the play.

A specter of contaminated intimacy gradually emerges and taints all that has happened up to 3.3. Something that, strangely, has never been said, a dark silence, slips belatedly beneath the floor of all prior interactions involving Othello, Desdemona, and Cassio. This is what haunts the play, and it haunts Othello's perception of and references to Desdemona in a manner that is unaffected by the frequently asked question "Did they or didn't they?"

Bradshaw was the first critic to give the specific consequences of this disclosure the attention they deserve. He argues compellingly that it can't be rationalized in terms of the theory of a double time scheme, which, he demonstrates, is redundant.[8] The double-time theory is symptomatic of an understandable interpretive anxiety aroused by apparent inconsistencies in the relation between what happens and how long it takes to happen. Reduced to its essentials, which I give in Joel Altman's paraphrase, the original justification for the theory is that "long time is needed to convince the audience that what Othello imagines has taken place could have taken place; short time is needed to make Othello's gullibility credible."[9]

The double-time hypothesis is a distorted response to a real problem. Critics who deploy it to make sense of inconsistencies overlook the fact that the belated disclosure puts into play an entirely different structure of temporality: the structure of *preposterity* or *the preposter-*

7. Graham Bradshaw, *Misrepresentations: Shakespeare and the Materialists* (Ithaca: Cornell University Press, 1993), 160.

8. Ibid., 156–63. His argument is especially damaging to those who think longer time is needed to make it feasible for Othello to suspect that Desdemona and Cassio have committed adultery. "What warrant," Bradshaw asks, "does the play provide for supposing that Othello is concerned only with what might have happened *after* his marriage? The answer is, none" (159).

9. Joel B. Altman, "'Preposterous Conclusions': Eros, *Enargeia*, and the Composition of *Othello*," *Representations* 18 (Spring 1987): 145.

ous, The preposterous is organized by the principle of inverse causality: "If A is the cause of B, then B is the cause that A is a cause; the effect is the cause of the cause; the cause is the effect of the effect."

This simple, lilting hypothesis lies at the root of the most influential criticism of the last century. It is the founding principle of deconstruction, and its basic premise is that the past is continuously recreated by or in the present. The principle draws its inspiration from a mix of now canonical sources (Hegel, Nietzsche, Foucault, Derrida, Lacan, to name a few). A staple of the hermeneutics of suspicion, it both presupposes and generates a skill of ironic reading.

In Shakespeare criticism, the various aspects of this structure have been brilliantly explored by Altman and Patricia Parker.[10] It's in terms of their explorations that I now turn to the question raised by the disclosure in 3.3. Why does it surface so belatedly and briefly, and then disappear, as if it has done its work? But what *is* its work? Is it only Iago who was looking for the opening it provides?

The idea that Othello is in Cassio's debt for premarital services shines a new light on his jumpy reaction to seeing Cassio leave Desdemona at 3.3.37 ("Was not that Cassio parted from my wife?"). Retroactively it invites us to reconsider earlier moments in the play. Recall Cassio's first appearance in 1.2, for example.

Like 1.1, the second scene begins in medias res. Iago has been inveighing against the animosity toward Othello of some unidentified "he"—whom we assume to be either Roderigo or Brabantio—and he then warns Othello that Brabantio is out to get him. Othello is in

10. Ibid., 129–57; Patricia Parker, *Shakespeare from the Margins: Language, Culture, Context* (Chicago: University of Chicago Press, 1996), chap. 1, esp. 48–52. See also the related discussion of "dilation" in *Othello* in chap. 7, esp. 248–52 and 268–70, and the earlier, more expanded version of these pages in "Shakespeare and Rhetoric: 'Dilation' and 'Delation' in *Othello*," in *Shakespeare and the Question of Theory,* ed. Parker and Geoffrey Hartman (New York: Methuen, 1985), 54–74. Altman and Parker focus on the grammatical, rhetorical, logical, genealogical, and chronological aspects of the preposterous—on linguistic, causal, and temporal inversions exemplified in hysteron proteron, metalepsis, and the larger structures of deconstructive historiography—also called "genealogy" in a restricted (and ironic) sense— associated with Nietzsche and Foucault. In what follows, my indebtedness to Altman and Parker will be obvious. But my attention will be directed toward a somewhat different aspect of *Othello*'s preposterous structure: the reinterpretation, necessitated by the disclosure in 3.3, of everything that occurred before it.

the midst of defending his pedigree with studied diffidence and hauteur when Cassio enters "with Officers and torches," at 1.2.28. He tells Othello the Duke and Senate require his presence "haste-post-haste" concerning some news from Cyprus,

As soon as Cassio enters, and before he can say a word, Iago brilliantly sees and seizes an opportunity for mischief. Speaking to Othello, he misidentifies Cassio's party as Brabantio's ("Those are the raised father and his friends," 1.2.29). He thus shifts Cassio from the martial to the marital context and from the party of Othello's public supporters to the party of his private enemies. This wicked misdirection is underlined twenty-five lines later, when Brabantio's party does indeed appear, again "with Officers and torches."

Since Cassio adds to his message from the Duke the news that "three several quests" have been sent to find Othello (1.2. 36–38 and 39–47), his must be the first of the three parties to make contact. Presumably he knew where to look. Othello responds, "'Tis well I am found by you," that is, "by *you* rather than by the others" outside the lovers' trysting place (1.2.47). This suggests that Cassio is in on the secret he pretends to hide.

Othello steps away briefly, and Cassio turns to Iago with a series of questions that seem disingenuous, intended to forestall any suspicion of his complicity in the elopement: "Ancient, what makes he here?," "I do not understand," married "To whom?" (1.2.49–52).[11] Cassio speaks once more in this scene: as the group headed by Brabantio and Roderigo enter, again "with Officers and torches," he tells Othello "Here comes another troop to seek for you" (1.2.54).[12] Cassio surely knows why. He then falls silent until 2.1.

"From the Renaissance to the end of the eighteenth century," Hayden White observes, "Europeans tended to fetishize the native peoples with whom they came into contact by viewing them simultaneously

---

11. "Certainly," Bradshaw notes, "no spectator watching the play for the first time could know that Cassio has reason to be discreet when he asks, 'To who?'" (*Misrepresentations*, 157).

12. Whether or not we're supposed to assume that this is one of the three "quests" sent by the Duke and Senate is not clear. The Duke's subsequent impatience with Brabantio and his insistence that he not interfere with state matters suggest that Brabantio's "quest" is a fourth party.

as monstrous forms of humanity and as quintessential objects of desire."[13] One of the achievements of Stanley Cavell's classic essay on *Othello* is to have posed the question of this divided view precisely in terms of the problem of Othello's self-representation. Cavell asks what Othello's blackness means "to him—for otherwise it is not Othello's color that we are interested in but some generalized blackness, meaning perhaps 'sooty' or 'filthy', as elsewhere in the play." He interprets Desdemona's "I saw Othello's visage in his mind" to mean "that she saw it as he sees it, that she understands his blackness as he understands it, as the expression (or in his word, the manifestation) of his mind." Then how, Cavell asks, does he understand it? And his answer is that Othello understands it as

> the color of a romantic hero. For he . . . is the hero of the tales of romance he tells, some ones of which he wooed and won Desdemona with, others of which he will die upon. It is accordingly the color of one of enchanted powers and of magical protection, but above all it is the color of one of purity, of a perfect soul.[14]

Cavell distinguishes Othello's interpretation from the pejorative one favored "elsewhere in the play," that is, among the Venetians. He argues that Othello tries to construe the thought of Desdemona's death as a sacrifice to "his image of himself and of her," a sacrifice that would "keep his image intact, uncontaminated; as if *this* were his protection from slander's image of him, say from a conventional view of his blackness."[15] But the problem for him is that he was "surprised by her, at what he has elicited from her; at, so to speak, a success rather than a failure"; surprised to discover that "she is flesh and blood," that she desires his desire and therefore that what she desires must be what the conventional view signifies.[16] What she desires must be the bestial qualities against which he defends.

---

13. Hayden White, "The Noble Savage Theme as Fetish," in *Tropics of Discourse: Essays in Cultural Criticism* (1978; rpt. Baltimore: Johns Hopkins University Press, 1985), 194.

14. Stanley Cavell, *Disowning Knowledge in Six Plays of Shakespeare* (Cambridge: Cambridge University Press, 1987), 129–30. In this context, the "vulnerable romanticism and epic grandeur" G. K. Hunter attributes to Othello take on the added force of defensive self-representation. See Hunter, "Othello and Colour Prejudice," *Proceedings of the British Academy* 53 (1967): 163.

15. Ibid., 137.

16. Ibid., 136.

My sole qualification of Cavell's reading is to emphasize the possibility that neither Desdemona nor Othello understands his blackness only as the color of the romantic hero. His effort to defend against "slander's image of him" and his inability to do so are evident in his language from the start.[17] They're especially evident in the way he describes his courtship to the Duke and the senators in 1.3.

While giving them an abstract of the tales he told Brabantio and Desdemona, Othello portrays himself primarily as a tested warrior, a heroic underdog, a survivor, a victim, a loner or outsider always on the move. As he runs through the stories he told of the places and peoples he encountered during his travels, he stresses by his examples the exotica of vast unpeopled regions and of fabled tribes, which he illustrates with "the Cannibals, that each other eat;/The Anthropophagi, and men whose heads/Do grow beneath their shoulders" (143–45).

Karen Newman claims that "Othello's stories of slavery and adventure are *precisely* a rehearsal of his origins, from his exotic tales of monstrous races to the story of the handkerchief's genealogy in witchcraft and sybilline prophecy."[18] But I don't think that his auditors are expected to identify members of these "monstrous races" with the "men of royal siege" he told Iago he was descended from. It is true that the emphasis on homophagy linking two of the three tribes he mentions may indicate sensitivity about "the vices of my blood," because in the public outcry reported to him by Iago in 1.2, predatory lust may have been among the "scurvy and provoking terms" spoken against his honor. Nevertheless, homophagy is a hyperbole, a caricature, of

17. In *Shakespeare's Scepticism* (1987; rpt. Ithaca: Cornell University Press, 1990), Graham Bradshaw focuses on the conflict between two versions of "Othello" that "follow from Othello's and Iago's mutually exclusive visions of the nature of nature" and on the tragi-comic effect produced by opposing to Othello's "tragedy of idealism" the corrosive "black parody" with which Iago mocks and tests it in order "to expose and exhibit the monster *within*" (16–18). Though it evokes shades of John Danby's discussion of the two natures in *Shakespeare's Doctrine of Nature: A Study of King Lear* (London: Faber and Faber, 1949), a discussion constrained by the limits of the particular genre of the history of ideas it instantiates, Bradshaw's analysis also supports a different, and much more specific, notion of what he calls "double vision" (14): the double vision of blackness and Othello's relation to it that emerges in the analysis of his language that follows.

18. Karen Newman, *Fashioning Femininity* (Chicago: University of Chicago Press, 1991), 83.

predatory lust, while its removal to far-off places and its monstrous embodiment in far-off races have the force of a decontaminating gesture, a trope of exorcism.

Desdemona's reminder to Othello that Cassio "came a-wooing with you" (3.3.71) is news to Iago as well as to spectators and readers. It gives him the opening he was looking for after Desdemona appeared to defuse his previous attempt to encourage Othello's suspicion some thirty lines earlier (3.3.37–54). There, Othello nervously wondered whether the man who so abruptly left Desdemona on his entrance (sneaked "away so guilty-like," as Iago put it at 3.3.39) was Cassio.

After Desdemona leaves with Emilia, Iago pointedly and mischievously asks Othello whether Cassio was aware of the courtship. Othello says yes, and speaks a little more about it later in the scene. Why does it surface so belatedly and briefly, and then disappear, as if it has done its work? But what is its work? Is it only Iago who was looking for the opening it provides? Some of the interlocutory moves in the early part of 3.3 may speak to these questions.

The statement that Cassio "came a-wooing with you" has an edge to it. Since Cassio has done so much for you, her argument runs, why can't you simply reciprocate and reinstate him, instead of "mammering on" so? Why indeed? The argument implies that Othello is partly indebted to Cassio for the gift of Desdemona. "Prithee no more," Othello breaks in, "let him come when he will,/I will deny thee nothing." No more talk about what he owes Cassio. He (not Cassio) will bestow the favor, and Desdemona will be the recipient.

She recognizes and immediately fends off this threat ("Why, this is not a boon," 77) with a counter-protestation. She is only entreating him to do what is in his best interest. *She* is doing *him* a favor, rather than the other way round.

The idea that Othello is in Cassio's debt for his premarital services introduces a new wrinkle. It folds together his jumpy reactions to seeing Cassio leave Desdemona a few lines earlier with his curt deferrals of her requests to give Cassio an audience (3.3.38–60). In these exchanges, Desdemona's interlocutory deftness justifies her confident assurances to Cassio that she would henpeck Othello until he gave in (3.3.19–28).

She may not have succeeded in this mission. But she successfully counters Othello's efforts to seize the rhetorical advantage by occupying the donor's position ("I will deny thee nothing"). As we'll see, in this stretch of dialogue her argument about his indebtedness to Cassio is closely linked to her interlocutory power.[19]

When Iago probes the new wrinkle and tries to deepen its crease, Othello shows no diffidence in speaking of the courtship. He freely divulges that Cassio knew of their love "from first to last," was well acquainted with Desdemona "and went between us very often," and "was of my counsel,/In my whole course of wooing" (3.3.95–97, 101, 115–16). It is apparently no secret. Yet it isn't something he has mentioned before, and it was not part of his narrative to the senators in 1.3.

Well—someone might object—it just didn't come up. But when it does come up, his previous silence becomes retroactively audible. It contrasts with the openness of his disclosure to Iago, especially because Iago's strategies of insinuation (3.3.95–109) quickly draw from Othello the suspicion glimpsed earlier in the scene when he worried whether it was Cassio leaving Desdemona.

The contrast between silence and openness surrounds the disclosure with a haunting aura. It's as if Othello is eager to give Iago precisely the information he is looking for. He trusts honest Iago to know what to do with it—to know how to build around Othello the structure of self-incarceration that will bring him and Desdemona down without his lifting a finger. Othello need only follow the lead he has given Iago, and wait for the ocular proof he trusts him eventually to provide. Giving Iago that information is like laying the cornerstone of the structure. But what corpse has been buried under the cornerstone to guarantee the structure's efficacy?

To begin with Cassio's first appearance, the belated disclosure alters the meaning of his display of bewilderment when Iago tells him of Othello's marriage (1.2.50–52). It also alters the meaning of Othello's response to Cassio's message from the Duke in the same stretch of dialogue: to Cassio's report that the Senate sent people all over town

19. See Chapter 26, below.

looking for Othello, he replies, "'Tis well I am found by you" (1.2.47), that is, "found by *you* rather than by the others" outside the lovers' trysting-place. As I note above, this suggests that Cassio is in on the secret he pretends to hide.

The disclosure in 3.3 also sharpens the earlier impression that Othello's tale of his courtship (1.3.129–70) was selective and had a defensive function. More was involved in winning Desdemona than telling stories about himself in her father's house. Why was it that Cassio not only "came a-wooing with you" but also "went between us very oft" (3.3.72, 100)? Why was Cassio's role in the courtship elided from Othello's narrative to the senators? Could this role be imagined to have any bearing on Othello's choosing Iago and Emilia instead of Cassio to escort Desdemona to Cyprus?[20]

Iago's exposition in 1.1 suggests that Othello gave Cassio his commission during roughly the same period that Cassio was his go-between and second in the courtship. Temporal relations in this play are studiedly—and famously—vague or inconsistent, and for that very reason they assert a claim on interpretive attention. Did Othello choose Cassio as his officer before or after he chose him as a go-between? The implications both in Iago's irritable report and in Othello's account of the courtship suggest that it was after, and this is supported by circumstantial logic.

A lieutenant is second in command, a substitute or surrogate, a "placeholder." This position is roughly comparable in the domain of Mars to that of the go-between and second in the domain of Venus.

---

20. At 1.3.121, with Cassio present Othello asks Iago to conduct messengers to the inn because he best knows the place. In preposterous perspective, it seems noteworthy that he didn't give Cassio this task. Was this to conceal Cassio's knowledge of and role in the courtship? Was it to insure that Cassio is not to have anything to do with Desdemona? Here, as later in 1.3, Othello keeps a distance between them. Muir's reflection on Shakespeare's arrangements and intentions becomes more interesting if they are redirected to Othello: "As she travels to Cyprus on one boat and Cassio on another, there was no possible occasion between her elopement and her reunion with Othello when she could have committed adultery with Cassio. Shakespeare could have arranged for Desdemona and Cassio to travel to Cyprus on the same boat" (26–27). But Othello could have arranged this, too. He could have had them travel together either because he trusted them or because he wanted to set up the possibility of their being attracted to each other.

The difference is that in the military hierarchy the lieutenant is safely subordinate to his superior—there can be no rivalry between them—but the suitor's friend is traditionally, notoriously, a site of concealed rivalry and betrayal.[21]

It's plausible to assume that, if Othello promoted Cassio some time after his service as go-between, it was to reward him. But it's also true that (whatever Othello intended) the effect of this reward would be to place Cassio more firmly under his control in the order of Mars. This would compensate for the structurally induced precariousness of Othello's control over his placeholder in the order of Venus.

23. OTHELLO'S EMBARRASSMENT IN 1.2 AND 1.3

Othello's apparently impetuous act of elopement places him in a familiar contradiction. It is manly to overcome a virtuous woman's resistance to your sexual advances. It is effeminate to succumb to your lust and hers.

Both sides of the problem are implicit in the accusations Brabantio levels against Othello. He wonders whether Othello "abused" Desdemona with magic (1.1.69–71), and he later charges that she wouldn't run to his "sooty bosom" unless charmed by drugs or spells (1.2.65–81). According to the code, a conquest is manly only if it is "honest"—only if the fortress of virtue is frontally assaulted using techniques that accord with the rules of international erotic warfare. It is unmanly to sap or undermine the virtuous will with potions, spells, and charms, for that, as Brabantio twice reiterates (1.2.63–79, 1.3.64–66), is to use "witchcraft."

Brabantio's accusations are not consistent. He has in effect been jilted by his daughter, who throws him over for Othello. Occasionally, his language and Othello's betray something like a united front against Desdemona. He spends his last words onstage warning Othello that "She has deceived her father, and may thee" (1.3.294). "My life upon her faith," Othello replies (295), but the sense of her "faith" that lurks

---

21. Iago's "honesty" may have a suggestion of lower rank as well as serving Othello's purposes.

in his previous speeches is a little cloudy. In any event, to make his "life" depend upon "*her* faith" is already to hold her responsible for anything that may happen.

We don't learn until much later in the play that the only equivalent to the potions, spells, and charms Othello used in courting Desdemona was Cassio. But "witchcraft" is the specific charge he rebuts (1.3.169). This is itself embarrassing, since witchcraft is woman's work.

Othello's problem is compounded not only by the "sooty bosom" factor but also by his role as a leader, which demands soldierly restraint in affairs of the heart. The pressure his dilemma imposes on his effort to represent himself is established during his first appearance in the play. Act 1 Scene 2 opens in the middle of a conversation in which Iago is displaying indignation at the way Roderigo "prated / And spoke such scurvy and provoking terms" against Othello's honor (1.2.6–8).

Brian Vickers, who quotes both Iago's and Roderigo's "slanderous words" about Othello in 1.1, oddly claims that in 1.2 Iago is "recounting some imaginary slanders on Othello."[1] Why imaginary? Since Roderigo and Iago used "scurvy and provoking terms" several times in 1.1, it's more likely that as 1.2 opens Iago has just given Othello a sample and is concluding his doctored account of the preceding scene.[2]

"Are you fast married?" Iago's question at 1.2.11 is probative. It is also very wicked: "How tight are you two? How firmly attached? How close-fitting? Is there no opening? No way to untie your knot?" Under the question slips another related to it: "Did you marry in a hurry?" For Brabantio, he warns, "will divorce you" or seek redress (1.2.14–17).

Othello doesn't appear surprised by what he hears. He begins his reply with dismissive confidence ("Let him do his spite; / My services . . . / Shall out-tongue his complaints," 1.2.17–19). But his next

1. Brian Vickers, *Appropriating Shakespeare: Contemporary Critical Quarrels* (New Haven: Yale University Press, 1993), 313.

2. The "scurvy terms" used by Iago and Roderigo in 1.1 occur in lines 65, 87–88, 110–12, 114–15, 124, 133–35.

words reveal that whatever he has heard provokes him to a vaguely plaintive apologia:

> 'Tis yet to know—
> Which, when I know that boasting is an honour,
> I shall promulgate—I fetch my life and being
> From men of royal siege, and my demerits
> May speak unbonneted to as proud a fortune
> As this that I have reached.   (1.2.19–24)[3]

He leaks privileged information with the embarrassment of someone who doesn't want to appear to be blowing his own horn. The information is studiedly generalized. From what men of what royal siege? And if indeed his pedigree and status are at least equal to those of the family he is marrying into, why does he speak of "this" fortune as one he has "reached"?[4]

Any hint that his marriage is something he *reached for* is countered by the earnest explanation that follows:

> For know, Iago,
> But that I love the gentle Desdemona
> I would not my unhoused free condition
> Put into circumscription and confine
> For the sea's worth.   (1.2.24–28)

He is giving up a lot, and all for love. "'Tis yet to know— . . . for know, Iago": essential secrets and truths about himself are being confided, as if to a confessor.

But it is confession in reverse. Othello mentions later that he has confessed "the vices of my blood" to heaven (1.3.124–25). Here he confesses the virtues of his blood to Iago, and this is difficult for him because one of the virtues is that he is no braggart, no *miles gloriosus*.

---

3. Ridley's rationalization for preferring "provulgate" to "promulgate" is unconvincing in a useful way: "*promulgate* has a certain connotation of publication by official authority which is not particularly appropriate to Othello's hypothetical action as a private individual in presenting the common people (*vulgus*) with the facts" (Arden *Othello*, 16). That connotation is precisely the one Othello labors to activate in clinging to his threatened role as an official military authority.

4. The fortune of marrying Desdemona, of marrying into Brabantio's noble family, and into his money.

"[Father,] I have not sinned. I am better than they think." It is important that Iago understand this, that Othello's honesty be acknowledged by honest Iago, reflected back to him in Iago's honesty, entrusted to honest Iago along with Desdemona: "Honest Iago,/My Desdemona must I leave to thee" (1.3.295–96).

What must be acknowledged, entrusted, and reflected back is a particular story about himself, as opposed to some other story. His noble blood is a guarantee that he is not marrying up and that he won't afflict Brabantio with "coursers for cousins, and gennets for germans" (1.1.112).[5] His "unhoused free condition" talks back to Roderigo's "extravagant and wheeling stranger,/Of here, and everywhere" (1.1.134–35). It is because these arguments speak so directly to the slanders and accusations uttered in 1.1 that we can reconstruct what Iago must have been saying to Othello just before their entrance in 1.2.

Othello continues to deposit his story in Iago's purse when Iago advises him to make himself scarce and avoid the approaching Brabantio:

> Not I, I must be found.
> My parts, my title and my perfect soul
> Shall manifest me rightly.
>
> (1.2.30–32)

As James Calderwood cogently puts it, "the word *parts* turns false and takes on a theatrical cast," betraying the histrionic basis of this antitheatrical claim to transparency.[6]

During the remainder of 1.2, Othello displays the coolness, tact, and verbal economy of the model soldier. When Brabantio and his armed retainers accost him, he responds with chilly disdain and with flashes of wit sorely lacking from his later appearances: "Keep up your bright swords, for the dew will rust them" (1.2.59); "Were it my cue to fight, I should have known it/Without a prompter" (1.2.83–84). He is secure

---

5. At 1.2.50–51, Iago remarks to Cassio that if the "land carrack" Othello "hath boarded . . . prove lawful prize, he's made for ever." Othello's implied protestation in 1.3 that his marriage was not an expedient alliance strategy but all for love recalls this comment and reflects awareness that such comments are to be expected.

6. James Calderwood, *The Properties of* Othello (Amherst: University of Massachusetts Press, 1989), 104.

in the assumption that, since his services are urgently needed, Braban-tio's appeal to the Duke will fail.

The assumption proves correct. Throughout his interchange with Brabantio in 1.3, the Duke is curt and impatient. To paraphrase: "you'll get personal attention in due time, but let's now move on to the pressing affairs of state" (1.3.66–71); "your evidence is thin and your charges of witchcraft implausible" (107–10); "Othello's tale is persuasive, so you'll just have to make the most of 'this mangled matter'" (172–75). The Duke subsequently moves into rhymed couplets for ten sententious lines telling Brabantio to get over it (200–210). Brabantio bitterly responds with five matching couplets that have the force of echoic mockery: "thanks for nothing; let's now turn to what, for you if not for me, are the more pressing concerns" (211–21).

At this point the Duke shows Brabantio his back and shifts into prose to give Othello his marching, or sailing, orders (222–29). That this is the first prose passage in the scene—and the only one until the last part of the scene, when Iago and Roderigo are alone—is significant. It cuts off the emotionally cadenced airing of private grievances, and it makes them seem diversionary and self-indulgent in a time of impending war. The effect is sharpened when the Duke concludes with a phrase whose sarcastic edge betrays his own impatience about the elopement: "You must therefore be content to slubber the gloss of your new fortunes with this more stubborn and boisterous expedition" (227–29).

Othello slubbers the gloss with a defensive response in high heroic pentameters. The lines betray his sensitivity to any suggestion that his "new fortunes" will untune his soldierly timbre:

> The tyrant custom, most grave senators,
> Hath made the flinty and steel couch of war
> My thrice-driven bed of down. I do agnize
> A natural and prompt alacrity
> I find in hardness, and do undertake
> This present war against the Ottomites.
> Most humbly therefore, bending to your state,
> I crave fit disposition for my wife,
> Due reverence of place, and exhibition,
> With such accommodation and besort
> As levels with her breeding.   (1.3.230–40)

"I do agnize / A natural and prompt alacrity" is a mouthful even for Othello, and such Big Talk betrays the embarrassment involved in having to negotiate a demeaning quid pro quo that involves sleeping arrangements. His emphasis on "hardness" aims to mitigate the softness of his request.

Othello's statement in 1.3 that he isn't much at making peacetime speeches is a substantive part of his defense against Brabantio's charge that he charmed Desdemona into submission. The problem with the statement is not only that it is too eloquently expressed but also that it is phrased in a manner calculated to disparage and humiliate Brabantio:

> Most potent, grave, and reverend signiors,
> My very noble and approved good masters:
> That I have ta'en away this old man's daughter
> It is most true; true, I have married her.
> The very head and front of my offending
> Hath this extent, no more.   (1.3.77–82)

To follow the courteous upscale address of the first two lines with a brusque confession, uttered in Brabantio's presence, that he literally raped not "Desdemona" but "this old man's daughter" is harsh. Does "I have married her" mitigate or increase the harshness? The final sentence tops it off: "That's all I did; not very offensive" is truly offensive.

After this, his apology for rhetorical inadequacy is rhetorically more than adequate:

> Rude am I in my speech
> And little blest with the soft phrase of peace,
> For since these arms of mine had seven years' pith
> Till now some nine moons wasted, they have used
> Their dearest action in the tented field,
> And little of this great world can I speak
> More than pertains to feats of broil and battle,
> And therefore little shall I grace my cause
> In speaking for myself.   (1.3.82–90)[7]

7. The implied target of this rudeness appears later, when Othello speculates on the motives for Desdemona's unfaithfulness: his blackness, age, and lack of "those soft parts of conversation that chamberers have" (3.6.268–69), a facility easy to associate with what

He then proceeds to grace his cause by pumping up his rude speech with anaphoristic fury:

> I will a round unvarnished tale deliver,
> Of my whole course of love, what drugs, what charms,
> What conjuration, and what mighty magic—
> For such proceedings am I charged withal—
> I won his daughter.   (1.3.91–94)

Early in the first scene Iago complains to Roderigo about the manner in which Othello turned down the mediators who recommended his ancient's promotion: "he, as loving his own pride and purposes,/Evades them, with a bombast circumstance/Horribly stuffed with epithets of war" (1.1.11–13). Whether Iago is lying or merely exaggerating, he tells Roderigo what he thinks the latter will accept—what it's plausible to say about Othello. By 2.1.221, when Iago urges Roderigo to mark "with what violence" Desdemona "first loved the Moor, but for bragging, and telling her fantastical lies," we've already heard enough from Othello in 1.3 to know that, although Iago may exaggerate, the statement contains a grain of truth. The Othello of Acts 1 and 2 likes to hear himself talk.

Etymologically embedded in the phrase "bumbast Circumstance" (Folio) are meanings that disclose themselves in two stages. The rhetorical stuffing with which Othello pads out and inflates his appearance is defensive in 1.2 and 1.3. But from 3.3 on it modulates into something more self-flagellatory (bum-basting), something closer to a bitter self-parody that all but solicits contempt from its auditors, chief among whom is its speaker.

Othello's rhetorical performance in 1.2 and 1.3 is flamboyant, but it is also guarded. Emily Bartels observes in a luminous essay that, as "Brabantio's accusations induce him to explain himself to the court, he anticipates and attempts to assuage any doubts that his marriage will conflict with his public service." But in spite of himself he reveals that for him "domestication is the enemy (and the military metaphor is his)

---

the perplexed Brabantio refers to as "the wealthy curled darlings of our nation" (1.2.68) whom Desdemona unaccountably rejected for Othello. The difference Othello insists on he articulates in the categorical opposition between the rudeness of the simple unspoiled soldier and the decadence of overcivilized and "super subtle" Venetians.

to his martial role."[8] This seems exactly right to me, though the anxiety Bartels describes extends beyond marriage to sexuality and therefore includes Othello's uneasiness about the Venetian view of him as a black, a Moor, and a monster.[9]

Karen Newman persuasively argues that Othello is not only "the representative and upholder of a rigorous sexual code that prohibits desire and defines it even within marriage as adulterous." He is also "the sign of a different, unbridled sexuality."[10] Reading this phrase through Bartels's comment leads me to rewrite it as Othello's divided sense of himself. He is, in effect, on trial from the moment he appears with Iago in 1.2, and so he can be expected to take care to represent himself in the best light not only to the Venetians but also to himself.

Critics have well described the conditions that motivate Othello's effort of defensive self-representation: his "energetic guilelessness is perhaps compensatory, . . . a counterstrategy to the Venetian racism that, in its more benign but still humiliating form, imagines Othello as a white man unaccountably lodged inside a black body"; he shares the Venetians' "ambivalent attitudes toward his person"; "his identity" is theatrically constructed in the "constant performance . . . of his 'story,'" resulting in the "loss of his own origins, an embrace and perpetual reiteration of the norms of another culture."[11] If his conquest of Desdemona ratifies that "embrace," the terms in which he describes it in 1.3 make it a potential threat to the embrace, a potential restoration of his "origins."[12] But just what are those origins?

Newman takes issue with the reference to Othello's loss of origins because it implies that "somehow anterior to identity-as-performance"

8. Emily C. Bartels, "Making More of the Moor: Aaron, Othello, and Renaissance Refashionings of Race," *Shakespeare Quarterly* 41 (1990): 451.

9. For more on the figure of the Moor in late Elizabethan texts, see Emily C. Bartels's stimulating *Speaking of the Moor: From "Alcazar" to "Othello"* (Philadelphia: University of Pennsylvania Press, 2008).

10. Newman, *Fashioning Femininity*, 84.

11. Katharine Eisman Maus, "Proof and Consequences: Inwardness and Its Exposure in the English Renaissance," *Representations* 34 (1991), 42; Judd D. Hubert, *Metatheater: The Example of Shakespeare* (Lincoln: University of Nebraska Press, 1991), 74; Stephen Greenblatt, *Renaissance Self-Fashioning: From More to Shakespeare* (Chicago: University of Chicago Press, 1980), 245.

12. For more on this topic, see Chapter 27, below.

Othello has "an essential self, an ontological subjectivity, an Edenic moment of black identity prior to discourse." She insists that

> Othello doesn't lose "his own origins": his only access to those "origins" are the exotic ascriptions of European colonial discourse. Othello's stories of slavery and adventure are *precisely* a rehearsal of his origins, from his exotic tales of monstrous races to the story of the handkerchief"'s genealogy in witchcraft and sybilline prophecy. Othello charms by reiterating his origins even as he submits and embraces the dominant values of Venetian culture. His successful courtship of Desdemona suggests that those origins are not simply repressive but also enabling.[13]

The "not simply . . . but also" form of Newman's argument gestures toward a duality of origins. In doing so it suggests an analysis that differs from hers, one in which the "Edenic moment of black identity" is represented not prior to discourse but in discourse, the discourse of European colonialism, where it is placed in opposition to another moment: "From the Renaissance to the end of the eighteenth century, Europeans tended to fetishize the native peoples with whom they came into contact by viewing them simultaneously as monstrous forms of humanity and as quintessential objects of desire."[14]

A truncated version of the continuum that connects these poles informs the double view of Caliban in *The Tempest*. He is, according to Greenblatt, "anything but a Noble Savage. Shakespeare does not shrink from the darkest European fantasies about the Wild Man; indeed he exaggerates them: Caliban is deformed, lecherous, evil-smelling, idle, treacherous, naive, drunken, rebellious, violent, and devil-worshipping."[15]

Nevertheless, as Stephen Orgel argued more than a decade ago, "criticism has generally seen much more in Caliban than Prospero does," and the attempt "to humanize and domesticate him, to rescue him from Prospero's view of him" is "prompted by the play itself."[16]

13. Newman, *Fashioning Femininity*, 83.

14. White, "The Noble Savage Theme as Fetish," 194.

15. Stephen Greenblatt, *Learning to Curse: Essays in Early Modern Culture* (New York: Routledge, 1990), 26.

16. Stephen Orgel, introduction to *The Tempest*, The Oxford Shakespeare (Oxford: Oxford University Press, 1987), 25–26.

Similarly, Othello's language reveals an embarrassed attempt to rescue or defend his self-representation from "the darkest European fantasies" glimmering diffusely through the utterances of Venetian speakers in the first three scenes. After all, Desdemona's "I saw Othello's visage in his mind" (1.3.253) suggests, among other things, that she didn't see it in his face.[17]

24. DESDEMONA ON CYPRUS:
ACT 2 SCENE 1

As the venue shifts from Venice to the tempest-tossed isle of Cyprus in 2.1, we learn that the storm has destroyed the Turkish fleet and separated the Venetian ships. One of those ships carries Cassio, another Othello, and a third Desdemona, Emilia, Iago, and Roderigo. Cassio enters first, followed by the company of four, whom he hails.

The storm itself is otherwise a disappointment. Its bark is worse than its bite; it fails to live up to its symbolic promise. It produces nothing more serious than a pause in the action, a comic interlude, a parade of happy reunions. But this "nothing more" is critical: with the destruction of the Turkish fleet, the balance of dramatic power shifts from war to love, from Mars to Venus. The end of the storm leaves the stragglers stranded on Venus's island with nothing to do but celebrate victory, make trouble, feel jealous, and murder their wife.

"News, lords, your wars are done," the Third Gentleman announces twenty lines into 2.1, and at the end of the series of reunions Othello repeats this message almost verbatim: "News, friends, our wars are done" (2.1.201). Thus he has it backwards when he later blames Desdemona for his farewell to the "mortal engines whose rude throats / Th'immortal Jove's dread clamours counterfeit" (3.3.358–59). On the contrary, it was Jove's clamor that put the engines out of play and engendered the situation, enabling Iago to help Othello bid Desdemona farewell.

17. See the excellent essay by Dorothea Kehler, "'I Saw Othello's Visage in His Mind': Desdemona's Complicity," *Weber Studies* (Ogden, Utah), 5.2 (1988): 63–71. Kehler's reading is briefly discussed in Chapter 31, below. On the Internet, the essay can be found at http://weberstudies.weber.edu/archive/archive%20A%20%20Vol.%20110.3/Vol.%205.2/5.2%20Kehler_s.htm.

Venus's influence dominates the banter that precedes Othello's entrance in this surprising scene—Desdemona's banter with Iago, Emilia, and Cassio. The scene is surprising because of the confidence with which Desdemona orchestrates the dialogue. She manages both men with the aplomb of someone who knows herself worthy of praise and attention, "a deserving woman" confident in the fidelity of her love but confident also in the power of the sexuality she controls.

In fact her behavior in the interval between her appearance on stage and Othello's is anomalous. The anomaly is obvious and has often been remarked. Cavell reads "that difficult and dirty banter between her and Iago as they await Othello" as an index to the desire Othello "has elicited from her."[1] Desdemona's part in all this is a bit much for the Arden editor: "It is distasteful to watch her engaged in a long piece of cheap backchat with Iago, and so adept at it that one wonders how much time on the voyage was spent in the same way."[2]

What seems to trouble the Arden editor no less than it troubles Desdemona's father is her transgressive way with the stereotypes of lady, wife, and daughter. Ridley imagines the captain's captain, the general's general, spending hours at the ship's rail trading indelicate quips with Iago. This reaction may be neurotic, but it apprehends a truth.

In this scene Desdemona appreciates male attentiveness and enjoys the different styles of verbal puffery that convey it. So, repeatedly, to Iago: "What wouldst thou write of me, if thou shouldst praise me?"; "Come, how wouldst thou praise me?"; "but what praise couldst thou bestow on a deserving woman indeed?" (2.1.117, 124, 144–45). She encourages his mildly salacious epigrams and pronounces his mockery of a woman inhibited by virtue a "most lame and impotent conclusion" (2.1.161). Then she turns to draw in Cassio, who has been listening on the sidelines: "how say you, Cassio, is he not a most profane and liberal counsellor?" (2.1.162–64).

Cassio responds with the mixture of approval and disapproval the question calls for: "he speaks home, madam, you may relish him more in the soldier than in the scholar" (165–66). That is, his bluntness is refreshing but he lacks class. The lieutenant proceeds to demonstrate the

---

1. Cavell, *Disowning Knowledge*, 136.
2. Ridley, Arden *Othello*, 54.

more mannerly behavior of a true scholar and counsellor, or, in one word, a courtier, by walking Desdemona upstage and going through the sequence of gallantries that gives Iago, describing it from downstage, a vivid preview of Othello's nightmare.

Before 2.1 we see little more than the lieutenant in Cassio's appearances. His other side is glimpsed only in Iago's conspicuously biased characterization—"A fellow almost damned in a fair wife" (1.1.21), "He has a person and a smooth dispose/To be suspected, framed to make women false" (1.3.396–97). But on Cyprus Cassio's "smooth dispose" comes into its fatuous own. The Petrarchan connoisseur of fine women struts his hyperboles and commands genuflection before the "divine Desdemona" as if she were the Cyprian goddess stepping forth from her beached scallop (2.1.82–87).

He goes on to engage Emilia in a little courtly *baciamano* while assuring Iago he has nothing to worry about:

> Let it not gall your patience, good Iago,
> That I extend my manners; 'tis my breeding
> That gives me this bold show of courtesy.
>
> (2.1.97–99)

"Kissing," Kenneth Muir feels compelled to explain, "was a normal method of greeting, and does not imply that Cassio was flirting with Emilia." But if Muir is right, why does Cassio himself feel compelled to explain he isn't flirting? The utterance offers any speaker of Cassio's part a variety of tonal possibilities to choose from: apology, swash, aggression, condescension, and anxiety about overstepping boundaries. Here, after doing obeisance to Desdemona, he busily extends his manners downward.

When Bianca comes on the scene in 3.4, he will extend them downward even further. His reaction to her will shift from worship through condescension to contempt. But the *politesse* of erotic insinuation remains the active core of all Cassio's graduated performances.

His apology to Iago, for example, is interpretable as a signal to the husband that he *could* carry on with his wife if he wanted to. And the stage directions embedded in Iago's aside indicate that Cassio redirects his extended manners from Emilia to Desdemona, paddling palms and kissing fingers until Othello appears on stage: "He takes her by the palm. . . . Ay, smile upon her, do: . . . good, well kissed. . . . Yet again, your fingers at your lips?" (2.1.167–76). Sneering villainously at his pathetic victims, showing excitement at the improving prospects of his plot, Iago whets his audience's appetite for the spider's inevitable triumph ("with as little a web as this will I ensnare as great a fly as Cassio," 168–69).

What Iago describes in these words, the actors playing Cassio and Desdemona would probably exhibit in gestures that are conspicuously more innocuous—more conventionally courtly—than his description. The idea that there may be something going on between Desdemona and Cassio is no doubt ridiculous: it is Iago himself who will devilishly turn this unpromising raw material into the stuff of tragedy. It's nevertheless interesting that a couple of scenes later, Cassio replies guardedly to the insinuations with which Iago ferrets out signs of his sexual desire for Desdemona (2.3.15–26).

Susan Snyder's paraphrase highlights the edge of defensiveness with which the gentleman doth protest: "He resists strongly when Iago's conversation puts her in a sexual context, refusing to speculate about the wedding night, insisting on her modesty."[3] But this resistance *does* reflect his own tendency to put her "in a sexual context." His references to the "divine Desdemona" and "our great captain's captain" receive an erotic charge from his subsequent references to Othello's "tall ship" and "quick pants in Desdemona's arms" (2.1.79–80). There is a hint of courtly condescension in these phrases, a sidelong glance, perhaps, at "our great captain's" uxoriousness.

This is something Iago glances at directly at 2.3.336–39, and it is an impression we have already seen Othello taking care to defend against when he tells his story in 1.3. At this point in the play we're not encouraged—or not yet encouraged—to worry about Cassio and Desdemona. Rather, the question that enlivens these glances and vibrates through these passages has to do with whether anything is going on between Desdemona and Othello, and just what it may be.[4]

---

3. Susan Snyder, "*Othello*: A Modern Perspective," in William Shakespeare, *Othello*, ed. Barbara A. Mowat and Paul Werstine (New York: Washington Square Press, 1993), 295. This deeply insightful essay is the source of many of the ideas developed in the present chapter.

4. Commentary on the issue has been thoroughly canvassed, and critically but generously assessed, by Janet Adelman in one of the many brilliant footnotes (mini-essays,

This question sails into view in their reunion on Cyprus. Desdemona meets Othello's "O my fair warrior!" with a more reserved "My dear Othello!" and Othello comes back with eleven lines of ecstatic gush concluding in a fantasy of *Liebestod*:

> If it were now to die,
> 'Twere now to be most happy, for I fear
> My soul hath her content so absolute
> That not another comfort like to this
> Succeeds in unknown fate. (2.1.187–91)

Like to what? *What* is he talking about? Is he only expressing relief that they both made it through the storm? "Nothing good that happens to us in the future can match this orgasmic moment." What about the comfort of sex?—the enjoyment of which they're still looking forward to in 2.3.

Beneath the hyperbolic intensity of expression is an ominous prospect that prompts the captain's captain to issue a mild rebuke: "The heavens forbid / But that our loves and comforts should increase, / Even as our days do grow" (191–93). She sensibly redirects him toward a future of love-making, affection, and family life. Is that the anticlimax he fears?

Othello acknowledges her correction ("Amen to that, sweet powers!") and goes on: "I cannot speak enough of this content, / It stops me here, it is too much of joy," a too-much that irrupts in kisses: "And this, and this, the greatest discord be / That e'er our hearts shall make!" (194–97). But if this is said to his "fair warrior," and kisses are part of their warfare, shouldn't he look forward to greater and more pleasurable discord? Isn't that what it means to be "fast married" (1.2.11)?

He calms down a few lines later, announces that the Turkish "wars are done," assures Desdemona she will "be well desir'd in Cyprus," and confesses that "I prattle out of fashion, and I dote / In mine own comforts." He then settles down to business with a pair of orders to Iago (2.1.189–211). Finally, turning back to Desdemona, he reasserts his authority with an exit line that displays more restraint: "come, Des-

---

really) that make her studies of Shakespeare remarkable, make them absolutely essential reading for anyone in the field. See her *Suffocating Mothers: Fantasies of Maternal Origin in Shakespeare's Plays*, Hamlet *to* The Tempest (New York: Routledge, 1992), 271–73. The entire section of footnotes to Othello, 269–81, is a critical treasure trove.

demona, / Once more, well met at Cyprus" (210–12). But his rhetorical fluctuations dramatize the problem that confronts him on Venus's isle: to contain his joy and preserve his importance to the Venetians as a figure of martial authority after "our wars are done."

This isn't a private conversation but a public performance. Does he say what he feels or what he thinks he ought to say?—or has been taught to say? Othello's words are uttered before several onstage auditors, including Cassio, and there are some family resemblances between Cassio's and Othello's hyperbolic utterances to and about Desdemona in this scene. In fact, Othello and Desdemona are never sequestered on stage until late in the play. They are alone for 62 lines of bitter talk in 4.2, and for 83 lines before he smothers her in 5.2. Prior to that time he conducts his relation to Desdemona in public, as if before an audience whom he seems anxious to assure that he's doing it right.

After Cassio compliments Desdemona and extends his manners to Emilia, Iago treats his wife to a standard misogynist putdown. Before she has spoken a word in the play, he describes her as a scold (2.1.100–105). "Alas," Desdemona interjects, "she has no speech" (2.1.102). She responds to another misogynist salvo, this time extended to wives in general, with "O, fie upon thee, slanderer!" (109–13).

Desdemona warms to the spirit of this repartee, if not to its particular focus on Emilia. She uses Emilia's "You shall not write my praise" to replace her as Iago's target: "What wouldst thou write of me, if thou shouldst praise me?" (116–17). He offers to demur ("I am nothing if not critical") and she urges him to "assay." She then interrupts herself to ask whether "there's one gone to the harbor" (119–20) and to explain:

> I am not merry, but I do beguile
> The thing I am by seeming otherwise.
> Come, how wouldst thou praise me?
> (2.1.122–24)

These words are often taken to express Desdemona's attempt to divert herself from her underlying anxiety about storm-tossed Othello. But they could well tug in the other direction. That is, she may just as easily appear to be enjoying herself and apologizing for her enjoyment. That she *displays* anxiety doesn't mean she isn't anxious; it only means she is having a good enough time to be moved to remind the others of the concern from which she now diverts herself. So she reminds them she is really anxious, and continues to play.

I don't share Cavell's sense that the "banter between her and Iago" is "difficult and dirty," nor do I agree with Ridley that it is a "piece of cheap backchat."[5] For me, the primary effect of the dialogue is its striking contrast to anything that takes place between Desdemona and Othello, and the contrast, as I see it, is all on the side of the interchange in 2.1. Desdemona seems to appreciate not merely Iago's wit per se but his ability to meet her interrogatory challenges with well-rhymed misogynist witticisms about woman's sexual cunning. His truisms in that line obviously counterpoint Cassio's gynephilic arias and may offer relief from the latter's more subversive, because veiled, genre of misogynist discourse.

When we learn in 3.3 that Cassio has been Othello's go-between, it retroactively affects our sense of what went on in the earlier scenes. It means that since Desdemona was party to his intervention before the play started, her present relation to Cassio and Othello is constrained, and she can't expect to look to either of them for the truths of male fantasy she urges Iago to divulge. She appears to find it refreshing to hear the bad news about what it is to be both "a deserving woman" and a good wife in the eyes of a pretender to conventional misogynist wisdom. How would Iago praise someone who knows herself to be proof against dispraise—who "in the authority of her merit did justly put on the vouch of very malice itself" (2.1.145–47), and is doing it now in assaying the malicious Iago?

If I were Desdemona, I might be a little shaken by his reply, but I would feel that I had learned something about the possibilities, and more about the constraints, of my new condition. I might even be grateful that my new husband's arrival was delayed long enough to give me the chance to hear it:

> She that was ever fair and never proud,
> Had tongue at will, and yet was never loud,
> Never lacked gold, and yet went never gay,
> Fled from her wish, and yet said "now I may,"

5. Cavell, *Disowning Knowledge*, 136; Ridley, Arden *Othello*, 54.

She that, being angered, her revenge being nigh,
Bade her wrong stay, and her displeasure fly,
She that in wisdom never was so frail
To change the cod's head for the salmon's tail,
She that could think, and ne'er disclose her mind,
See suitors following, and not look behind;
She was a wight, if ever such wights were—

DESDEMONA

To do what?

IAGO

To suckle fools, and chronicle small beer.

DESDEMONA O, most lame and impotent conclusion!

(2.1.148–61)

A woman would be a fool to rein in her tongue and her desires and submit in self-abnegating obedience to the domestic servitude called marriage. Iago isn't sure such a woman can be found ("if ever such wight were")—men aren't that blessed or lucky.

Are these Iago's opinions? The end-stopped rhymed couplets make it appear more likely that he is ventriloquizing preformulated opinions, giving voice to a readymade Venetian discourse about women and marriage. It's the same discourse that finds its way into his words on other occasions:

I hate the Moor
And it is thought abroad that 'twixt my sheets
He's done my office. I know not if't be true,
But I for mere suspicion in that kind
Will do as if for surety.... (1.3.385–89)

...I do suspect the lusty Moor
Hath leaped into my seat....
For I fear Cassio with my night-cap too.

(2.1.293–94, 305)

In Venice they do let God see the pranks
They dare not show their husbands; their best conscience
Is not to leav't undone, but keep't unknown.

(3.3.206–8)

What Iago believes is less apparent than what he shows he thinks Venetian husbands and wives believe, less apparent also than his delight in playing the expert and critic. More to the point is that these are opinions he wants Desdemona to hear. The force of his utterance is obviously directed toward disrupting relations between Desdemona and Othello. She should spread her wings, be receptive to suitors (Cassio, for example), not refuse to take her justified revenge or pleasure, and, above all, not let the disease of matrimony unsinew the vibrant assertiveness she displayed in contracting it.

How does Desdemona hear the utterance? What does her subsequent behavior show her to have heard? Does her "O most lame and impotent conclusion" impugn only the fate and final state of the paragon of self-restraint Iago mockingly profiles, on the grounds that she deserves much better? Or does it speak to the whole of his argument? If so, does it pronounce its verdict on the extremism of the outrageous alternatives proposed in the wife's fantasy or on the bitterness of the suspicious husband's fantasy of that fantasy?

"Lame and impotent" denote shortcomings normally associated with the Cyprian goddess's husband. If the angry husband's voice is heard through Iago's couplets, Vulcan's epithets gravitate toward him. But if the couplets are heard as praise of "bad" women, then it is the dutiful wife whose fate attracts those epithets and whose submission is understood as a degendering equal to that of a husband castrated by his bad wife.

Loosely held together in Iago's couplets are the two contending sides or fantasies of the discourse of marriage marked by what Susan Snyder calls "a deep-seated sexual pathology in Venice": "In an ideology that can value only cloistered, desireless women, any woman who departs from this passivity will cause intense anxiety."[6] The discourse consequently gives pride of place both to departures and to anxieties. Desdemona represents her relation to this discourse in a manner the discourse itself doesn't allow for, and therefore a manner that neither Iago nor Othello could predict.

It isn't only that she represents herself and her marriage as exceptions to the discursive rule. It is also that her performance in 1.3 gives

6. Snyder, "*Othello*: A Modern Perspective," 296–97.

a clear indication of a set of concerns different from those Iago raises in his couplets. My sense of what she hears in his words is influenced by the premise that she is not interested in sexual adventures. She desires Othello and is "loyal" to him. Whatever messages the play sends about the question of consummation, it is a problem for him rather than for her.

This premise shifts the focus of concern from sexual to gender politics. Thus I imagine that, in responding to Iago's argument, Desdemona splits the difference. She takes to heart the implied encouragement to assertiveness and the warning about abject submission. But she also receives the message about husbandly anger from the misogynist discourse Iago exploits, and she combines these with her own commitment to fidelity.

That commitment might well induce her to countenance the misogynist critique of female promiscuity. It could lead her to resent any imputation of promiscuity. If she were stubborn enough, she might even persuade herself that nothing she did could possibly be misconstrued as promiscuous, however it might appear to others. As she has already suggested, she knows herself to be "a deserving woman" who "in the authority of her merits did justly put on the vouch of very malice itself"—though, on reconsidering this utterance in the light of what I have just been saying, I now detect the hint of a challenge in her words, the hint, that is, of a dare to the malicious to do their worst.

Desdemona's subsequent behavior in 3.3 conveys no sense that she might be misunderstood, might be suspected of concealing desire. Rather, it conveys the sense that she shouldn't and couldn't possibly be so misunderstood, regardless of what anyone who knows about her premarital relations with Cassio might think. Her doggedness in this regard maddens many readers and spectators of the play.

To interpret her language and behavior thus is to suggest they may be setting up the conditions that enable her at some point to ensconce herself in the discourse of injured merit. In suggesting this, I take my cue from the odd construction of one of Iago's couplets: "She that, being angered, her revenge being nigh,/Bade her wrong stay, and her displeasure fly" (2.1.152–53). Ridley's interpretation of "Bade her wrong stay" is plausible—"[bade] her sense of injury cease"—as is the slightly different reading of the Folger editors, "endured her injury . . . with patience."[7]

The Folger gloss invites a more interesting paraphrase, produced by the effect of "fly" on "stay": it changes the meaning of "stay" from "stop" or "cease" to "remain." The statement that results is: "while getting over her displeasure or anger, she stifled but nursed the wrong that caused it. Instead of discharging her anger in revenge, she silently kept her sense of injured merit alive and in place." We'll see that Desdemona's behavior from 3.3 on is illuminated by this paraphrase and, more generally, by the lessons and expectations about marriage she has gleaned from Iago. But the most striking feature of her performance in this brief interlude is its atypicality. Desdemona retains her spiritedness and independence of viewpoint to the end, but her playful enjoyment of men's company and attention shuts down when Othello enters.

25. THE PROCLAMATION SCENES:
ACT 2 SCENES 2 AND 3

"Are you fast married?" Iago had asked Othello in their first conversation, and he still wonders in Act 2 whether Othello and Desdemona remain eligible for a *pro*thalamion. The question is kept alive in 2.2 when Othello formalizes the shift from Mars to Venus by inviting everyone to celebrate not only the "perdition of the Turkish fleet" but also his "nuptials." Because I'll discuss this scene and the opening lines of 2.3 in some detail, I quote the passage in full:

> [2.2] *Enter Othello's* Herald, *with a proclamation.*
> HERALD [*Reads.*] *It is Othello's pleasure, our noble and valiant general, that, upon certain tidings now arrived, importing the mere perdition of the Turkish fleet, every man put himself into triumph: some to dance, some to make bonfires, each man to what sport and revels his addiction leads him. For, besides these beneficial news, it is the celebration of his nuptial.*—So much was his pleasure should be proclaimed. All offices are open, and there is full liberty of feasting from this

7. Arden *Othello*, 57; Folger *Othello*, 70.

present hour of five till the bell have told eleven. Heaven bless
the isle of Cyprus and our noble general Othello!   *Exit.*

[2.3]   *Enter* OTHELLO, CASSIO *and* DESDEMONA.

OTHELLO

> Good Michael, look you to the guard tonight.
> Let's teach ourselves that honourable stop
> Not to outsport discretion.

CASSIO

> Iago hath direction what to do,
> But notwithstanding with my personal eye
> Will I look to't.

OTHELLO.   Iago is most honest.

> Michael, good night. Tomorrow with your earliest
> Let me have speech with you. Come, my dear love,
> The purchase made, the fruits are to ensue:
> That profit's yet to come 'tween me and you.
> Good night.   *Exeunt Othello and Desdemona.*

The terms of the invitation are seductive: each man is to pursue
whatever "sport and revels" he prefers, and as if to make it easier for
everyone to overdo it Othello guarantees six hours of "full liberty"
with "all offices . . . open." To be more precise, it isn't Othello himself
who invites them to carouse. He sends a Herald onstage to read from
a proclamation. This is a cue to any director to rummage through
company props for some parchment and a signet that would ritually
objectify the invitation to celebrate and the provision of celebratory
means.

Why stage it in this manner? Why enclose the proclamation in a
scene of its own? The unruly sequel could just as easily have been ini-
tiated by any speaker's suggesting that the sudden end of the Turkish
threat called for a little celebration. Or Othello could have made the
announcement himself and then paused at the end to savor the affection with which he would be regarded by his men. Instead, he eschews
the personal touch and communicates through an official go-between,
who increases the distance by adding information in his own voice
after reading the proclamation.

The effect is to dissociate the order from Othello, amplify its au-
thorization of liberty, and make it seem less informal or spontaneous,

more like a command issued from the office of the military governor. And it could be expected to stir up trouble—just the sort of trouble the governor would have to handle even if (especially if?) it interrupted his nuptial pleasure.

As the Herald exits, Othello himself enters with Cassio and Desdemona, and immediately qualifies the command by reminding his lieutenant to stay sober: "Let's teach ourselves that honourable stop / Not to outsport discretion." The reflexive plural that tactfully includes everyone ("let's [all of us] teach ourselves . . .") makes the statement innocuous and conventional. These are the limits of celebratory license everyone, including Cassio, should observe, and just to make sure they will, Othello puts his trusty lieutenant in charge of the night watch.

It turns out that, in this celebratory atmosphere, being on duty presents no obstacle to bibulous indulgence. Because Othello commanded "All offices" to stay open for six hours, the wine flows so easily that with a little prodding from Iago the watch are as quick to raise a glass as those they watch. Thus Cassio's less than enthusiastic response to his assignment may signal not the desire to celebrate more freely but a wary presentiment that even being on duty would not keep him from giving in to the peer pressure of companionly invitations to indulge.

When Cassio mentions his drinking problem to Iago a few lines after Othello's warning, the warning becomes less innocuous and reveals something about Othello's sense of the proclamation: he suspects it might induce disorderly behavior, at least in Cassio, and he assigns him guard duty as a precaution. Cassio's response suggests that he had already delegated Iago to oversee the watch and may have had other plans.[1] At the same time, the response is defensive. His forceful adversative ("But notwithstanding") tells us that, although he may be disappointed, he accepts the assignment as a challenge, and he assures Othello that he can be counted on.

---

1. It appears that Cassio's assignment to the liberty watch had been arranged earlier, for at 2.1.216–17 Iago remarks to Roderigo that "the lieutenant to-night watches on the court of guard," and this information was the basis of his scheme to "have our Michael Cassio on the hip" (2.1.300). One could ask whether Iago knew this before Cassio, and whether Othello's opening remark is a reminder rather than a new instruction. But questions about the pragmatics of the imaginary situation may not be relevant if they don't affect our sense of the state of the triangle at that moment.

For me, there is a touch both of pathos and of prideful self-credentiation in Cassio's phrase "with my personal eye / Will I look to't," and so when Othello brushes by this avowal with another reference to Iago's honesty, I can feel Cassio's pain. The tension in their exchange is heightened by Desdemona's presence. For one thing, it appears that the other members of the play's major triangle know about Cassio's problem. For another, her presence as auditor alters my sense of the tone of Othello's advice to his military and amatory placeholder—adds a performative and competitive edge to it, makes it a little condescending.

When Iago appears a moment later, Cassio greets him with an imperative—"Welcome, Iago, we must to the watch" (12)—that Iago interprets as a sign of disappointment. He responds by rubbing in the fact that the lovesick Othello has just gotten rid of them: it isn't time to go on duty yet, "Our general cast us thus early for the love of his Desdemona—whom," he adds wickedly, "let us not therefore blame; he hath not yet made wanton the night with her" (13–16). "Don't blame Desdemona for depriving us of Othello's company and the chance to enjoy the liberty; blame the lustful Othello."

His next words transfer the blame to Othello's "fair warrior" and Cassio's "great captain's captain," whose warfare is more effective than the Turk's: she is "full of game," her eye "sounds a parley to provocation," and "when she speaks is it not an alarum to love?" (19–24). Donning Mars's armor, Iago's Desdemona threatens to unman Othello. "Iago's pruriency about Desdemona," Kenneth Muir remarks, "is contrasted with . . . [the] chaste admiration" of Cassio, who does his best to fend off the innuendoes."[2] That Iago's comments may reflect his pruriency doesn't prevent them from reflecting the same response in Othello. And as Othello's disclaimers in 1.3 suggest, he could be imagined to resist the "parley to provocation" by telling himself what Cassio tells Iago ("a most exquisite lady," "a most fresh and delicate creature," "An inviting eye; and yet methinks right modest"; 2.3.18, 20, 23).

After his cautionary remark to Cassio, Othello bids him goodnight, tells him to report back early the next day, and then steers Desdemona off stage with a promise that lets Cassio hear how the bride and groom

2. Muir, *Othello*, 196–97.

plan to spend the intervening time: "The purchase made, the fruits are to ensue:/That profit's yet to come 'tween me and you" (2.3.9–10). Apart from the fact that it oddly depicts elopement in the language of arranged marriage, there is something both showy and pathetic in this jingly utterance. It seems aimed at Cassio: "How'm I doing?" But it indicates that he and Desdemona haven't yet gotten around to doing much of anything. And why does he make a point of inviting Cassio for a talk early the next day—on the morning after the night before (2.3.7–8)? The whole of this brief interchange crackles with sparks of the mini-competition performed before Desdemona: Othello thrusting at Cassio in the first speech, Cassio parrying in the second, Othello running him through in the third.

Taken together, Othello's proclamation and admonitions are simultaneously permissive and preemptive. They give Cassio the opportunity to "outsport discretion" but they also anticipate the unpleasant event they encourage and move to deter it. The pressure this dangerous gift of liberty exerts on Cassio is similar to the pressure exerted on Desdemona by the gift of the handkerchief. Both gifts illustrate the strategy made explicit by Portia in *The Merchant of Venice* when she bestows the ring on Bassanio:

> I give . . . this ring,
> Which when you part from, lose, or give away,
> Let it presage the ruin of your love,
> And be my vantage to exclaim on you.
> (3.2.171–74)

The proclamation and warning work together as speech acts. They make it possible for Othello's nuptial bliss to be not only celebrated but also interrupted. They seem calculated to produce a crisis that will bring the General storming forth from the conjugal bed "to exclaim on" whoever stirred up trouble. And, after a little arm-twisting by Iago, he goes to it with real zest—almost, you might say, with relief at the chance to reactivate his occupation:

> Zounds, if I once stir,
> Or do but lift this arm, the best of you
> Shall sink in my rebuke. Give me to know
> How this foul rout began, who set it on,

And he that is approved in this offence,
Though he had twinned with me, both at a birth,
Shall lose me. What, in a town of war
Yet wild, the people's hearts brimful of fear,
To manage private and domestic quarrel?
In night, and on the court and guard of safety?
'Tis monstrous.   (2.3.203–13)

The figure of the guilty twin reveals that, even before Iago's laboriously indirect accusation (2.3.216–42), Othello was prepared to make
an example of someone he is very close to. Dividing himself from the
instigator of this monstrous brawl, he reminds the offenders that the
town remains, psychologically, in a state of siege.

We hear nothing more about the people and their fearful hearts.
Iago's statement that the watch includes three prickly and arrogant
Cypriots, "The very elements of this warlike isle" (2.3.52–54), sug-
gests a different view of the town. Against lingering anxiety about the
Turkish threat implied by Othello, the prior events of the scene sug-
gest that, if people have something to fear, it is likely to be the result
of the monster produced by the coupling of Iago's machination with
Othello's proclamation.

The idea that Othello sets up the need for him to intervene is supported by one of the many stimulating passages in James Calderwood's
The Properties of Othello. He argues that "whether or not there is a *coitus
interruptus* in the play there is certainly a *miles interruptus* when the anticipated battle with the Turks fails to materialize." Thus "deprived of
satisfaction," Othello finds that "random drunken swordplay between
Cassio and a few Cypriots is no substitute for the Turkish wars."[3]

My point is that there is a close relation between the two forms of
interruptio. Othello makes the most of the slender opportunity to ensconce himself in the martial function that justifies another separation
from Desdemona. Is the nuptial "profit" everyone has been raucously
celebrating *still* "to come 'twixt me and you"?

This is a question the play conspicuously poses and refuses to answer. It is a question to which Iago twice draws his interlocutors' attention. First, he mischievously apologizes to Cassio for our general's

3. Calderwood, *The Properties of* Othello, 126–27.

early retirement ("he hath not yet made wanton the night with her," 2.3.16–17). Later, and more mischievously, in replying to Othello's "From whence ariseth this?," he reminds everyone in the street of the private bliss that occasioned their celebration and has just been interrupted by it. What do we suppose Iago wants Othello to hear in these words?

> I do not know, friends all, but now, even now,
> In quarter and in terms like bride and groom
> Divesting them for bed; and then, but now,
> As if some planet had unwitted men,
> Swords out, and tilting one at other's breasts
> In opposition bloody.   (2.3.175–80)

Cassio and Montano were as friendly as Othello and Desdemona undressing for bed. The next minute they're at war, and Cassio stabs Montano. Iago couples Cassio with Othello and Montano with Desdemona in a figure that simultaneously leers at Othello's nuptial activity, anticipates his aggression against Desdemona, and inserts Cassio into the surrogate lover's position.

"Like bride and groom" conjures up for all in earshot, including Othello, a possibly embarrassing image of what the actual bride and groom could have been doing when so rudely interrupted. The best comment on this move is by Julia Genster. Iago, she writes, transposes "Othello's interrupted bridal . . . into the terms of the brawl, artfully mingling sexual anxieties . . . with social and military ones."[4]

Othello fends this off by throwing himself into the role of Commanding Officer and going after Cassio: "How comes it, Michael, you are thus forgot?" (2.3.184). He pushes quickly by Cassio's predictable answer, "I pray you pardon me, I cannot speak," to a more polite, even courtly, interrogation of Montano (181–87), who redirects him to Iago. Iago's long response (211–37) guides Othello discreetly into the safe harbor toward which the vessel of his proclamation had been sailing: "Cassio, I love thee,/But never more be officer of mine" (2.3.244–45). Acknowledging the appearance onstage of Desdemona—"Look if my

<hr />

4. Julia Genster, "Lieutenancy, Standing In, and Othello," *English Literary History* 57 (1990): 798.

gentle love be not raised up!"—he adds a final touch to his dismissal of
Cassio, "I'll make thee an example" (2.3.246–47).

Why enclose and formalize the proclamation in a scene of its own? To
the untrusting or suspicious mind, the Herald's announcement sets the
stage for Othello to intervene after the anticipated failure in self-control
he himself warns Cassio against. Cassio's is a weakness—maybe *the*
weakness—the proclamation is guaranteed to put to the test.

Thus one answer to the question is this: omitting the scene would
have left Iago as sole instigator of the plot against Cassio. Including it
makes Othello a hidden but essential co-motivator of that plot. Iago
has unknowingly lost the initiative of evil to Othello and become his
general's tool. This needs to be affirmed against the tendency to insist one-sidedly that the action takes place in "Iago's world," that "his
transformation of Cassio" in Act 2 is his "masterpiece," and that, since
Cassio "doesn't seem to have a chance against Iago . . . [w]hy should we
expect Othello to fare any better?"[5]

The proclamation makes it possible for Othello's nuptial bliss to be
not only celebrated but also interrupted. It sets up a situation that re-
quires nothing more than a little arm-twisting, a little elbow-bending,
by Iago to get the General out of the conjugal bed and into the street.
And when this happens, when Othello intervenes and promises
to punish the wrong-doer, his language is revealing: "he that is approved in this offence,/Though he had twinned with me, both at a
birth,/Shall lose me" (207–9). The care with which he affirms his im-
partiality shows that even before Iago's laboriously indirect accusation
(216–42), Othello entered the scene prepared to make an example of
someone he is very close to.

The example will teach others not to outsport discretion in their
pursuit of such pleasures as "the celebration of . . . nuptials." And of
course Cassio may have just provided Othello with an occasion to
impose "the honorable stop" on himself. From what has Desdemona
"been disturbed"? Her "balmy slumbers" (2.3.250)?

5. Edward Pechter, Othello *and Interpretive Traditions* (Iowa City: University of Iowa
Press, 1998), 75, 78.

Othello has already represented himself to the Duke and senators as one who can be trusted to observe that stop. He had assured them that Venus's "light-wing'd toys" would not lead him to "scant" the "serious and great business" of defending Cyprus from the Turks. Yet the phrasing of this assurance suggests that his occupational commitment to Mars functioned as a guarantee against the corruptions of those toys. Now that the "perdition of the Turkish fleet" threatens him with the perdition of his "occupation," it is appropriate that he repeat the lesson of the honorable stop to himself as well as to others.

Calderwood notes that, at the end of his exit speech in 2.3, Othello accepts "with remarkable equanimity a second arousal from bed":[6]

> All's well now, sweeting,
> Come away to bed.—Sir, for your hurts
> Myself will be your surgeon. Lead him off.
> Iago, look with care about the town
> And silence those whom this vile brawl distracted.
> Come, Desdemona: 'tis the soldier's life
> To have their balmy slumbers waked with strife.
>
> (2.3.248–54)

For the moment he is total soldier, the great leader efficiently spraying orders about the stage and graciously offering to make amends for his officer's unmannerly assault by acting as Montano's personal physician. General Othello is in his element. Honigmann glosses "balmy slumbers" as a euphemism for the intercourse they were having before the interruption.[7] But the question about Desdemona and Othello is pretty much the same as the question about Antonio and Bassanio.[8] Trying to give a definitive answer to the question Did they or didn't they"?, as Honigmann does, seems counterproductive.

"Come, Desdemona: 'tis the soldiers' life/To have their balmy slumbers wak'd with strife." Whether we read the lilt of this exit jingle as defensive or self-satisfied, it resembles nothing so much as the theme song of some heroic Disneyland dodo: "Hi diddledy dee, it's the

6. Calderwood, *The Properties of* Othello, 125.

7. Arden *Othello*, 197.

8. See Chapters 7, 14, 16, and 20.

soldier's life for me!" Othello marches offstage with an air of Mission Accomplished.

But what, exactly, was his mission? Its groundwork was laid by the proclamation and its sequel. They establish the conditions for both nuptial bliss and its interruption. Their objective seems to have been to stir up a new storm and produce new Ottomites to contend with—to have balmy slumbers waked with strife so that the perdition of the Turks would be succeeded by the perdition of Cassio. But why should this be? Why target Cassio? Why, in other words, is Othello already complicit with Iago and handing him the platter on which to put Cassio's head?

If, as Cavell argues, Othello has a use for Iago in 3.3, in 2.3 he has a use for Cassio. The ultimate objective of his mission seems to have been accomplished when he says, "Cassio, I love thee,/But never more be officer of mine." Significantly, this momentous utterance coincides with Desdemona's entrance and another reunion of the Girardian trio. Honigmann departs from both the First Quarto and the Folio in placing her entrance before rather than after the proscriptive "never more be officer of mine." His decision makes good theatrical sense because it allows Othello to see Desdemona watching him as he cashiers Cassio.

At the end of Act 2 Scene 1—just before the proclamation scene—Iago gives Roderigo a compressed (and therefore caricature) version of the line he plans to develop with Othello: Desdemona has a crush on Cassio and is getting tired not only of Othello's "fantastical lies" but also of his defects of appearance, age, and manners. Roderigo finds this hard to believe. But Othello will later find it easy to believe. In fact, as *we* find out later, he was probably ready to believe it when he decided to delegate Cassio the chamberer as his go-between.

"Who does the wolf love?," Menenius asks in *Coriolanus*, and the tribune replies, "The lamb" (2.1.6–7). The question is syntactically ambiguous: "Whom does the wolf love?" and "Who loves the wolf?" converge in the lamb. This registers the complicity that couples the victim and the villain. At one point in 3.3, Othello and Iago all but get married.

This must be terrifying for Othello. And exhilarating. He doesn't intend to actualize the apprehensions, suspicions, and potential conflicts built into the triangle of deceit and desire. But they come with its territory. They belong to its structure. The triangle has a will of its own. Until the disclosure in 3.3, Iago thinks he created the triangle. But it preexisted his wicked deeds and gave him his power well before he began to think of using it. How infuriating and humiliating it would be for him to discover the way his victims have used him!

26. DARK TRIANGLES IN 3.3

The idea that Cassio should appeal for help to Desdemona (2.3.309–20) was first suggested by Iago. It was he who planned to make Emilia "move for Cassio to her mistress" and to arrange for Othello to find Cassio "Soliciting" Desdemona (2.3.378, 382–83).[1] Act 3 opens with Cassio asking Othello's Clown to notify Emilia he'd like an interview and then reporting this to his honest friend, her husband. Iago obligingly offers "to draw the Moor/Out of the way" (3.1.37–38). Up to now, he has comfortably managed the campaign in which attempts at reparation will lead to tragic consequences. But this balance of power begins to change immediately.

After Iago leaves, Emilia enters and assures Cassio "all will . . . be well" because "The general and his wife" are already "talking of it,/And she speaks for you stoutly; the Moor replies" that although Cassio's offense was serious and can't be ignored, "he protests he loves you/And needs no other suitor but his likings" to find the opportunity to reinstate him (3.1.42–52).[2] Desdemona need not take on herself the role of Cassio's suitor: Othello loves him enough for both of them. The (still undisclosed) shadow of triangulated desire falls across Emilia's report.

The importance of this critical moment in the play has been vividly illuminated by Graham Bradshaw: one "effect of Emilia's report is to make Desdemona's subsequent appeals in 3.3 redundant, and even offensive." Another "is to suggest how, at this crucial moment, Othello is to be the victim not only of his ensign's brilliantly malignant improvi-

---

1. That Iago carried this plan out is indicated by Emilia's remark at 3.3.3–4: Cassio's plight "grieves my husband/As if the cause were his."

2. In view of subsequent developments centered on the handkerchief, it's worth noting that Emilia's complicity with Iago and distance from Othello are suggested here when she follows Iago in referring to Othello as "the Moor."

sations but also of the two people he most 'loves' and trusts." Had Cassio abandoned "his (or Iago's) plan of involving Desdemona as soon as he had heard Emilia's report . . . the play, or the play Iago is now staging, would stop."[3] As Bradshaw notes, Emilia's use of the present progressive tense indicates that the discussion she reports occurs as she speaks.[4] This means that Desdemona must just have come from her talk with Othello when she opens 3.3 by greeting Cassio with the promise that "I will do/ All my abilities in thy behalf."

Bradshaw's analysis makes what follows even stranger. In spite of the good news Cassio hears from Emilia, and in spite of "Othello's insistence that . . . [Desdemona's] role as 'Suitor' is . . . inappropriate," both Cassio and Desdemona persist.[5] First, Cassio implores Emilia to set up an interview "with Desdemon alone" (3.1.53–54). The interview takes place after the brief interval of a six-line scene (3.2) guarantees it will be undisturbed by showing Othello on his way to work. Desdemona vows to make Othello's life miserable until he agrees to reinstate Cassio: "thy solicitor shall rather die/Than give thy cause away" (3.3.27–28).

As Bradshaw notes, these requests and assertions seem gratuitous and even perverse. Having been advised by Othello to butt out, Desdemona "encourages Cassio to believe that she is the general's general" and that his reinstatement depends on her success in "overcoming Othello's resistance with her own eager and relentless suit."[6] From this moment on, the trouble the trio make for themselves facilitates and exceeds the trouble Iago makes for them.

No sooner does Desdemona promise lifelong solicitation than Othello enters with Iago. Cassio therefore turns down her invitation to "stay and hear me speak" (3.3.31) and skitters nervously away. Noticing this, Iago begins his direct assault with a stage mumble, "Ha, I like not that." Othello has also noticed it. A series of terse responses, four of them questions, registers his alertness and concern:

3. Bradshaw, *Misrepresentations*, 174–75.
4. Ibid., 149–50.
5. Ibid., 175.
6. Ibid. Strictly speaking, what Desdemona promotes and Othello resists is not reinstatement per se but simply a face-to-face interview.

OTHELLO
>What dost thou say?

IAGO
>Nothing, my lord; or if—I know not what.

OTHELLO
>Was not that Cassio parted from my wife?

IAGO
>Cassio, my lord? no, sure, I cannot think it
>That he would steal away so guilty-like
>Seeing you coming.

OTHELLO   I do believe 'twas he.

DESDEMONA
>How now, my lord?
>I have been talking with a suitor here,
>A man that languishes in your displeasure.

OTHELLO
>Who is't you mean?

DESDEMONA
>Why, your lieutenant, Cassio. Good my lord,
>If I have any grace or power to move you
>His present reconciliation take:
>For if he be not one that truly loves you,
>That errs in ignorance and not in cunning,
>I have no judgment in an honest face.
>I prithee, call him back.

OTHELLO   Went he hence now?

>(3.3.35–51)

We could imagine Othello's "What dost thou say?" to be uttered either sharply or absentmindedly: either Iago's "I like not that" makes him prick up his ears or else he is distracted because he has already noted what Iago hints at and is independently moving toward his next question. Some eighty lines later we learn that he *was* attentive: "I heard thee say even now thou lik'st not that/When Cassio left my wife: what didst not like?" (3.3.112–13). This actualizes the possibility that, in his second question, Othello was already fishing: "Was not that Cassio parted from my wife? Is that what you didn't like?"

The suspicion that begins to surface anticipates the imminent return of the repressed (or merely disremembered) triangle of mimetic desire. "I do believe 'twas he" does more than merely react to Iago's false denial. It identifies Cassio as one who "would steal away so guilty-like"— and "from my wife." Desdemona further fills out the picture: whoever stole away guilty-like is someone she views as "a suitor," someone who "languishes" in Othello's displeasure. The force of Othello's "Who is't you mean?" jumps precipitously beyond the limits of a real or even a rhetorical question. It is apprehensive and probative.

Of course he knows whom she means. But the perplexity that will soon become extreme stirs into life: will she answer truly or will she lie? The form of her answer ("Why, your lieutenant, Cassio") emphasizes its obviousness ("who else?"). "Went *he* hence now?" ignores the substance of her plea and in effect repeats the previous question: was it *Cassio* who just stole away so guilty-like? Desdemona, as if ignoring him in return but catching a hostile note in the brusqueness of his tone, takes Cassio's part in a figure that joins her to him in affective sympathy: he fled because he was "so humbled/That he hath left part of his grief with me/To suffer with him." And she begs him to call Cassio back (3.3.52–54).

In the series of brief exchanges that follows, Othello is affectionate and polite but laconically firm in his insistence on deferring an interview with Cassio to "some other time" (3.3.55). Desdemona, however, pertinaciously ratchets up her advocacy:

> When shall he come?
> Tell me, Othello. I wonder in my soul
> What you would ask me that I should deny
> Or stand so mamm'ring on? What, Michael Cassio
> That came a-wooing with you? and so many a time
> When I have spoke of you dispraisingly
> Hath ta'en your part, to have so much to do
> To bring him in? By'r lady, I could do much!
> (3.3.67–74)

Since Cassio has done so much for you, the argument runs, why can't you simply reciprocate and show your generosity, your appreciation, by receiving him, instead of "mamm'ring on" so? Why indeed?

The argument implies that Othello is partly indebted to Cassio for the gift of Desdemona. In a dazzlingly sudden yet casual disclosure, the residual bonds of triangulated courtship become fully visible, along with a hint of latent complications that will have been there all along. This revelation brings not one but two triangles into view. The first one formed around the practice of courtship. The second now forms around a question of military discipline.

In the first triangle, the outsider Othello presumably sought assistance from someone who was an insider, a practitioner, an authority, in the art of wooing. In the second, Cassio is the outsider and Othello the authority. But since the second triangle emerges as a reconfiguration of the first, Othello becomes the outsider again as Desdemona teams up with Cassio.

Othello is challenged by Desdemona's spirited reminder: "Prithee no more. Let him come when he will,/I will deny thee nothing" (75–76). No more talk about what he owes Cassio: he (not Cassio) will bestow the favor, and Desdemona will be the recipient. She recognizes and immediately fends off this threat ("Why, this is not a boon," 76) with a counter-protestation: she is only entreating him to do what is in his own best interest, ergo she is doing him a favor, rather than—as he suggests— the other way round.

Having countered his effort to seize the donor's position, Desdemona now claims that position for herself and her fellow sufferer, Cassio. Othello repeats his attempt at a magnanimous gesture ("I will deny thee nothing") but not the offer to see Cassio. Instead, he asks for respite from this encounter, "I do beseech thee, grant me this,/To leave me but a little to myself," to which she responds with an echo that belittles his gesture, "Shall I deny you? No, farewell, my lord." He makes amends for his rudeness, "Farewell, my Desdemona, I'll come to thee straight," but her leave-taking is impatient: "Be as your fancies teach you:/Whate'er you be, I am obedient" (3.3.83–89).

And that is the end of the affair: he will never come to her "straight" again. The next time they meet, Othello will have taught Iago to help him be as his fancies teach him. This lesson begins almost as soon as

Desdemona and Emilia make their exit, leaving him alone onstage with Iago. First, however, he reacts to what has just transpired with an aside:

> Excellent wretch! perdition catch my soul
> But I do love thee! and when I love thee not
> Chaos is come again.   (3.3.90–92)

Edward Pechter nicely distinguishes between what the language suggests and what the speaker means to say. He finds the aside "ominous, like Desdemona's assurance to Cassio just earlier that 'thy solicitor shall rather die/Than give thy cause away' . . . ; but whatever our premonitions, Othello's speech is an unqualified effusion of contentment and trust."[7]

Since the aside falls under the shadow of the triangle, I'd prefer to see it as a qualified effusion. "Our premonitions" are shared by a speaker who expresses admiring but perplexed affection rather than contentment. His words convey self-admonitory trepidation rather than trust. Three of those words, "wretch," "but," and "when," impart the qualifying wobbles to the effusion. If "excellent wretch" responds to Desdemona's spirited yet respectful resistance in the preceding exchange and to her unabashed display of loyalty to Cassio, it also carries a spark of the irritation or impatience ignited in Othello during that exchange.[8]

The spark flares into his two oaths and keeps them from being merely exclamatory. The first oath can be reduced to an exclamatory "I surely do love you!" by minimizing the function of "but." However, a sampling of editorial glosses reveals that the looseness of this idiomatic construction makes room for other shades of meaning: "I'll be damned if I don't love you"; "I'll be damned 'unless' I love thee"; "may I be damned if I don't love thee" or "if I stop loving thee."[9]

These don't exhaust the possibilities, and they glance at but don't fully confront an alternative that is, to use Pechter's term, more ominous: "I love thee even though I will be damned for it" ("I can't help

---

7. Pechter, Othello *and Interpretive Traditions*, 79–80.

8. "[W]retch could be a term of endearment or the opposite. Perhaps meant to imply both, playfully" (Honigmann's gloss, *Othello*, 214)—or perplexedly.

9. The glosses of the New Pelican, Folger, and Arden[3] editions respectively.

myself"), which slips toward the malediction, "May I be damned for loving thee."[10] This slippage in turn unsettles the succeeding "when" clause, so that the effusive force of "when" as "if ever" (with the counterfactual sense of "never") gives way to a darkly predictive anticipation of doom: there will be hell to pay, an acknowledgment, just before Iago gets to work, that hell lurks within the speaker as well as in his name.

The complex of implications building through the scene toward "Excellent wretch" steeps "wretch" in a profoundly moving pathos. For he is damned if he does and damned if he doesn't, and she is going to have to suffer for it, and she is not making it easier for either of them by going on so about Cassio. His language proleptically names her the wretch whose perdition will catch his soul. In this pause between Desdemona's departure and the onset of Iago's campaign, Iago's work is already done; the future has already exploded into view.

But doesn't Desdemona understand this? Why is she being such a wretch? What motives of self-representation drive the stubborn obtuseness with which she brings on her fate, the refusal that in fact will make it harder for Othello to turn back and resist the temptation Iago throws in his path?

During Othello's aside, as I imagine the scene, Iago will have been waiting at a respectful distance, ready to ask the money question. But by the time he asks it, Othello will have glimpsed in an instant the shape of the Perdition that lowers on the horizon of his love. So he is prepared for the money question, and he helps Iago draw forth its consequences by urging him on with his own relentless string of interrogatories:

IAGO
    My noble lord—
OTHELLO   What dost thou say, Iago?
IAGO
    Did Michael Cassio, when you wooed my lady,
    Know of your love?

10. Are the senses of these alternatives altered by the fact that "thee" can vary between the intimate and the inferiorizing (or impolite) senses?

OTHELLO He did, from first to last.
Why dost thou ask?

IAGO

But for a satisfaction of my thought,
No further harm.

OTHELLO Why of thy thought, Iago?

IAGO

I did not think he had been acquainted with her.

OTHELLO

O yes, and went between us very oft.

IAGO

Indeed!

OTHELLO

Indeed! Ay, indeed. Discern'st thou aught in that?
Is he not honest?

IAGO

Honest, my lord?

OTHELLO

Honest? Ay, honest.

IAGO

My lord, for aught I know.

OTHELLO

What dost thou think?

IAGO

Think, my lord?

OTHELLO

Think, my lord! By heaven, thou echo'st me
As if there were some monster in thy thought
Too hideous to be shown. Thou dost mean something,
I heard thee say even now thou lik'st not that
When Cassio left my wife: what didst not like?
And when I told thee he was of my counsel
In my whole course of wooing, thou criedst "Indeed?"
And didst contract and purse thy brow together
As if thou then hadst shut up in thy brain
Some horrible conceit.   (3.3.93–118)

"Did Michael Cassio, when you wooed my lady,/Know of your love?" Othello's answer, "He did, from first to last," is not merely confiding in tone. It also has the slightly aggressive or defensive edge of "So what?" He then seizes the interlocutory advantage by asking his own question, "Why dost thou ask?" What's on your mind? Iago back-peddles with "Oh, nothing, not to worry": "But for a satisfaction of my thought,/No further harm."

"No further harm": nothing to be suspicious about, which of course means, something to be suspicious about. Let's not make things worse than they already are. But "why of thy thought, Iago?" Because, Iago answers, he didn't think Cassio "had been acquainted with her." Once again Othello tosses him bait: "O yes, and went between us very oft." Oh yes. Of course. You didn't know? Can you do something with that? Make something of it?

Who diddles whom in this exchange? We have a better sense of what Iago is up to, partly because Othello hasn't yet had a chance to soliloquize. Iago is at the top of his game as he conspicuously hides secrets and pulls Othello along by the nose. Poor Othello, we say. But lines 112–13 show that he has had Cassio on his mind since the beginning of the scene and that it is he who drives the dialogue: "I heard thee say even now thou lik'st not that/When Cassio left my wife: what didst not like?" (3.3.112–13).

Othello's relentless volley of questions is rhetorical and aggressive, not interrogatory. He hunts down the monster in Iago's thought. But the echo-logic of his final speech in the passage leads toward a hypothesis different from the one he expresses in lines 109–10: "thou echo'st me/As if there were some monster in *my* thought." Swerving away from this alternative, his words formally transfer the "horrible conceit" to Iago's brain and, along with it, the power to actualize it. If it all happens with startling rapidity, that's because it has already happened. Poor Iago has to huff and puff to keep up with his victims. It is almost too late to do further harm. The rapidity with which they destroy their relation makes him all but belated and dispensable.

After Iago warns Othello of "the green-eyed monster," their exchanges begin to reverberate with echoes of the opprobrious language he, Brabantio, and Roderigo use about Othello in the early scenes ("the thicklips," "an old black ram," "a Barbary horse," "sooty bosom," "an erring barbarian"). To Iago's "Good God, the souls of all my tribe defend/From jealousy" (3.3.178–79), Othello huffily rejoins that he is proof against the monster:

> Exchange me for a goat
> When I shall turn the business of my soul
> To such . . . surmises. . . .
>
> . . .
>
> Nor from mine own weak merits will I draw
> The smallest fear or doubt of her revolt,
> For she had eyes and chose me.   (3.3.183–92)

"She had eyes and chose me": she knew what she was getting, a member of an alien nation. Is that what he ascribes his "weak merits" to? As if this moment, preserved in Iago's "all my tribe," knifes into his mind and stays there, he returns to it in his final speech: "like the base Indian [or Judean]," he had thrown "a pearl away/Richer than all his tribe" (5.2.345–46).

Iago picks up on the defensive edginess of "She had eyes" and plays off of it a few lines later. He suggests that Othello has replaced Brabantio as her dupe. Brabantio had expressed incredulity that Desdemona could "fall in love with what she feared to look on" (1.3.99), and Iago now echoes this: "She did deceive her father, marrying you,/And when she seemed to shake, and fear your looks,/She loved them most" (3.3.209–211).[11]

In 1.3, the threat posed by Brabantio was rudely brushed aside by the Duke's eagerness to send General Othello to the front. Now, in 3.3, Iago resurrects the spirit of Brabantio. He drives home the "truth," the authority, of Brabantio's final words in the play: "Look to her, Moor, if thou hast eyes to see:/She has deceived her father, and may thee" (1.3.293–94).

Iago directly broaches the issue of the "looks" Desdemona seemed to fear with his frontal assault on the blackness problem at 3.3.232–

---

11. In ratifying this assertion with "And so she did," Othello opens up another vista on the prehistory of the play—on conceivably furtive behavior enabling the courting couple to hide the truth of their goings-on from Brabantio. But once again, the active agent, the guilty party, is Desdemona. By phrasing it thus, Iago capitalizes on Othello's previous insistence that she was more than half the wooer and prepares to turn that against both his victims.

42.[12] This leads Othello, in the first of his three soliloquies, to speculate along lines that might induce someone in his position to enlist Cassio as a go-between:

> Haply for I am black
> And have not those soft parts of conversation
> That chamberers have, or for I am declined
> Into the vale of years—yet that's not much—
> She's gone, I am abused, and my relief
> Must be to loathe her.   (3.3.267–72)

He entertains two possibilities but immediately dismisses the second and rushes as if with relief to the conclusion, "She's gone" because he is black and lacks Cassio's manners. Cassio is now bitterly downgraded to a chamberer, a carpet-knight. But wasn't he always? Isn't that what Othello initially saw in him? Did he ever call him "honest Michael"?

"My relief/*Must* be to loathe her": This is his assignment and he tackles it by diving into the villain's discourse under Iago's supervision:

> Look here, Iago,
> All my fond love thus do I blow to heaven:
> 'Tis gone!
> Arise, black vengeance, from the hollow hell,
> Yield up, O love, thy crown and hearted throne
> To tyrannous hate! Swell, bosom, with thy fraught,
> For 'tis of aspics' tongues!

Look here, Iago: listen to my bombast. Watch me get into it.

IAGO   Yet be content.
Get into it, by all means.
OTHELLO
   O, blood, blood, blood! *Othello kneels.*

I'm getting into it.

---

12. Between lines 192 and 450 in 3.3, there are five direct or indirect references to his blackness, and another in his impassioned history of the handkerchief in 3.4 (57–77). In addition, goats, monkeys, horned beasts, and monsters reappear several times in his utterances (3.3.183, 398–99; 3.4.62, 263).

IAGO

Patience, I say, your mind perhaps may change.

Good! Keep going.

OTHELLO

Never, Iago: Like to the Pontic sea,
Whose icy current and compulsive course
Ne'er keeps retiring ebb but keeps due on
To the Propontic and the Hellespont:
Even so my bloody thoughts with violent pace
Shall ne'er look back, ne'er ebb to humble love
Till that a capable and wide revenge
Swallow them up. Now by yond marble heaven
In the due reverence of a sacred vow
I here engage my words.   (3.3.447–82)

How did you like that? But why this extravagant burst of regional color?

We now call the "Pontic sea" the "Black Sea," the "Propontic" the "Sea of Marmora," and the "Hellespont" the "Dardanelles." The Black Sea is the very large sea north of the Aegean, which is the northeastern arm of the Mediterranean. The Black Sea flows into the much smaller Sea of Marmora, which passes through the straits of the Dardanelles into the Aegean. Thus Othello compares the force of his hatred to the force of a huge body of water as it descends through a constantly narrowing passage.[13]

Again, why these particular bodies of water? What they all share is contiguity to Turkey. "Are we turned Turks?" Othello had exclaimed after Cassio's fight with Montano (2.3.166). Here, he himself turns Turk and confirms his enmity against himself.

If, according to the Quarto stage directions, Othello kneels at 3.3.454. When Iago drops to his knees ten lines later, it has the effect of a mordant parody like that of the Battle of the Bended Knee in *Richard II*, 5.3.[14] He swears to place himself under the revenger's command. At this point Othello confers on Iago the field commission he

13. http://www.shakespeare-navigators.com/othello/Water.html.

14. See my comments on this battle in *Making Trifles of Terrors: Redistributing Complicities in Shakespeare* (Stanford: Stanford University Press, 1997), 176–77.

had denied him before: "Now art thou my lieutenant" (3.3.481). But it is a commission in the wrong field, and Iago accepts it as if it were an offer of marriage: "I am your own forever" (3.3.482). He thus tightens the knot Othello began tying earlier with "I am bound to thee forever" (3.3.217).

27. DESDEMONA'S GREEDY EAR

If, as Cavell argues, Othello has a use for Iago in 3.3, we learn from the disclosure in the same scene that he has had a use for Cassio since before the beginning of the play. He seems to have used Cassio both to stir up Desdemona's desire and to keep his own distance from it. He desires her desire but is troubled by it. The marks of his diffidence are clearly inscribed in the courtship account he gives the senators in 1.3.

Let's turn to that passage and look at Othello's strangely twisted story of who does what to whom:

> Her father loved me, oft invited me,
> Still questioned me the story of my life
> From year to year—the battles, sieges, fortunes
> That I have passed.
> I ran it through, even from my boyish days
> To th' very moment that he bade me tell it,
> Wherein I spake of most disastrous chances,
> Of moving accidents by flood and field,
> Of hair-breadth scapes i'th'imminent deadly breach,
> Of being taken by the insolent foe
> And sold to slavery; of my redemption thence
> And portance in my travailous history;
> Wherein of antres vast and deserts idle,
> Rough quarries, rocks and hills whose heads touch heaven
> It was my hint to speak—such was my process—
> And of the cannibals that each other eat,
> The Anthropophagi, and men whose heads
> Do grow beneath their shoulders.

It's significantly at this point, following the reference to predatory homophagy, that Othello brings Desdemona into his story:

> This to hear
> Would Desdemona seriously incline,
> But still the house affairs would draw her thence,
> Which ever as she could with haste dispatch
> She'd come again, and with a greedy ear
> Devour up my discourse; which I, observing,
> Took once a pliant hour and found good means
> To draw from her a prayer of earnest heart
> That I would all my pilgrimage dilate,
> Whereof by parcels she had something heard
> But not intentively: I did consent.   (1.3.129–56)

Here is a rough paraphrase of the critical section, the characterization of Desdemona's response beginning at line 146 ("This to hear . . ."): observing her "rapacious appetite" for my discourse, I found means to persuade her to implore me to retell the whole story, only parts of which her household chores had allowed her to hear.[1] I then consented, and was often able to beguile her of her tears with my accounts of one or another bad thing that befell me in my youth. Othello displaces the perversions of Ignoble Savages (whose skin color might resemble his) to curiosities, freaks, monsters, totally unrelated and perhaps inimical to the speaker. But the decontaminating gesture fails almost as soon as he redirects attention from the monsters to Desdemona.

His story strangely positions Desdemona as an intruder who disrupts his idyllic relation to her father. The news of her intrusion affects our sense of Brabantio's response to their elopement.[2] His anger may be fueled by jealousy.

The unexpected vividness of the figure "greedy ear"—its reductiveness, its weight as a synecdoche—registers a moment of recoil. It glances back to his mention in line 144 of "the cannibals that each other eat," and since Othello's language also betrays his complicity in taking advantage of Desdemona's appetite, it binds them closely together in

---

1. The phrase "rapacious appetite" is borrowed from Greenblatt, *Renaissance Self-Fashioning*, 239.

2. See the brilliant comments on Brabantio by Edward A. Snow in "Sexual Anxiety and the Male Order of Things in Othello," *English Literary Renaissance* 10 (1980): 410 and by Girard in *A Theater of Envy*, 183–84 and 293.

mutual cannibalism. At least in the defiles of his rhetoric, their courtship falls under the shadow of the beast with two backs.

It is from this shadow that his narrative strives to escape by shifting the cause of their burgeoning desire from sexuality to stories: his
prowess as a raconteur combined with vivid little sketches of himself
as the victim of "most disastrous chances":

> I did consent,
> And often did beguile her of her tears
> When I did speak of some distressful stroke
> That my youth suffered. My story being done
> She gave me for my pains a world of sighs,
> She swore in faith 'twas strange, 'twas passing strange,
> 'Twas pitiful, 'twas wondrous pitiful;
> She wished she had not heard it, yet she wished
> That heaven had made her such a man. She thanked me
> And bade me, if I had a friend that loved her,
> I should but teach him how to tell my story
> And that would woo her. Upon this hint I spake:
> She loved me for the dangers I had passed
> And I loved her that she did pity them.
> This only is the witchcraft I have used:
>   *Enter* DESDEMONA, IAGO, *Attendants.*
> Here comes the lady, let her witness it.
>   (1.3.156–71)

His stories evoke from Desdemona not groans of lust but sighs of pity,
a proper Aristotelian response by a proper Venetian lady seated next
to a crackling fire, as if in some novella by Henry James. Nevertheless,
discernible beneath the appeal to the register of romance are traces of
the fear of monstrosity that give the appeal the value of defensive sub-
limation. The story betrays the presence of another triangle of mimetic
desire. First, Brabantio "loved me," then Desdemona "loved me" and
stole him from Brabantio.

If we revisit this speech after learning in 3.3 about Cassio's role as
mediator, new problems arise. First, Othello says nothing about that
mediation. Second, Cassio is among those on stage silently listening

to the narrative from which his part has been elided. Third, Othello reports a request by Desdemona that resonates through the indirect discourse of his conveyance as demurely coquettish but that contains the germ of the go-between idea:

> She wished she had not heard it, yet she wished
> That heaven had made her such a man. She thanked me
> And bade me, if I had a friend that loved her,
> I should but teach him how to tell my story
> And that would woo her.   (1.3.163–67)

As reported by Othello, Desdemona's "if I had a friend that loved her" seems at first glance to be similar in tone to her wish "That heaven had made her such a man." Both statements are coyly distanced acknowledgments that Othello is on the right track: his wooing is having its effect. But, since the statements are Othello's, they register his apprehension, repeated later in the scene, that she is more than half the wooer (1.3.261–75). The optative playfulness in which his report invests her suggestions doesn't prevent them from sounding like suavely aggressive innuendoes. This investment conforms with the diffidence that shades many of Othello's utterances in 1.3: an anxiety about her forwardness, an effort to protect or at least dissociate himself from her frank public avowals of desire.

"She . . . bade me, if I had a friend," can be construed figuratively or literally: either, "she urged me to act as a friend to myself" ("to do myself a favor") or else "she urged me to find a go-between." The former is obviously what Desdemona must have intended, since she referred to "a friend that loved *her*." The latter is a demonic inversion of the former, an erotic analogue of the lieutenancy whose potentially ironic structure has best been characterized by Julia Genster: "In choosing a subordinate a captain is, in effect, choosing a second self; he is empowering someone to play him, to be him in his absence."[3]

Had Desdemona intended the go-between suggestion to be taken literally, we'd expect Othello to report her as saying and implying "'If I [Othello] had a friend that loved *me*,' I would enlist him as my

3. Genster, "Lieutenancy, Standing In, and Othello," 786.

go-between." Oddly, then, and even perversely, Othello opts for the go-between plan in spite of the strange proviso, "a friend that loved her"[4]—or perhaps *because* of it? His decision produces the triangular instability that this proviso structurally and conventionally guarantees. The go-between will become the Friend/Rival whose threat reanimates Othello's potentiality to be victimized: defending against Desdemona's desire, he exposes himself to the danger of being betrayed and replaced by his courtly placeholder.

Othello uses his report to the senators to continue dealing with the fear. But he only half succeeds. The triumphant noblesse oblige of "I did consent" comically disowns responsibility for the manipulativeness betrayed in the statement that it was *he* who "found good means/To draw from her" a request for more of the stories which "often did beguile her of her tears" (157), and in lines 160–67 he savors his conquest by mimicking the labored coyness with which she archly invites him to pop the question.

What this performance registers is the speaker's sense of the deviousness and underlying horror of their mutual seduction, but a sense also of the gradual shift of power in which his narrative dilation strives both to satisfy and to domesticate the desires of her greedy ear. He redescribes their discourse in terms of prayer and pilgrimage. And all this happens with Cassio standing quietly by, along with Iago, whose subsequent comment on the performance is characteristically mordant and one-sided, but contains a grain of truth: "Mark me with what violence she first loved the Moor, but for bragging and telling her fantastical lies—and will she love him still for prating? let not thy discreet heart think it" (2.1.220–23).

An earlier comment, uttered by Iago in the soliloquy that concludes 1.3, floats one of the play's teasingly ambiguous pronominal references: "After some time to abuse Othello's ear/That *he* is too familiar with his wife" (1.3.394–95, my italics). In the context of Iago's planning, the referent of "he" is more likely to be Cassio than Othello. But the preceding interpretation suggests that whatever we think Iago intends

---

4. In Othello's version of this plan, as Desdemona implies in 3.3, he may have told Cassio his story, but he surely didn't teach him *how* to tell it.

to say, in the context of Othello's reaction to Desdemona's greedy ear, the "he" drifts in the Moor's direction.[5]

Looking back from 3.3, we're inclined to wonder about the silent presence of Cassio during this account, especially since the story Othello tells is selective and has a defensive function. More is involved in winning Desdemona than telling stories about himself in her father's house. Cassio's role in the courtship is not expressly mentioned. But it is clearly laid out, and it glides past like a dark shape in what is retrospectively the most uncanny utterance in the speech, and also the most disturbing, because it implies that the go-between idea was not Othello's but Desdemona's: she "bade me, if I had a friend that loved her, I should but teach him how to tell my story." Cassio listens silently. And at the end of the scene Othello chooses Iago and Emilia rather than Cassio to escort Desdemona to Cyprus.

"If she confess that she was half the wooer," Brabantio states when Desdemona appears, his "bad blame" will not fall on Othello: if she is half the wooer, the blame is wholly hers. And she proclaims from the start that she was and still is half the wooer. Critics who argue that Othello subscribes to Brabantio's misogynist article of faith are partly right: his language represents him representing her (to himself) as half the wooer. It already glances at the pornographic fantasy Iago will concoct later.

Yet there is more at stake. To punish the two-backed monster is always and unavoidably to punish both Othello and Desdemona. Her lust is entangled in his, and the two of them together jeopardize his effort to escape the stigma of the Venetian stereotype of the "lascivious Moor." This danger is already present in the comparison with which he prefaces his narrative:

> as truly as to heaven
> I do confess the vices of my blood
> So justly to your grave ears I'll present
> How I did thrive in this fair lady's love
> And she in mine. (1.3.124–28)

---

5. The reference to Othello is most tellingly justified by Greenblatt, *Renaissance Self-Fashioning*, 233. For an excellent critique of responses to the passage see Pechter, *Othello and Interpretive Traditions*, 94–95.

The element of difference is overcome by the similarity on which the grammar of analogy insists. "The buried identification here between the vices of the blood and mutual thriving in love" haunts everything that follows.[6] It sets the stage for the eventual displacement of vices from Othello's blood to Desdemona's. Punishment is what he seeks, and he empowers Iago to serve as the agent of retribution. Iago will help him procure the sinner's keen and bitter pleasure of hurting, punishing, destroying himself by hurting, punishing, destroying what, next to himself, he most loves.[7]

In making this argument I return, finally, to Cavell's basic insight. Othello's demand for ocular proof "was no purer a threat than it was a command, as if he does indeed wish for this outcome, as if he has a use for Iago's suspicions, hence a use for Iago that reciprocates Iago's use of him." Iago "offers Othello an opportunity to believe something, something . . . [he can] oppose to something else he knows."

What he knows is that Iago is lying, but he would rather believe Iago's slander than the "more terrible" truth of "her faithfulness," the fearful frankness of her desire for him, the freedom of her voluntary gesture of total submission. The danger of submitting to that submission is that what his blackness symbolizes will shift from the isolated splendor, the "unhoused free condition," of the romance hero to the circumscription of the two-backed beast.[8] But the possibility that he

6. Greenblatt , *Renaissance Self-Fashioning*, 245.

7. My reading of the Othello/Iago relation offered in this study is intended to complicate the relatively simple-minded interpretation, put forward by Brian Vickers, that Othello is a "lunkhead" and Iago a genius. See Vickers, *Appropriating Shakespeare: Contemporary Critical Quarrels* (New Haven: Yale University Press, 1993), 74–91. "Lunkhead" is Stanley Cavell's term (used in *Disowning Knowledge*, 133), cited by Vickers in a characteristically meanminded critique of Cavell's *Othello* essay (*Appropriating Shakespeare*, 308–20), which Vickers—dismissing Cavell's focus on the problematics of skepticism as unhistorical—incorrectly treats as an example of "psychocriticism." Vickers has a point in claiming that Cavell contradicts himself on the question whether Othello and Desdemona consummate their marriage, but Cavell's inconsistency is more understandable than Vickers's confident "we are left in no doubt that Othello and Desdemona consummate their marriage on Cyprus" (314).

8. Cavell's reading is more powerful and persuasive than the theater-of-envy interpretation Girard develops by cranking Othello through his mimetic-desire machine. Girard, with his usual tone of excitement at his own originality, comes up with the well-worn insight that Iago makes "explicit the thoughts" of jealousy "that Othello is vainly

might *accept* the danger, not flinch from it, not disown his knowledge of Desdemona's faithfulness: Shakespeare's play is about Othello's refusal of this possibility, and about the self-loathing that results and is registered in his flaying of the two-backed beast.

That he is the sole object of Desdemona's desire and she is so eager to publish the fact only makes matters worse. She insists on accompanying Othello to Cyprus because if she should be left behind when he goes to war "The rites for which I love him are bereft me" (1.3.257). Even as he seconds her request, he's at pains to emphasize that the sexual "will" motivating the request is hers, not his, and the very phrase he later uses to affirm her faithfulness also reaffirms his insistence that Desdemona of the greedy ear was the primary mover in their relation: "For she had eyes and chose me" (3.3.192).

This is what throws Othello off balance and perplexes him "in the extreme."[9] In Cavell's words, Othello is surprised "at what he has elicited from her; . . . Rather than imagine himself to have elicited that, or solicited it, . . . [he] would imagine it elicited by anyone and everyone else."[10] It's the role he imagines for Cassio, the role he had, so to speak, *pre*-selected Cassio to play in choosing him as go-between and advocate. Cassio is his alibi, ready in the wings along with honest Iago should the need arise for Othello to persuade himself it wasn't he who stained her.

Cassio, Iago, Othello: this too is a Girardian triangle, one of envy rather than jealousy, with Othello choosing to promote the outsider Cassio instead of Iago. But the choice was arbitrary only to Iago. His exposition in 1.1 suggests that Othello gave Cassio his commission during roughly the same period that Cassio was his go-between and second in the courtship.

Because temporal relations in this play are famously vague, they assert a claim on interpretive attention. Did Othello choose Cassio as his officer before or after he chose him as a go-between? The implications both in Iago's irritable report and in Othello's account of the courtship

---

trying to repress" (*A Theater of Envy*, 292). Girard is nevertheless helpful in pointing us toward the structural conditions of a discourse of heterosociality that introduces heteroerotic elements of desire into the language and situation of the hero's wife and of the lieutenant who was recently his surrogate and go-between.

9. A. D. Nuttall, *A New Mimesis: Shakespeare and the Representation of Reality* (London: Methuen, 1983), 138–39.

10. Cavell, *Disowning Knowledge*, 136.

suggest that he was a go-between before Othello gave him his commission. The disclosure throws an ironic shadow over Iago's complaint in 1.1 that Othello "Nonsuits my mediators" (1.1.15–16). Iago didn't know that Othello has a mediator of his own to reward.

This scenario is supported by positional logic. A lieutenant is second in command and a substitute or "placeholder" roughly comparable in the domain of Mars to that of the second or go-between in the domain of Venus. The difference is that in the military hierarchy the lieutenant is safely subordinate to his superior—there can be no rivalry between them—but the suitor's friend is traditionally, notoriously, a site of concealed rivalry and betrayal.

It's interesting that the triangle Cassio/Iago/Othello is featured by Iago in skewed form after the disclosure. For Othello's benefit, he pictures himself in bed with the sleeping Cassio, who kissed him and boarded him because he dreamed Iago was Desdemona. Iago as Othello's beloved getting screwed by Cassio; Iago, soon after, replacing both Desdemona and Cassio in Othello's affection and being rewarded with a field commission, albeit a commission in the wrong field: "I greet thy love . . . with acceptance bounteous. . . . Now thou art my lieutenant." Iago submits: "I am your own for ever" (3.3.472–82).

As Genster finely puts it, they celebrate "their newly wrought alliance as sexual avengers within the structures of military rank."[11] "Othello's occupation" has been revived in the field of domestic warfare, in which his new lieutenant has also appropriated the spousal role. At the end of the play, when Iago says, "I bleed, sir, but not killed," he strangely represents himself as a truer Desdemona, one whom Othello has deflowered but lets live.

28. IMPERTINENT TRIFLING: DESDEMONA'S HANDKERCHIEF

—that's but a trifle here. . . .
—we make trifles of terrors. . . .

Too much attention has been paid to the symbolic meanings of the famous handkerchief and too little to such considerations as its puta-

11. Genster, "Lieutenancy, Standing In, and *Othello*," 788.

tive size and the odd circumstances of its appearance and removal. Just when Othello's rage has reached a first climax, Desdemona enters to tell him he is keeping his dinner and dinner guests waiting (3.3.283). "I am to blame," he replies, and her next questions ("Why is your speech so faint? are you not well?") tell us to hear something more in the reply than an apology for delaying dinner.

"I am to blame" is at the same time a logical response to the thought that concludes the soliloquy he has just uttered, "If she be false, O then heaven mocks itself,/I'll not believe't" (282–83). "Haply," he is to blame "for I am black,/And have not those soft parts of conversation/That chamberers have," therefore "She's gone" (267–71). Seeing Desdemona approach, he veers away from that dread conclusion and, in effect, blames himself for believing it possible. But perhaps he is to blame for having aroused her desire in the first place.

What allows him to share the blame with Desdemona is the idea that "this forked plague is fated to us" (280)—"us" males, husbands, and especially "great ones" (277), not to mention great ones who are black, don't have extended manners, are somewhat "declined" in years (269). This idea, manured by Iago, leads him to answer her questions by hinting at his imaginary horns,

> OTHELLO
>> I have a pain upon my forehead, here.
>
> DESDEMONA
>> Faith, that's with watching, 'twill away again.
>> Let me but bind it hard, within this hour
>> It will be well.
>
> OTHELLO   Your napkin is too little.
>> Let it alone. Come, I'll go in with you.
>
> DESDEMONA
>> I am very sorry that you are not well.
>>> *Exeunt Othello and Desdemona.*
>>> (3.3.288–93)

This is the most problematic of problem scenes. It has to be decelerated and visualized. Let's start with the handkerchief. Is it small as a kleenex or big as a flag? Has it been seen on her person before? At what point does she drop it? Before or after his "Let it alone"? Arden[3] follows Rowe's 1709 edition and places the stage direction before, a decision that blurs and broadens the sense of "Let it alone." It could then mean, "don't bother to pick it up," which would accord with H. C. Goddard's idea that Othello's pushing her hand away causes it to drop.

I would stage it differently. As I see it, the question everyone asks—Is it his forehead or her handkerchief he tells her to let alone?—is not only a question for them both. It is also a test for them both. If he means to indicate his forehead, he is being petulant: he doesn't want to be nursed or coddled by *her*. But if he means to indicate the handkerchief, he is being serious: he is, in effect, asking her to part with the very token he had insisted she always keep about her. "Let it alone," he says. His challenge. Her choice. She chooses. The handkerchief flutters to the ground.

To seal the meaning of that gesture, he quickly walks her away from where it lies. For one moment they flare into a fury of mutual rejection. From then on, regardless of what she claims, she understands his words. "Let it alone," he says. And she does. Let nobody blame him. She has heard and shared the fury.

The crucial object makes its appearance modestly and anonymously as a "napkin." That is what Emilia also calls it before she enlarges on its significance and Iago's interest in it, after which she teasingly offers it to Iago as "that same handkerchief" (310). Thus, almost as soon as it appears, we learn that it had already been the topic of much conversation and observation, fetishized by Othello as a token of her love and fidelity, and loved by her for this reason.

To learn this is to realize that an extraordinary event has just taken place. Othello's "Let *it* alone" is teasingly laconic, but whether "it" denotes his forehead or the napkin, the result of his command is that Desdemona drops the napkin, and this tells us how she heard the statement. Yet he had "conjured her she should ever keep it," and "she reserves it evermore about her" (Emilia, at 3.3.298–300).

This precious token could hardly go unrecognized, and it would be perverse to stage the episode in a manner that concealed it from Othello (for example, by having Desdemona wad it up in her hand). She, at any rate, knows what she is dropping. To represent him as recognizing it before he tells her to drop it makes him perceive what she offers to bind his head with. She hears him countermand his general conjuration by ordering her to drop it. This is the high gestural melodrama of interlocutory warfare.

When Othello points to his forehead and Desdemona says "that's with watching," she obviously refers to his staying up too late, working too hard, and so on. Yet listening to the phrase with Othello's ears may give it a different ring, for it comes after a stretch of dialogue with Iago in which much had been made of perceiving, observing, seeing, scanning, and noting (3.3.245–56). "Watching" may, like standing the watch, mean protecting against trouble, and it may also mean looking for trouble. Desdemona's "'twill away again" then has the force of a shallow consolation, like his "If she be false . . . /I'll not believe it" (3.3.283). Her repeating the sentiment in the next line may sound suspiciously dismissive to him: perhaps the offer to "bind" his head is an offer to hide his horns and seel up his eyes—and with the very handkerchief that signifies the power of the gift that binds her to him in loving obligation.

If she has abused and soiled the gift, if she is doing so now with this brazen gesture, it makes sense for him to protect himself by refusing the offer. He will not let her touch him with it and his command is so phrased as to persuade her he wants her to drop the fetish and leave it behind. But doesn't he notice that she drops the precious keepsake? Only a little later in the same scene he explodes when Iago, who has not left the stage and still has the handkerchief, all but gives him the ocular proof he demanded, telling him that "today" he saw "Cassio wipe his beard" with it (440–57).

Presumably Iago doesn't know that Othello had seen the handkerchief several minutes earlier. Emilia neglects to tell him when or under what conditions she found the handkerchief. But doesn't Othello remember? It is evidently useful to him to disremember in order to set up the possibility of her losing it. On the one hand, she does not deserve to keep it if she has violated what it represents; on the other hand, if she loses it despite his conjuration, she violates what it represents. Thus, by helping Desdemona lose it and by disremembering the episode, Othello facilitates the production of the ocular proof that will give him vantage to exclaim on her.

If Desdemona normally keeps the handkerchief "evermore about her," why doesn't she pick it up before going offstage? Emilia tells Iago she "let it drop by negligence" (3.3.315), and at 3.4.23 Desdemona wonders, "Where should I lose that handkerchief, Emilia?" What could cause such unexpected negligence and forgetfulness? What motivates Desdemona's act of disremembrance?

The gesture that interprets Othello's "Let it alone" as a command to let go of the handkerchief signals a double rejection. In his rejection of her offer to soothe him, she hears the message that she does not deserve and should not have the handkerchief. Dropping it may be read simultaneously as an act of obedience and as a contestatory gesture rejecting his rejection—he doesn't deserve the love and fidelity her possession of the handkerchief symbolizes. Dropping the handkerchief enables her to be in the position of losing it, and losing it, she knows, would be "enough/To put him to ill-thinking" if he were capable of jealousy, which of course he isn't (3.4.25–31). So (one is tempted to say), knowing this, she loses it. And later, having elicited from him all the signs of jealousy, she ignores the signs and stubbornly denies that she lost the handkerchief (3.4.85–90). Her stubbornness in this exchange is closely linked to the maddening stubbornness with which she changes the subject from the handkerchief to Cassio. In spite of her devotion to Othello, her sense of injured merit keeps her from acknowledging his jealousy, even as she pursues a course of rhetorical action that aggravates it.

Othello and Desdemona work closely together to lose the handkerchief and to disremember its loss. In the playing-through of disowned desires and apprehensions, they cooperate with Iago by losing the handkerchief. They make the kind of trouble for themselves, for each other, that each is motivated to make. "Give me the ocular proof," Othello commands Iago (3.3.363), but not until after he has helped provide a likely candidate for that function.

Her dropping the handkerchief is already ocular proof. If she is unfaithful she should not have it; if she does not have it she is unfaithful. For Desdemona, his rejection of her offer to soothe him with the handkerchief is ocular proof that he has rejected her. Losing the handkerchief puts her in a good position to test the force and meaning of his rejection.

My sense of what she hears in his words is influenced by the premise that she's not interested in sexual adventures. She desires Othello and is "loyal" to him, and whatever messages the play sends about the question of consummation, it is a problem for him rather than for her. But it's also a problem for Emilia and for the cynical Venetian ideology of marriage she and Iago share.

Why won't she tell Desdemona about the handkerchief? Partly, no doubt, out of loyalty to Iago; partly because it enables her to put pressure on Desdemona to acknowledge both the truth about Othello and the larger truth that their marriage is not the exception Desdemona thinks it is—that it is as difficult, as precarious, as frangible, as any other. Emilia may be moved by the voyeuristic curiosity that servants entertain toward their betters. She may want to prove that not even the divine Desdemona can avoid being victimized by the misogynist discourse governing relations between men and women, wives and husbands, in and out of marriage in Venice.

Near the end of *The Tempest*, Prospero says of Caliban: "This thing of darkness I/Acknowledge mine." In *The Underside of Innocence*, his marvelous study of Norman Rockwell and the innocence industry, Richard Halpern uses this statement to exemplify what he calls "disavowal," and he distinguishes it from "innocence." He defines "innocence" as "a choice not to know something," and he defines "disavowal" by contrasting it to Prospero's act of acknowledgment. Disavowal is "a refusal to acknowledge those things of darkness that are ours."[1] If disavowal is a refusal, at some level it involves Saying No. As a result, Halpern argues, the practice of disavowal is stained by residual awareness of the dark things disavowed.

"A choice not to know"; "a refusal to acknowledge." These definitions of innocence and disavowal are tellingly similar: both are framed in the rhetoric of intention. Yet Halpern describes and employs them as operations of what I've been calling practical unconsciousness. Both apply equally well to Desdemona's interlocutory resistance—her disremembrance—in the scenes under discussion.

---

1. Richard Halpern, *Normal Rockwell: The Underside of Innocence* (Chicago: University of Chicago Press, 2006), 4.

The fruits of disremembrance are harvested in 3.4. Desdemona initiates the action by sending the Clown in search of Cassio (1–22), then pauses to wonder about the handkerchief and to assure Emilia Othello is incapable of jealousy. Seeing Othello approach, she says "I will not leave him now till Cassio/Be called to him" (32–33).[2] Othello barges in with a series of broad hints about her lechery that hark back in tone to Iago's quips and his comments on hand-paddling in 2.1. To his angry variations on the topic of her moist and liberal hand, she responds at first with reserve (33), then more tartly (40–41), and finally, as if to put an end to this nonsense and get back to *her* topic of choice, "I cannot speak of this. Come, now, your promise"— "What promise, chuck?"—"I have sent to bid Cassio come speak with you" (48–50).

Viewers who have watched Othello get upended by Iago in 3.3 may become understandably apprehensive when Desdemona enjoins him to keep his promise. This is the first of the two occasions on which Othello addresses her as "chuck." The other occurs at 4.2.25, after he has cross-examined Emilia and ordered her to fetch Desdemona. "Chuck" is normally a term of endearment, but here both instances express the anger with which he acknowledges the foolish affection that made him a cuckold.

I find it hard to imagine that Desdemona, who earlier engaged Iago in what the Arden editor disapprovingly calls "cheap backchat," grasps the meaning of Othello's little disquisition on her hot hand (3.4.36–47) less clearly than that editor: "The palm, if hot and moist, was taken to be an indication of 'hot' desires"; "[liberal] free, and so 'too free' and so 'loose.'"[3] The Desdemona who displayed acquaintance with humoral theory just before Othello's entrance in 3.4 (30–31) and who, according to Iago, flirtatiously paddled palms with Cassio (2.1.167–68) knows whereof she "cannot speak," or will not speak. It is she, after all, and not Emilia, who first brings up the possibility of "ill-thinking" and jealousy at 3.4.25–31, but only to rule it out in advance. Immediately

2. Keeping the Arden line count but replacing M. R. Ridley's First Quarto reading with the Folio variant adopted by several other modern editors.

3. Ridley, Arden *Othello*, 54, 125.

after she does so, Othello enters displaying all the signs of ill thinking and jealousy.

Far from appearing ingenuously unaware of the jealousy with which he confronts her from this point on, she shows rather that she refuses to acknowledge it. She refuses to acknowledge that he has any cause, therefore any right, to be jealous, refuses to acknowledge even the possibility of behavior on her part that could be misinterpreted. As Thomas Rymer huffily and astutely observes, "Othello's Jealousie, that had rag'd so loudly and had been so uneasie to himself, must have reach'd her knowledge. . . . And yet she must still be impertinent in her suit for *Cassio*."[4]

After 3.4 her refusal to acknowledge his jealousy modulates into a desire to rise above it—or, to put it more precisely, a desire to show herself rising above it. Yet her ability to ignore or rise above Othello's jealousy depends on his expressing it. From 3.4 on, she secures that ability by pushing the button that lights up Othello's angry-husband display. She acts in a manner calculated to evoke from him the signs of ill thinking that denote the jealousy she won't acknowledge.

The battle between them is joined when Othello, armed (as he thinks) with his ocular proof, prepares to establish the guilt that will justify the sentence of death he has already passed on her.[5] His preparation—in effect, the argument for the prosecution—consists in conferring the broadest possible significance on her betrayal. He interprets it as misuse of the generous gift of power he has bestowed on her, the apotropaic power to ward off the contamination of their coupling by moderating the sexuality she arouses.

This gift, this alienated power, together with the sexuality he both desires and fears, makes Desdemona her captain's captain and her general's general. It is to insure against the risk this involves—the risk (let us say it now) of castration—that Othello reifies gift and power together in the second gift of the handkerchief. Thus he tries to reclaim some of the control he has alienated by making Desdemona

4. Thomas Rymer, "A Short View of Tragedy . . . ," in *Critical Essays of the Seventeenth Century*, ed. J. E. Spingarn, vol. 2, *1650–1685* (1957; rpt. Bloomington: Indiana University Press, 1963), 246.

5. "I will withdraw/To furnish me with some swift means of death/For the fair devil" (3.3.479–81).

both responsible for the power she has and potentially guilty for its misuse. In its structure this tactic resembles Portia's bestowal of the ring on Bassanio after she admits that "Myself and what is mine to you and yours/Is now converted" (*The Merchant of Venice* 3.2.166–67). The compensatory function of the ring is identical to that of the handkerchief:

> I give . . . this ring,
> Which when you part from, lose, or give away,
> Let it presage the ruin of your love,
> And be my vantage to exclaim on you.
> (*The Merchant of Venice* 3.2.171–74)

Like Othello's courtship, the gift of the handkerchief is introduced as part of the prehistory of the play. Desdemona has been apprised of and has embraced the general tenor of the gift since before her arrival at Cyprus. Yet if we recall this when Othello parries Desdemona's "I have sent to bid Cassio come speak with you" with his handkerchief attack, we may be puzzled about the status of the Egyptic narrative he tells. Is he now filling in details omitted when he first gave her the handkerchief? His meticulous exposition and her puzzled responses suggest this is the case.

It's idle to wonder whether he had such a narrative in mind from the beginning, but the fantasy he unfolds is obviously parabolic, and the parable is consistent with the divided attitude his language displays toward sexuality and blackness in 1.2 and 1.3. In Carol Neely's excellent formulation, the narrative represents "something of Othello's . . . imagined relations to . . . the myth of African men's sexual excess." He makes the handkerchief symbolize first the wife's sexual power over her husband (3.4.58–65) and then the chastity that the husband demands as an always inadequate placeholder for the virginity she lost when she subdued him to her love (67–73).[6] The burden of the parable

---

6. Carol Thomas Neely, "Circumscription and Unhousedness: *Othello* at the Crossroads," paper delivered at the meeting of the Shakespeare Association of America in Kansas City, April 1992, p.10. I'm grateful to Professor Neely for sending me a copy of the paper. See also Neely's *Broken Nuptials in Shakespeare's Plays* (New Haven: Yale University Press, 1985), 128–29. For a similar and equally stimulating interpretation, see Janet Adelman, *Suffocating Mothers: Fantasies of Maternal Origin in Shakespeare's*

is that, if the exotic blackness of the romantic and heroic stranger gives way to the monstrous blackness of the Barbary horse, it will be—it already is—her fault.

Desdemona's two puzzled responses in 3.4—"Is't possible?" punctuates the parable's first thesis (70) and "I'faith, is't true?" the second (77)—are themselves puzzling. Given what we have already heard from her, it isn't clear that these questions express the simple wide-eyed bewilderment of the naive auditor. They may suggest that she realizes for the first time how serious he was when "he conjured her she should ever keep it," and realizes also that the conjuration contained as an admonitory nucleus his "vantage to exclaim on you." I hear as much anger as perplexity in the placement and voicing of her questions: "Can he really be holding me responsible and setting me up this way? Is my noble Moor going mad? Is he actually going to make a Thing out of this, threaten me with matchless 'perdition', over my losing the handkerchief? 'Then would to God that I had never seen it' (79)."

To measure the intensity of her recoil, let's set it against the fetishistic attachment described by Emilia: "she so loves the token/ . . . /That she reserves it evermore about her,/To kiss and talk to" (3.3.297–300). What she cherished as a token of his love she now rejects as a token of his bad faith. The terms of his threat are themselves revealingly muddled: the implied perdition she faces is that *he* will "hold *her* loathed" and "hunt/After new fancies" (3.4.64–65). But since the Egyptian parable follows his harping on her moist hand, the threat has the hapless ring of the betrayed victim's desire for revenge: if she loses the handkerchief or gives it away it will not only symbolize but also actualize both her failure to moderate his desire and her success in moderating another's.

I imagine Desdemona to be capable of hearing this message in Othello's words, and to be offended by his aggressive yet devious power plays. She is dismayed by his unstable behavior and the ground-

---

Plays, Hamlet *to* The Tempest (New York: Routledge, 1992), 68–69. Adelman lays more emphasis on the parable's strange conjunction of maternal power with virginity as representing "the impossible condition of male desire, the condition always already lost" (69).

less accusation he all but makes. For it isn't fear and trembling alone that her three mendacious utterances convey:

DESDEMONA
It is not lost, but what an if it were? . . .
I say it is not lost.
OTHELLO   Fetch't, let me see't.
DESDEMONA
Why, so I can, sir; but I will not now.
This is a trick to put me from my suit.
Pray you, let Cassio be received again.

                              (3.4.85–90)

Her tone is at first defiant and truculent, and then dismissive, as she counterattacks with her own weapon and continues to rub Cassio in his face:

OTHELLO
Fetch me that handkerchief, my mind misgives.
DESDEMONA
Come, come,
You'll never meet a more sufficient man.
OTHELLO
The handkerchief!
DESDEMONA   I pray, talk me of Cassio.
OTHELLO
The handkerchief!
DESDEMONA   A man that all his time
Hath founded his good fortunes on your love,
Shared dangers with you—
OTHELLO
The handkerchief!
DESDEMONA   I'faith, you are to blame.

                              (3.4.91–98)

The concluding utterance echoes his "I am to blame" and has the same indeterminate reference. He is to blame for what? His treatment of Cassio? His treatment of her? Her losing the handkerchief? She ducks away from Emilia's second question about jealousy and contin-

ues to make excuses for Othello later in the scene, attributing his "pud-
dled . . . spirit" to state matters (3.4.141–46). "Pray heaven," Emilia responds, that "it be / State matters, as you think, and no conception / Nor
no jealous toy, concerning you," at which Desdemona exclaims, "Alas
the day, I never gave him cause" (155–58).

That note of rueful but defiant self-exoneration underlies her interlocutory moves in 3.4: Othello is not the sort of man to be jealous (and
if he were, it would be the result of humoral imbalance, 30–31). If he
is jealous, it must be because of the handkerchief's magic or its loss
(101–3). Perhaps, as Emilia helpfully suggests later, he is jealous because he is jealous (jealousy is a self-begotten monster, 161–62). At any
rate, it has nothing to do with her. All she can do is implore heaven "to
keep that monster from Othello's mind" (163). He can't—that is, he
shouldn't—be jealous because she never gave him cause, and it would
be unworthy of him to imagine something unworthy of her. Therefore she will ignore the signs of jealousy.

Her way of ignoring them is to deny she lost the handkerchief in
order to deny his interpretation of the loss. If the loss of the token signifies or actualizes the loser's infidelity, it signifies or actualizes falsely
with respect to her and she rejects its lie. If she has to lie in order to
maintain the truth, he is to blame for that as for so many other things:
for evading the Cassio problem, for making her badger him about it,
and for mistreating the man who shared with him the dangers not
only of war but also of courtship.

Desdemona's heated exchange with Othello displays an interest in
keeping him angry, but angry on her terms, not his. She brushes past
his demands for the handkerchief and irritates him by switching to a
topic entirely unrelated to jealousy, a topic she has already seen him
reluctant to deal with, the topic of Cassio. There is no indication in
her language that she associates Cassio with Othello's display of jealousy, much less that she is angrily taunting him with the possibility of
adultery. She frames the Cassio Project as an enterprise that has everything to do with gender—with the struggle of will between her and
Othello—and nothing to do with sex.

This strategy is consistent with and reinforces her refusal to acknowledge Othello's jealousy. Yet the refusal is perversely self-blinding.
It accompanies behavior that seems, even more perversely, to arouse

and intensify the jealousy she refuses to acknowledge, the jealousy that gives her vantage, if not to exclaim on Othello, then to dramatize her injured merit: "I never gave him cause," "you are to blame," "poor Barbary." To view it from this standpoint is to throw the harshest light on her motivation: if encouraging his unjustified jealousy is important to her own self-justification, what better way to do this than couple her refusal to acknowledge the jealousy with her persistence in rubbing the salt of Cassio into its wound?

This is no doubt too harsh a light. It's enough to say that ignoring Othello's jealousy allows Desdemona to defend herself and even seize the offensive in 3.4. It gives her permission to bring up Cassio as often as she likes without for a moment having to entertain the not improbable possibility that Othello suspects a liaison between her and this most "sufficient man" who helped bring them together. Yet the Cassio Project remains the instrument of her anger, and she is not unaware of its effect. "I have spoken for you all my best," she tells Cassio at 3.4.128, "And stood within the blank of his displeasure/For my free speech."

In 4.1 her persistence in this line produces the predictable climax of the collision course on which she and Othello have set themselves. Speaking to Lodovico in Othello's presence, she tells him of the "unkind breach" between Othello and Cassio, and predicts that Lodovico will "make all well" (4.1.220–21). Othello, who is reading about his replacement as governor by Cassio, interjects, "Are you sure of that?" Desdemona's "My lord?" indicates that she is aware he is listening. Her next comment seems meant to be overheard by him. To Lodovico's inquiry about the breach she replies that it is "most unhappy" and that she "would do much/T'atone them, for the love I bear to Cassio" (4.1.231–32).

This piece of "free speech" draws "Fire and brimstone!" from Othello. Why shouldn't she expect that? She harps on what she knows displeases him, and her comment is itself a continuance of her effort to "atone" Othello and Cassio. Moreover, their exchanges are now being monitored by Lodovico and his attendants, which affects the way her response to Othello—another "My lord?"—can be played and heard: not only, "What did you say? I didn't hear you," but also "Say that again, so everyone can hear it."

By the end of the skirmish that follows, Lodovico has shifted from a bystander to Desdemona's partisan:

OTHELLO

    Fire and brimstone!

DESDEMONA   My lord?

OTHELLO   Are you wise?

DESDEMONA

    What, is he angry?

LODOVICO   Maybe the letter moved him.

    For, as I think, they do command him home,

    Deputing Cassio in his government.

DESDEMONA

    By my troth, I am glad on't.

OTHELLO   Indeed!

DESDEMONA   My lord?

OTHELLO

    I am glad . . . to see you mad.

DESDEMONA   Why, sweet Othello?

OTHELLO

    Devil!   *[Striking her]*

DESDEMONA

    I have not deserved this.

LODOVICO

    My lord, this would not be believed in Venice

    Though I should swear I saw't. 'Tis very much;

    Make her amends, she weeps.   (4.1.233–43)

Desdemona's second question has demonstrative or even exclamatory force because directed to Lodovico: "What, is he angry?" equals "Look, he's angry!" Her reply to Lodovico's news is ambiguous. She is truly glad because they will return to Venice and leave the Cassio problem behind them; she is glad to hear Cassio will be not merely reinstated but promoted; perhaps also, since she has just heard Lodovico speculate that the letter may have caused Othello's anger, *she* is glad to hear the news even if *he* isn't.

Given this choice of targets, Othello's "Indeed!" is relatively restrained, only a warmup, and Desdemona's third "My lord?" challenges him to speak his mind. He does not directly meet the challenge but throws "I am glad" back in her face and muffles his meaning, if not his aggression, enough to confuse several commentators and elicit another inquiry from Desdemona. "Why, sweet Othello?" is, again, ambiguous in its reach, and the work done by "sweet" is affected by the scope of "Why?"[7]

Because Othello's utterance is more than an ejaculation or mutter, because it redirects attention from the letter to her, and because it is a cryptic nonsequitur, I take Desdemona's question to be asking for a more explicit restatement: What are you getting at? Why do you call me—or how am I—mad? Why are you talking and behaving this way? I see that you're angry, but why take it out on me?

Her words contain something like a challenge to him to come clean. She solicits accusation and he withholds it. But this is a drama she, more than he, is displaying for Lodovico's benefit. Her "sweet Othello" may be no more than a gesture of affection and concern, an attempt to soothe him (comparable to her earlier offer to bind his head with the handkerchief). Nevertheless, it can't escape the aggressiveness of the context or the performative edge given it by the presence of onstage spectators.

"Sweet Othello" displays her love and concern to Lodovico, and asks him to join her in wondering why Othello is being so hostile: "See, I love him, why is he talking to me this way?" Even in terms of Desdemona's preferred interpretation of her "for the love I bear Cassio," she may be expected to know why. In her terms, Othello clearly overreacts and enables Desdemona to offer Lodovico the spectacle of an unjustly battered wife.

To return for a moment to Othello's "I am glad . . . to see you mad," the most satisfactory gloss on the utterance is the one M. R. Ridley proposes. He reads it together with "Are you wise?": "'are you in your right wits?' (i.e. thus openly to speak of love for Cassio). . . . 'I am glad to see that you have so manifestly taken leave of your senses, and betrayed yourself publicly.'"[8] But if this is what Othello insinuates, he refrains from saying it outright, and the gap between insinuated message and cryptic utterance is important as part of a withholding

7. "Why?" in the Quarto; "How?" in the Folio.
8. Ridley, Arden *Othello*, 148.

pattern: Othello never mentions Cassio by name to Desdemona until 5.2.48–49. After 3.3.76 he makes no pronominal reference to him in her presence.

This is especially noticeable in the accusation scene, 4.2, during which, as Muir points out, "he does not give her a chance of defending herself by naming her supposed lover, her accuser, or the evidence against her."[9] When he finally mentions Cassio in 5.2 (and mentions him together with the handkerchief), he does so on the mistaken assumption that Cassio has been killed. I conclude from this that he doesn't want to give her a chance to clear herself by confronting him together with Cassio.

Othello has a use for his jealousy. But Desdemona also has a use for it. Her insistence on mentioning Cassio in the martial context of her project has the same effect as—and reinforces—his refusal to mention Cassio in the venerean context. She departs from her withholding pattern only once, responding in a justifiable moment of weakness to Othello's "thou art false as hell" with "To whom, my lord? with whom? how am I false?" (4.2.41).

He avoids the questions ("Ah Desdemon, away, away, away!"). She obediently veers away through "Am I the motive of these tears, my lord?" to the hypothesis that he may be unhappy because he suspects her father had a hand in his recall to Venice—therefore, "Lay not your blame on me: if you have lost him,/Why, I have lost him too" (4.2.40–48). After this Othello and Desdemona collaborate in redirecting blame from the third party, steering it back to her so that he can continue belaboring her as if she is the sole offender and she can continue protesting her honesty and injured merit (4.2.49–96).

Their collaboration is founded and dependent on the losing of the handkerchief. The handkerchief in turn has its potential meanings preinscribed by the terms of Othello's gift, terms he mystifyingly displaces or injects into "the web of it" as its "magic." Karen Newman observes that this "snowballing signifier . . . first appears simply as a love token given by Othello to Desdemona and therefore treasured by her," but it would be more accurate to say that it first *disappears* as a

9. Kenneth Muir, ed., *Othello*, The New Penguin Shakespeare (London: Penguin Books, 1968), 209.

love token, and that at its appearance or disappearance what it represents is not so simple.

Newman herself remarks on its "doubleness": "when the handkerchief is first given, it represents her virtue and their chaste love, but
it later becomes a sign, indeed a proof, of her unfaithfulness."[10] Yet
Emilia's "he conjured her she should ever keep it" (3.3.298) places the
representational emphasis less on *her* virtue and *their* chaste love than
on *his* desire to test her fidelity. Whatever the object symbolizes must
be something he entrusts to her safekeeping—this something could
include his reputation—and the point of the gift is that it transfers
accountability from him to her. Should she lose it she will bear the
culpability of losing all that he has decided to make it stand for.

The sense that Othello presented the handkerchief not only as a gift
but also as a threat or warning is reinforced in 3.4, after it has become
a sign of her unfaithfulness. There he blusters that the gift of chaste
desire to be entrusted to and safeguarded by the woman is the man's.
The "Egyptian . . . charmer" told his mother that

> while she kept it
> 'Twould make her amiable and subdue my father
> Entirely to her love; but if she lost it
> Or made a gift of it, my father's eye
> Should hold her loathed and his spirits should hunt
> After new fancies.   (3.4.60–65)

If we had only Emilia's and Othello's comments to judge by, we might
conclude that "when the handkerchief is first given" the anticipation of
betrayal is already woven into the web of the gift: its terms express an
anxiety about, a potential proof of, Desdemona's unfaithfulness. Its apotropaic function glows in the underbrush of an earlier exchange:

BRABANTIO

> Look to her, Moor, if thou hast eyes to see:
> She has deceived her father, and may thee.

OTHELLO

> My life upon her faith. Honest Iago,
> My Desdemona must I leave to thee.
>   (1.3.293–96)

---

10. Newman, *Fashioning Femininity* , 91.

The handkerchief transfers responsibility for his life to her faith. In 3.4, having, as he thinks, proved her unfaithful, he makes it represent both the power she has lost (the power of prophetesses, mothers, wives, virgins) and the power he has lost because of her.

It is in this gestural drama more than in the reified web of the handkerchief that symbolic action resides. The action is not merely iconographic — not merely elicited from a description of the object ("a handkerchief,/Spotted with strawberries," 3.3.437–38). The handkerchief becomes the medium of a motivational conflict between agents who displace or alienate their agency from themselves to it as to a scapegoat or a fetish. The poison in Othello's gift is mystified as the magic in the web. But the handkerchief itself is, as Emilia says, only "a trifle" (5.2.226), the word picked up by Rymer in his notorious critique of "the *Tragedy of the Handkerchief*" as little more than the "Tragedy of this *Trifle*."[11]

When Desdemona can no longer justify Othello's behavior she justifies her own. Indeed, after Othello has struck and bewhored her she more insistently affirms her difference and uniqueness not only against his slander but also against Emilia's worldly norm. In 4.3 she appropriates the childlike and wounded bewilderment of poor Barbary to put questions to the Emilian voice of experience: Can there be women who abuse their husbands as grossly as Barbary and I were abused? Would you do such a deed?

Unlike the run of women described by and including Emilia, she would never dream of cheating on her husband. And as if to dramatize her innocence by a show of unworldly ignorance, she goes so far as to claim not to believe "there is any such woman" (4.3.60–78). Thus, where Iago wants to prove to himself that he can make Othello jealous, and where Emilia wants to prove to Desdemona that Othello is jealous, Desdemona seems intent on showing she can rise above his jealousy when she can no longer deny it.

Given the predicament she is placed in by her position, at the juncture where "in one line" the "crafts" of Iago, Emilia, and Othello "directly meet" (*Hamlet* 3.4.212), what can she do? For she *is* being unjustly victimized. That needs to be emphasized in the face of the argument that she won't let Othello victimize her all by himself but will

---

11. Rymer, "Short View," 2: 251, 254.

get herself victimized, make him do it, be his partner even in crime. At one tender moment she all but acknowledges the anger behind her militantly nonviolent resistance when, after rationalizing his rage as a reaction to state matters, she says,

> Beshrew me much, Emilia,
> I was, unhandsome warrior as I am,
> Arraigning his unkindness with my soul,
> But now I find I had suborned the witness
> And he's indicted falsely. (3.4.151–54)

"Unhandsome warrior" is like a lifeline of self-accusation thrown from the "O my fair warrior!" (2.1.180) it remembers. But if this makes for tenderness of tone, the legalistic rhetoric that follows resonates more harshly. Desdemona concedes that she persuaded herself to misinterpret the behavior she witnessed, but hers remains the prerogative of judgment, the power of indictment. She derives that power from "the authority of her merits" as the "deserving woman" she knows herself to be. Those merits measure Othello's unkindness, which is still the defendant and may still undergo a new trial in her "soul's court of justice."[12] She will give him another chance.

Desdemona is indeed a warrior, a trooper, who defends against the fate predicted by Iago in 2.1. It is possible to be a good wife and yet to avoid being reduced to a suckler of fools and chronicler of small beer. When the man she loves begins very soon, and unaccountably, to abuse her, she turns the other cheek. She makes excuses for him. She forgives him. Finally, when all else fails, she reduces herself to "poor Barbary," who, forsaken by her mad lover, dies singing the willow song.

From one line of this song, "Let nobody blame him, his scorn I approve" (4.3.51), she gets the idea for her death scenario in 5.2: after reviving to announce that she is "falsely, falsely murdered" and that "A guiltless death I die," she answers Emilia's "who hath done / this deed?" with "Nobody, I myself. Farewell: / Commend me to my kind lord—O, farewell!" (115–23). Thus she bids "her wrong stay and her displeasure fly." "Let nobody blame him" solicits pity and praise for the innocent victim who has the charity to forgive. But at the same

---

12. Gloss from the New Folger Library edition of *Othello*, 162.

time the phrase arraigns his unkindness by creating the presupposition that he *is* to blame and is *being* blamed by others, so that her charity only intensifies the sense of the wrong he did, and the instruction coded in her speech act is, "Let everyone blame him."

The same effect is serially produced in her final three utterances. The complex balance of the final gesture is testified to by the diverse and sensitive reactions of several critics. On the one hand, Desdemona "effectively authorizes" Othello's view of the murder as a sacrifice, "allowing him to have the last word"; "her last breath is a protective lie"; she is thus "fully in collusion with Othello's destruction of her," for "[i]f she did not actually kill herself, she unwittingly invited death through the nobility of a love that platonically (and foolishly) refused to register Othello's metamorphosis."[13]

On the other hand, in this emphasis on her ennobling if suicidal power lurks the suggestion that her final utterance disempowers Othello, arraigns and indicts him. It was she who drove him to it and made him less than himself. If she dies helping him live his lie about her, it is to intensify his sense of her value and of his loss. He couldn't have killed her without her complicity. They remain partners to the death.

It must be obvious that this account of Desdemona has taken an odd but not unusual critical turn. In spite of my effort to portray Desdemona as a strong and admirable figure, a true member of the sisterhood that includes Rosalind, Helena, Portia, and Hermione, my use of free indirect discourse snidely exposes her utterances and motives to the rhetoric of moral disapproval. The message this procedure conveys is, "let nobody blame her." It is as if in my delight to find Desdemona complicit in her undoing, I equate her complicity with moral culpability rather than with discursive responsibility.

A less tendentious view might begin with the observation that Desdemona's final words allow a paraphrase which amounts to a refutation of her earlier claim, "I never gave him cause": to say "Nobody, I

---

13. Bartels, "Making More of the Moor," 454; Eamon Grennan, "The Women's Voices in *Othello*: Speech, Song, Silence," *Shakespeare Quarterly* 38 (1987): 290; Adelman, *Suffocating Mothers*, 280, which is a paraphrase of Kay Stockholder 's argument in "Form as Metaphor: *Othello* and Love-Death Romance," *Dalhousie Review* 64 (1984–85): 744–45; Calderwood, *The Properties of* Othello, 36.

myself" is to acknowledge that she gave him cause. As a confessional gesture, this edges toward self-accusation. But if a glimmer of the sinner's discourse is discernible, it remains faint: "falsely murdered," she dies a "guiltless death," not, however, as one who *was* victimized but as one who *got* victimized. She accepts responsibility, not culpability.

Can her words signify that she accepts responsibility *for* his culpability? Isn't that what "my kind lord" may suggest if you imagine it uttered with no trace of bitterness, sarcasm, or reproach? This reading, however, doesn't neutralize the more tendentious interpretation developed above.

Desdemona can only sustain her self-representation as a deserving woman of spirit, the subject of her own desire, by performing or behaving in a manner that leads perversely to her undoing. And so, in spite of herself, she helps Othello and Iago recuperate the values of the misogynist discourse of virgin power and marriage. In spite of herself she helps them affirm the discourse that expresses the structure of suspicion and castration known in Venice as manhood. She helps them recuperate and affirm the discourse that she herself rejects—except for its qualified commitment to the values of chastity and sexuality as signifiers of fidelity and true love. It's in support of those values that she runs up her flag and runs down her chances to escape from the deadly horns of Othello's wrath.

She acknowledges that she gave him cause and even perhaps that she deserves what she got. But her performance of the victim's discourse culminates in her reduction of herself to poor Barbary, who saintlike forgives her tormentor. And this is what vibrates through her last words: he will discover too late what a jewel he has thrown away. Thus "I gave him cause" struggles with "I never gave him cause," and "I deserve what I got" struggles with "he'll deserve what he gets," and in my reading of Desdemona, these combatants remain locked in mortal embrace.

29. ON THE EMILIAN TRAIL

Othello and Desdemona are not alone in promoting the loss of the handkerchief. Someone else is complicit with them and makes it possible for them to capitalize on its loss later. In 3.3, after Iago has, as he put it, "a little dashed" Othello's spirits, he leaves and Othello shakily deliver his first soliloquy (3.3.261–81).

At this point Emilia accompanies Desdemona onstage. She listens as Desdemona worriedly asks, "Are you not well?" and Othello complains of "a pain upon my forehead." She hears Desdemona respond to this portentously allusive remark by offering to "bind" his forehead with her handkerchief. She then hears Othello reject the offer with an ambiguous command, "Your napkin is too little./Let it alone" ("it": his forehead or the handkerchief?). Desdemona has chosen to interpret "Let it alone" as a command to drop what Othello had conjured her she should ever keep about her. She responds defiantly by taking him at his word. Emilia watches as Desdemona lets the handkerchief fall.

After Othello escorts Desdemona offstage Emilia snaps it up:

> I am glad I have found this napkin,
> This was her first remembrance from the Moor.
> My wayward husband hath a hundred times
> Wooed me to steal it, but she so loves the token
> —For he conjured her she should ever keep it—
> That she reserves it evermore about her
> To kiss and talk to. I'll have the work ta'en out
> And give't Iago: what he will do with it
> Heaven knows, not I,
> I nothing, but to please his fantasy.
>
> (3.3.294–303)

To hear that the handkerchief has special value as a keepsake is to realize that something momentous may have flown across the field of vision, no sooner glimpsed than gone.

Emilia's final line in the First Quarto variant reads "I nothing know, but for his fantasy; Arden³ gives the Folio reading. The elided verb in the Folio version could be "do" or "wish," but the influence of the preceding phrase suggests the Quarto's "know." Emilia actively disowns knowledge in a manner that recalls Brakenbury's demurral in Richard III: "I will not reason what is meant thereby,/Because I will be guiltless from the meaning" (1.4.94–95).[1] Her "because" is more

---

1. On this, see my "Conscience and Complicity in *Richard III*," in *Richard III*, ed. Thomas Cartelli, A Norton Critical Edition (New York: W. W. Norton, 2009), 400–17.

indirect: "my husband is a little weird ('wayward') and is probably up to some mischief, but it's none of my business; he has odd fancies or whims, and my job is to humor him and keep him happy."

When she offers the handkerchief to Iago, she wonders what he will do with the object he has "been so earnest / To have me filch," and she has a moment of hesitation:

EMILIA

> If it be not for some purpose of import,
> Give't me again. Poor lady, she'll run mad
> When she shall lack it.

IAGO   Be not acknown on't,
> I have use for it. Go, leave me

(3.3.320–23)

This is enough to overcome the scruple: Emilia promptly, obediently, and wordlessly leaves the stage. According to Edward Pechter, she "passes the handkerchief to Iago but doesn't know what she is doing."[2] Better to say she doesn't want to know, or wants not to know. The very phrase Pechter cites as evidence for his opinion, "I nothing, but to please his fantasy," enacts in its noticeably syncopated or stifled syntax the complex self-censorship recommended in Iago's "Be not acknown on't."[3] In the following comments on Emilia, my discussion is deeply indebted to Michael Neill's wonderful characterization of Emilia's "cowed compliance." Her "deference to her husband's will" conceals "a bridling rebelliousness that parallels his own secret resentment of service," and her "denunciation of husbandly oppression is in many ways the equivalent of Iago's denunciation of the iniquity of masters and the humiliations of service."[4]

"Poor lady, she'll run mad" sounds a note of pity verging on condescension, as if for a child who has been imposed upon by the Moor's

2. Pechter, Othello *and Interpretive Traditions*, 116.

3. Pechter cites the syncopated Folio variant. The First Quarto reads, "I nothing know, but for his fantasy." Russ McDonald's New Pelican gloss, "I *do* nothing but please his whims" (my italics), is a possible expansion of the Folio line. I prefer the constrictedness of the Folio line because it makes more vivid the difficulty of the move Emilia is trying to negotiate. But both versions equally convey a touch of moral embarrassment, the apologetic nuance, that reflects anything but mindlessness or thoughtlessness.

4. William Shakespeare, *Othello*, ed. Michael Neill (Oxford: Oxford University Press, 2006), 174–75.

strangely demanding act of donation. Desdemona will have to suffer the consequences not only of her negligence but also of the enthusiasm with which she embraces the odd conditions attendant on his gift. Momentarily distanced from Desdemona by her own acquiescence in Iago's "fantasy," Emilia expresses the mixture of curiosity, sympathy, and censure with which members of the serving class scrutinize the follies of their (often less worldly) betters.

Emilia, then, anticipates trouble but blinkers herself and throws in her lot with Iago. The dramatic crescendo of threats that concludes 3.3 enhances our sense of Desdemona's vulnerability and of Emilia's contribution to it. In 3.4 Emilia remains mum during the whole stretch of dialogue in which Othello spins out his history of the handkerchief and hectors Desdemona about its whereabouts.

After he leaves, Desdemona expresses her unhappiness "in the loss of it" and thus gives Emilia a chance to make her less unhappy by speaking up. Her refusal is therefore all the more blatant. She responds with an evasively general witticism about men's mistreatment of women (3.4.96–103).

This pattern of nondisclosure continues into the fourth act. At the beginning of 4.2 Emilia learns from Othello himself that he suspects Cassio. She stoutly defends Desdemona against his misguided suspicion in words that carry the true Desdemonan pitch: "if she be not honest, chaste and true / There's no man happy" (4.2.17–18). Then she leaves the stage at Othello's request to summon Desdemona.

Returning with her five lines later, Emilia is curtly dismissed again as if she were Desdemona's procuress (27–30). She reenters just in time to hear Othello ranting about "that cunning whore of Venice" (91). "Alas," she exclaims, "what does this gentleman conceive?" and, a moment later, "what's the matter with my lord?" (97, 100). Has she forgotten the discussion that opened the scene?

Critics comment on the dramatic irony and heightened suspense of Emilia's all but fingering Iago in this scene (131–35, 141–49), yet her failure to mention that discussion is equally damaging and of a different order of complicity. The former is strictly part of a negotiation between the play and its audience: her failure to associate the scoundrel she describes with Iago is a venerable mechanism for driving spectators/readers wild by conspicuously blocking and deferring anagnorisis until too late. But her failure to mention the discussion is part of her negotiations with Desdemona and Iago. Twice she fails to report something she has seen or heard though in both cases she is well positioned to know that her failure can increase Desdemona's jeopardy along with Othello's jealousy. These lapses are deeply problematic; they haunt the interchange between Emilia and Desdemona from the handkerchief episode on.

None of this should be construed as reflecting adversely on Emilia's loyalty and devotion to Desdemona, any more than Desdemona's passive/aggressive reactions to Othello reflect adversely on her loyalty and devotion to him. It is just that Emilia's behavior in the play is charted along, and straddles, two different trajectories, one dominated by Desdemona and the other by Iago. In the first she is a faithful attendant, in the second a closemouthed watcher. The relation between these trajectories is textually underdetermined, and therefore open. It wants, in other words, to be motivated, and several motivational cues present themselves as candidates for inspection to anyone imagining or staging the speaker of Emilia's language.

1. In the context of socioliterary allusion, Emilia occupies a well-stenciled and recognizable position, that of the servant or attendant who innocently or corruptly helps betray her mistress in order to humor her lover—for example, Pryene in the tale told by Phedon in *Faerie Queene* II.14 and Margaret in *Much Ado About Nothing*. According to the notoriously inconsistent stage directions of *Much Ado*, Margaret is not among the dramatis personae listed in the Folio for the repudiation scene (4.1). The possibility that she might be present, watching but not exposing the slander of Hero, is not thereby foreclosed, but it is not thematized.

Emilia's collusion with Iago (over the handkerchief) differs from the charade Don John and Borachio get Margaret innocently to perform, because it involves her in a voyeuristic exercise of the power of nondisclosure. Among the motives imaginable for Emilia is a socially coded pleasure in watching one's betters misbehave and suffer, a pleasure Don John and Iago vigorously pursue in their self-appointed roles as performers of the villain's discourse.

2. Does Emilia remain silent because she is afraid of Iago? Because she is interested in finding out what her weird husband is up to? Be-

cause in such matters a wife should obey her husband? Her silence about the handkerchief is not something Iago explicitly enjoins; it appears to be Emilia's decision. In the interchange at 3.3.305–13, she offers the handkerchief as a gesture that seems partly an attempt to surprise and please him, partly a rebuke to his brusque and chiding manner.

The gesture suggests that she finds his manner more a challenge than a threat. At 4.2.146–48 she rattles him by mocking his idle jealousy. Her discomposure at discovering his villainy in 5.2 suggests that she has previously humored him as a kind of crank, a buffoon, that is, a husband, like herself an exemplary player in the Venetian game of marriage—a game that reflects and reproduces the cynical norms they both articulate as conventional wisdom.

3. This is the game depicted for Desdemona by Iago in 2.1 and by Emilia in 4.3. It is the game Desdemona refuses to play, and her anomalous marriage to Othello promises at first to flout its rules. After he finds a use for the game, she continues to represent herself as an exception, and to buttress her claim by denying their marriage could be jeopardized by suspicion for which there are obviously no grounds.

I can imagine an Emilia who expects husbands to be jealous, who is intrigued by the possibility of Othello's conforming to the rule, and who may even be willing to prove her point to Desdemona by the silence that facilitates his conformity. In 3.4 Emilia disingenuously puts Desdemona to the test. After she has watched Othello go on about the handkerchief, Desdemona defy him with her lies and talk of Cassio, and Othello storm off stage, she asks, "Is not this man jealous?" (3.4.100).

This is scarcely reducible to a request for information. The inquiry has the force of a rhetorical question soliciting Desdemona's assent. It's as if Emilia has just run off an experiment that proves Desdemona's marriage is no more impervious than hers to the slings and arrows of outrageous husbands.

The demonstration is set up at the beginning of 3.4:

DESDEMONA

Where should I lose that handkerchief, Emilia?

EMILIA

I know not, madam.

DESDEMONA

> Believe me, I had rather lose my purse
> Full of crusadoes; and but my noble Moor
> Is true of mind, and made of no such baseness
> As jealous creatures are, it were enough
> To put him to ill-thinking.

EMILIA   Is he not jealous?

DESDEMONA

> Who, he? I think the sun where he was born
> Drew all such humours from him.

$$(3.4.23-31)$$

At the end, when Emilia archly repeats her question, Desdemona swerves from a direct answer and steers her perplexity toward the handkerchief:

EMILIA

> Is not this man jealous?

DESDEMONA

> I ne'er saw this before,
> Sure there's some wonder in this handkerchief;
> I am most unhappy in the loss of it.

$$(3.4.100-103)$$

Her refusal to enlighten Desdemona puts pressure on her to acknowledge both the truth about Othello and the larger truth that their marriage is not the exception Desdemona thinks it is. It is as difficult, as precarious, as frangible, as any other. Not even the divine Desdemona can avoid being victimized by the misogynist discourse that governs relations between men and women, wives and husbands, in and out of marriage in Venice.

Emilia's "I am glad I have found this napkin" soliloquy has been characterized as thoughtless and mindless.[5] Yet she speaks as if she understands something important has just occurred, and also as if she feels a conflict between the token's value to Desdemona and Iago's importunate demands. Either he's been after it for a longer period of

---

5. "The thoughtfulness [of her utterances in 5.2] . . . is directly opposed to the thoughtlessness—indeed, mindlessness: 'I nothing, but to please his fantasy'—at the beginning of her story": Pechter, Othello *and Interpretive Traditions*, 119.

time than seems plausible, or else Emilia's "a hundred times," like her subsequent "That which so often you did bid me steal" (3.3.313), is an exaggeration that registers his importunity.[6]

During her final confession, she acknowledges that she noticed this and thought it was odd: "often, with a solemn earnestness/—More than indeed belonged to such a trifle—/He begged of me to steal't" (5.2.225–27). In her soliloquy she attributes this to his waywardness. But "wayward" is a term with a broad range of meanings (mischievous, wrong-headed, perverse, weird), and Emilia's usage is extenuative: her husband is a practical joker, a trickster, and although he's probably up to no good, she prefers to remain in the dark about his intentions. "Be not acknown on't."

Nevertheless, she is also curious enough about the possible effect of those intentions to act as his accomplice. She not only gives him the handkerchief. She keeps Othello and Desdemona ignorant of its whereabouts.[7]

"I am glad I have found this napkin,/This was her first remembrance from the Moor." What sort of soliloquizing is this? Does it resemble Iago's in performative intention? Is it merely an informational aside? An exposure of her thought process as in the convention we now call a voice-over? Her proposal to have "the work ta'en out"—that is, copied—before giving it to Iago suggests a more complex function.[8]

Why have it copied unless to return either the original or the copy to Desdemona? And why do that if not to hide the theft? Granted, she doesn't get around to copying it, because at that moment Iago enters and, in her effort both to please and to tease him, she dangles it be-

---

6. The first alternative has narrative force and presupposes the "long time" interval hypothesized by the double-time theory. The second alternative has rhetorical force and registers the speaker's reaction to the pressure of a persistent demand. Many of the dilemmas that get resolved by resorting to double time would disappear if expressions were treated as rhetorical and reflexive signifiers of *pathos* in discourse time rather than as narrative and objective signifiers of *mythos* in story time.

7. On this episode, see Chapter 28, above.

8. Ridley's Arden[2] gloss suggests that "ta'en out" could also mean "removed," but both in Cinthio's novella and in the other occurrences of the idiom at 3.4.180 and 4.1.153, "copied" is clearly the intended meaning.

fore him. When he snatches it away, she gives voice to the scruple behind her intention to have "this napkin" copied: "Poor lady, she'll run mad/When she shall lack it." His response, "Be not acknown on't,/I have use for it. Go, leave me" (3.3.321–23), is enough to overcome the scruple: she promptly, obediently, and wordlessly leaves the stage.

Edward Pechter thinks that, in passing the handkerchief to Iago, Emilia "doesn't know what she is doing."[9] But of course she knows. To answer the question about Emilia's soliloquizing, it is a theatrical device for representing acts of ethical self-representation. It expresses a desire for an assurance the speaker can't give herself and needs others to confer on her: justification rather than judgment. She soliloquizes to get off the hook: "what he will do with it/Heaven knows, not I,/I nothing, but to please his fantasy."

In other words, she acknowledges that she doesn't want to know (that she wants not to know) what he'll do with it. But she has a suspicion. If she plans to have it copied so the theft or loss won't be noticed, that means she doesn't expect the handkerchief to be returned right away. The very phrase Pechter cites as evidence for his opinion, "I nothing, but to please his fantasy," enacts in its noticeably syncopated or stifled syntax the more complex discursive behavior Iago urges on Emilia twenty lines later: "Be not acknown on't." Honigmann is more mindful of the tonal diffidence of Emilia's phrase: "Emilia . . . prefers not to ask too many questions, fearing to discover things as they really are."[10]

"Be not acknown on't": "Forget about it. Disremember it." Honigmann notes that this occurrence of "acknown" is "unique in Shakespeare," but its resonance is familiar. Both in form and meaning, the usage resembles Thomas More's in a passage of *The History of King Richard III* that deeply impressed the author of Shakespeare's *Richard III*. Describing the bad faith of London's citizens in acquiescing in Richard's seizure of the crown, More writes that "menne must sommetime for the manner sake not bee a knowen what they knowe."[11]

---

9. Pechter, Othello *and Interpretive Traditions*, 116.

10. Honigmann, *Othello*, 47.

11. Thomas More, *The History of King Richard III*, ed. Richard S. Sylvester (New Haven: Yale University Press, 1963), 80.

Emilia's "Heaven knows, not I," marks her soliloquy as an example of this technique, the technique of ethical evasion Cavell calls "disowning knowledge." The soliloquy has illocutionary force as a speech act. It an act of preemptive self-auscultation. By this I mean that it's the act of a speaker who undertakes morally dubious action and then positions herself so as to minimize the effect of this undertaking on her self-respect.

The awareness of collusion and of divided loyalties nevertheless vibrates uneasily in Emilia's utterance. She uses her words to soothe a ruffled conscience. But in the scenes that follow she continues in the course of action that ruffles it, refusing to tell the beleaguered couple what she knows as she voyeuristically watches their relation evaporate. "Where should I lose that handkerchief, Emilia? / I know not, madam" (3.4.23–24).[12]

But we know she knows. And we can follow the path the handkerchief takes down the Emilian trail marked by a chain of echoing signifiers:

> I'll have the work ta'en out
> And give't Iago.   (3.3.300–301)

> I will in Cassio's lodging lose this napkin
> And let him find it.   (3.3.324–25)

> Have you not sometimes seen a handkerchief
> Spotted with strawberries, in your wife's hand? . . .
>   . . . such a handkerchief,
> I am sure it was your wife's, did I today
> See Cassio wipe his beard with.   (3.3.437–42)

CASSIO
>   Take me this work out. . . .
BIANCA
>   . . . Why, whose is it?

---

12. This is the Lie Direct. Later in the scene we encounter the Lie Indirect. "Sure there's some wonder in this handkerchief," Desdemona muses after Othello's Egyptic parable, "I am most unhappy in the loss of it." Emilia continues to stonewall, responding with a nonsequitur, a standard wisecrack about male appetites: "They are all but stomachs, and we all but food" (3.4.102–5).

CASSIO

>I know not neither, I found it in my chamber.
>I like the work well enough: ere it be demanded,
>As like enough it will, I'd have it copied.
>Take it, and do't, and leave me for this time.
>
> (3.4.180–91)

>[*Bianca to Cassio.*] I must take out the work! . . . I must take out the
>work? . . . I'll take out no work on't!   (4.1.149–54)

The Emilian trail is a series of recurrent echoes of the act that enabled Iago to secure the ocular proof Othello demanded, and of the silence that remains the necessary condition of his success. The most interesting of these is the hand-in-glove relation of Emilia's and Cassio's motives for having the work copied. Hers, unstated, is to keep it from being missed. His is to have it copied because he assumes the original will sooner or later be missed and "demanded." Honigmann thinks Cassio "might be expected to recognize it" as Desdemona's.[13] What makes this thought compelling is that it highlights Cassio's diffidence: like Emilia, he in effect follows Iago's advice: "Be not acknown on't."

The Emilian trail of silent complicities winds through this and the next Cassio-Bianca episode in 4.1. These episodes show Cassio at his worst. The chamberer in him comes out, and once again we wonder about Othello's taste in go-betweens and his sense of what would impress Desdemona. Cassio's hurried command to Bianca to take the handkerchief is part of his effort to get rid of her because he doesn't want Othello to see him "womaned" (3.4.192–94). Her spirited refusal to copy the work in 4.1 provides a parodic commentary on the more deeply infolded double rejection signified by Desdemona's dropping the handkerchief.

Emilia might well apply to herself and Iago what she heard the Clown say about Cassio: "To tell you where he lodges is to tell you where I lie" (3.4.8–9). On this point, Honigmann's reflections about Emilia are consistently enlightening. He thinks she "should have suspected her 'wayward husband.'" He judges from her discussion with Desdemona and Iago in 4.2 that by then she probably did suspect him. In support

---

13. Honigmann, *Othello*, 71.

of this opinion he notes her subsequent reference back to this scene at 5.2.188–89: "I think I smell't it, O villainy!/I thought so then."

Acknowledging her complicity, Honigmann wonders how guilty she is of acting as a passive accomplice in Iago's plot? The question arises when Desdemona asks "Where should I lose that handkerchief, Emilia?" and she lies, "I know not, madam" (3.4.23–24). "Just four words, yet momentous in their implications. Had she not been afraid of Iago the truth might have come out and Iago's plot would have collapsed."[14] There's a difference, however, between "fearing to discover things as they really are" and fearing Iago. Honigmann's decision to focus on the latter throws too much away. It ignores Emilia's prolonged investment in the strategy of bad faith described above. It keeps us from appreciating the extent to which her refusal to enlighten Desdemona and Othello is a source of her power over Iago: it ratifies and preserves his power over them.

At the end of the play, she belatedly exercises this power in the accusation that undoes Iago and leads to her death at his hands. But there is an earlier episode in which the power struggle between them flashes briefly into view. It occurs in 4.2, the scene that follows the embarrassing clash witnessed by Lodovico.

In this scene, Emilia seems as truly upset and perplexed by Othello's behavior as she is concerned about and protective of Desdemona. But the incompatibility between her loyalties to Iago and to Desdemona presses insistently up to the surface in her outburst against whomever Desdemona was slandered by. The outburst activates the full range of the word she had previously applied to Iago, "wayward": "some eternal villain/Some busy and insinuating rogue,/Some cogging, cozening slave" (4.2.132–34; see also 141–42).

"Emilia *senses* that someone like Iago is responsible, and may suspect him."[15] This is a psychological speculation, but since Iago is present along with Desdemona, a rhetorical gloss would be more relevant: "Emilia hints that . . . ," or, better still, "Iago hears Emilia hinting,

---

14. Honigmann, *Othello*, 46, 44. Honigmann simply adopts the motivation mentioned by Cinthio: "The Ensign's wife . . . did not dare, for fear of her husband, to tell her anything" (ibid., 381).

15. Ibid., 282, my italics.

in Desdemona's presence, that. . . ." Regardless of what we think the speaker of Emilia's language means to say, the language itself seeks out Iago like a guided missile to remind him of something she knows and of the power over him which that knowledge guarantees.

The missile grazes Iago. He reacts curtly: "Speak within doors" (146). As if to oblige, Emilia redirects her accusation toward an un-identified third person, and aims a safer, more conventional, reproach at Iago: "some such squire he was/That turned your wit the seamy side without/And made you to suspect me with the Moor" (147–49). Iago lightens up. She has capitulated. He is relieved. His rejoinder is more relaxed: "You are a fool, go to" (150).

But after the murder, capitulation is no longer possible. Emilia im-plores Iago to disprove Othello's charge that he had slandered Desde-mona: "I know thou didst not, thou'rt not such a villain./Speak, for my heart is full." Iago's dogged refusal to satisfy her compels her, she says, "to speak:/My mistress here lies murdered in her bed," and, she adds, "your reports have set the murder on" (5.2.170–83).

She then fixes everybody's attention on Iago's culpability, recalls her earlier suspicion ("I thought so then"), and joins the chorus of his ac-cusers, only to learn the one fact that could make the terrible deed more terrible. She hears Othello confess that what drove him over the brink was "the pledge of love/. . . I saw . . . in his hand" (212–13); the "ocular proof" made possible, first, by her provision of the handker-chief and, second, by her silence about it:

EMILIA
    O God, O heavenly God!

IAGO   Zounds, hold your peace!

EMILIA
    'Twill out, 'twill out! I peace?
    No, I will speak as liberal as the north.
    Let heaven and men and devils, let them all,
    All, all cry shame against me, yet I'll speak.

IAGO
    Be wise, and get you home.

EMILIA
    I will not.   *[Iago tries to stab Emilia.]*

GRATIANO   Fie! Your sword upon a woman?

EMILIA

    O thou dull Moor, that handkerchief thou speak'st of
    I found by fortune and did give my husband,
    For often, with a solemn earnestness
    —More than indeed belong'd to such a trifle—
    He begged of me to steal't.

IAGO   Villainous whore!

EMILIA

    She give it Cassio? No, alas, I found it
    And I did give't my husband.

IAGO   Filth, thou liest!

EMILIA

    By heaven I do not, I do not, gentlemen!
    O murderous coxcomb, what should such a fool
    Do with so good a wife?   (5.2.216–32)

"Let them . . . cry shame against me": why? Because "what I did and didn't do made me an accessory to murder"? That message flashes briefly across the listener's mind before being pushed aside by the next clause, "yet I'll speak." Now the message slides from "I am guilty" to "I am brave": "let them cry shame against me for not holding my peace and disobeying my husband, or worse, for accusing him. But I will speak out at all costs"—as she had just done a few minutes earlier, "You told a lie, an odious, damned lie!" (5.2.176)—"and I will tell the truth." And the truth she tells—"fearing," as Honigmann puts it, "to discover things as they really are"—is that she found the handkerchief and gave it to Iago, who put it to deadly use. End of truth.

I can be expected to keep Emilia from getting off the hook, to insist that she fudges a little, that it's less than the whole story to say she "found [it] by fortune," that "shame" may be more, or less, than she deserves. But even in my bitter book this moment is too sad for moral casuistry. If she fudges it must be because she perceives and acknowledges what she helped happen, because she anticipates my criticism enough to stand up to it and brave this moment out the best she can.

Emilia owes me less than she owes Desdemona. Why shouldn't she drown her silence at the end and draw as close to Desdemona as she'll ever get?

> What did thy song bode, lady?
> Hark, canst thou hear me? I will play the swan
> And die in music. [*Sings.*] Willow, willow, willow.
> —Moor, she was chaste, she loved thee, cruel Moor,
> So come my soul to bliss as I speak true!
> So speaking as I think, alas, I die.   (5.2.246–49)

She speaks as she thinks at last (alas) and not in time. The act of silence remains deafening.

30. IAGO'S SOLILOQUIES

In every act of utterance dramatic speakers *give themselves to be heard or seen*. This implies that they represent themselves to themselves as well as to others and that they monitor these performances of themselves. They mark how their performances are being received and judged, and what their auditors and observers want or expect.

At the same time they are not only the subjects *of* their performances; they are subject *to* them—subject to what their language, whether verbal or postural, shows about them, what it says to us, and what it conveys about them regardless of what they mean to convey. In spite of Hamlet's claim to "have that within which passes show," there is inwardness not only inside the body, behind doors, hidden in an unobservable and inaudible faculty of soul or mind. There is also inwardness in discourse. Performers express themselves in media that independently convey information about their performances. This holds not only for the mimetic genre of dialogue but also for the non-mimetic genre of soliloquy, whose deployment by Iago is the subject of the present chapter.

Iago delivers nine soliloquies in verse, in addition to the two prose asides he utters in Act 2 Scene 1.[1] Four of the soliloquies occur be-

---

1. Verse soliloquies: 1.3.381–403, 2.1.284–310, 2.3.45–60, 2.3.331–57, 2.3.377–83, 3.3.324–36, 4.1.44–48, 4.1.94–104, 5.1.11–22, 5.1.129–30. The two prose asides occur at 2.1.167–78 and 2.1.198–200. Arden³ and the 1622 Quarto format the second aside as verse, but I follow the Folio in treating it as prose. Of the two verse versions, which differ from each other, the Quarto makes more sense both metrically and rhetorically because its line divisions (a hendecasyllable sandwiched between two iambic trimeters) accentu-

fore Act 3 Scene 3 and five after. The first four vary in length from sixteen to thirty-two lines and stand out as rhetorical performances because they are islands of verse in a sea of prose. The remaining five are shorter and less clearly set off. With one exception, they are surrounded by verse.

The speaker of the first four soliloquies is in performative heaven. He seasons them with a generous salting of explanations, progress reports, psychological profiles of his victims, plot projections, and even little demonstrations of hands-on plot cookery. And all the while he coaxes, cajoles, confides, confesses, gloats, and sneers.

In 1.3, after Iago and Roderigo hear Othello and Desdemona proclaim their love for each other in the presence of the assembled Duke and senators, the bereft Roderigo threatens to drown himself. This draws from Iago a series of contemptuous harangues spanning some sixty lines and filled with the clichés of misanthropic discourse (1.3.312–73). Even as he tries to restore Roderigo's self-confidence and hope, he seems to enjoy rubbing Roderigo's unmanliness in his face and increasing the sense of impotence that binds him to his diabolical savior.

Since Roderigo's threat of suicide seems little more than a melodramatic whine, the energy and volume of Iago's response are gratuitous. This he all but acknowledges when, just after Roderigo's exit, he steps forward and delivers his first soliloquy:

> Thus do I ever make my fool my purse:
> For I mine own gained knowledge should profane
> If I would time expend with such a snipe

---

ate the phrasal structure: "O, you are well tun'd now,/. But I'll set down the pegs, that make this music,/. As honest as I am." I prefer the prose version on situational grounds: this and the preceding aside differ from the soliloquies in being more spontaneous outbursts directly triggered by actions taking place on stage and in being partly or wholly addressed to participants in those actions. The longer first aside begins as a commentary to the audience, but after two sentences it changes into a threat aimed at Cassio. All the speeches I call "soliloquy" are characterized by direct and formalized audience address that interrupts the action.

Neither the Quarto nor the Folio text of *Othello* uses the words *aside* or *solus* (or such alternative indicators as *Manet*) to distinguish these performances. Consult the discussions of those terms in Alan Dessen and Leslie Thomson's invaluable *A Dictionary of Stage Directions in English Drama, 1580–1642* (Cambridge: Cambridge University Press, 1999).

But for my sport and profit. I hate the Moor
And it is thought abroad, that 'twixt my sheets
He's done my office. I know not if 't be true,
But I for mere suspicion in that kind
Will do as if for surety. He holds me well,
The better shall my purpose work on him.
Cassio's a proper man: let me see now,
To get his place, and to plume up my will
In double knavery. How? How? let's see:
After some time to abuse Othello's ear
That he is too familiar with his wife.
He hath a person and a smooth dispose
To be suspected, framed to make women false.
The Moor is of a free and open nature
That thinks men honest that but seem to be so,
And will as tenderly be led by th' nose
As asses are.
I have't, it is engendered! Hell and night
Must bring this monstrous birth to the world's light.

(1.3.382–403)

The opening "Thus" refers to the preceding eighty lines of dialogue with Roderigo, and the words that follow make Iago sound apologetic. He defends against the imagined charge that his misanthropic outburst (in lines 312–73) was sententious overkill wasted on "such a snipe" as his only onstage auditor. Is it for Roderigo alone that he has been pumping up his wickedness with the rhetorical verve of someone impersonating the stage villain?

Iago speaks as if to the audience before which he's been performing throughout the scene. This must be a discriminating audience. He addresses a collective interlocutor more qualified to appreciate the fine points of his villainy than anyone in the Venetian community of his potential victims. David Denby's recent comment on Johnny Depp and Robert Downey applies equally well to Iago: "in the most grossly frivolous and commercial projects" they "found a way of remaining hip" by their ability to convey the impression that they realize "it's all nonsense."[2]

---

2. David Denby, "Going Native," *New Yorker*, January 4, 2010, 77.

The suspicion that he performs for another and better audience than Roderigo carries back to the first sixty-five lines of 1.1, which also feature his delight in rhetorical overkill:

> For when my outward action doth demonstrate
> The native act and figure of my heart
> In complement extern, 'tis not long after
> But I will wear my heart upon my sleeve
> For daws to peck at: I am not what I am.[3]
>
> (1.1.60–64)

Iago monopolizes this conversation with similar bits of spooky blather about himself, and with generous dollops of cynicism that exceed Roderigo's interlocutory demands. He seems enchanted by the rhetoric of villainy and by a discourse whose basic theme is not that of the victim, as in Lear's "I am a man / More sinned against than sinning," but that of the villain, "I am a man / More sinning than sinned against."

Since he treats Roderigo with disdain, you begin to wonder why he confides in him and why he enjoys pushing him around. It is as if he has been using him not only as a factor in his revenge but also as a kind of stand-in or dummy against which to bounce a performance of the villain's discourse destined for an invisible gallery of more discerning spectators—the gallery implied, addressed, and constructed by Iago's soliloquies. From now on I'll refer to this audience as "supervisors," borrowing a term Iago himself uses later in the etymological sense of "onlookers," or, more accurately, "spectators looking down from above."[4]

---

3. Since we expect "I am not what I seem," "I am not what I am" doesn't merely replace it but is defined by it: "What I seem *is* what I am."

4. "Would you, the supervisor, grossly gape on, /. Behold her topp'd?" (3.3.398–99). "Supervisor" is the term in the first Quarto, and it is preferable to the Folio's "supervision." I use "gallery" in the Elizabethan sense of "lords' rooms" in the upper level of the public stage, not in the demotic sense of the peanut gallery or space for groundlings.

Edward Snow remarks that the Quarto term "neatly condenses the watching, controlling, and judging functions that Freud defines as the superego's three attributes ("Sexual Anxiety and the Male Order of Things in *Othello*," *English Literary Renaissance* 10 [1980]: 396). Later in this stimulating essay, Snow claims that Iago fulfills the function "within Othello's psyche . . . [of] the punitive, sex-hating superego" (409). Snow's Freudian spin tends to diminish the context-specific force of the way Shakespeare uses the ethical discourses to redistribute complicities. Nevertheless, the idea of an imaginary audience fulfilling that function in Iago's fantasy makes good sense.

"I am not what I am." Iago protects his absence—his freedom—from the honest Iago confined in Venice by pretending he is like an actor on a stage (which, of course, he isn't). He clings parasitically to the fantasy that he performs his villainies before the imaginary supervisors whose hero is dishonest Iago. Picking up where Richard III left off, he hogs the platea and continuously solicits their admiration.[5]

Brian Vickers misses the point by taking the direct address of Shakespearean villains personally and then getting huffy about it: Iago, he grumbles, thrusts his intentions on us, and this makes Vickers nervous because it "leads to an intimacy which we would willingly avoid, if we could. There is no one in the world whose confidence I would rather less share than Iago's."[6] But, first, the audience constituted by the soliloquy of a character preexists—and thus can't be identical to—any particular theater audience addressed by the actor who plays the character. Iago is not forcing himself on Vickers any

---

5. On Richard III, see my "Conscience and Complicity in Richard III," 400–17. On the needy actor as a model, see, in general, Meredith Skura's remarkable *Shakespeare the Actor and the Purposes of Playing* (Chicago: University of Chicago Press, 1993). On the meaning and significance of the *platea* and the *locus* as, respectively, a downstage area reserved for interactions between characters and an upstage area where self-contained action among fictional characters occurs, see Robert Weimann, *Shakespeare and the Popular Tradition in the Theater: Studies in the Social Dimension of Dramatic Form and Function*, ed. Robert Schwartz (Baltimore: Johns Hopkins University Press, 1978), 73–85 and passim.

Weimann correlates these two stage areas with the different orientations of stage presence ("Figurenpositionen"), by which the actor connects with "his fellow actors, the play, or the audience, even when direct address has been abandoned" (230). But he goes on to insist that, in moments of direct audience contact, the character and the actor both address the same audience, the one consisting of the actual spectators in the actual theater. This means that the character at least intermittently behaves as if he or she knows he or she is in a theater performing before an audience (and if the character is a "she," does she know she is a "he"?).

I want to modify this premise, not reject it. In my version, if such participatory episodes as prologues, epilogues, and soliloquies are scripted, the audience they engage must be a fiction. It's a virtual audience constituted by the direction and express motivation of address. The main difference between Weimann's notion and mine is this: for Weimann, when characters like Hamlet, Iago, and Richard III address the audience, they function *as* actors. For me, they function *like* actors. See my "The Prince's Dog: Falstaff and the Perils of Speech-Prefixity," *Shakespeare Quarterly* 49 (1998): 40–73, esp. 47–50.

6. Brian Vickers, *Appropriating Shakespeare: Contemporary Critical Quarrels* (New Haven: Yale University Press, 1993), 79.

more than on me. And second, I, for one, very much enjoy Iago's confidential nasties and can't get enough of them. I would be tickled to be a member of the ideal audience of supervisors he addresses, and, in addressing, constructs.

What Iago bestows on the supervisors after the opening apology is unexpected. It has nothing to do with motiveless malignancy. As A. D. Nuttall well expresses it, Iago "is not just motivated, like other people. Instead, he *decides* to be motivated."[7] The very arbitrariness of the decision puts his manliness and autonomy on parade, even as it mischievously airs a possible threat to them in the suspicion of cuckoldry. He dares the imaginary audience to accuse him of defeating his "favor with an usurp'd beard" (341–42) and then proceeds to disarm the threat by converting the mere suspicion to a sufficient motive for revenge.

With Roderigo alone among his onstage interlocutors, Iago honestly flaunts his dishonesty, taking the calculated risk that at some point the poor snipe might expose him. He stages this risk for the approval of the audience that could appreciate his intrepidity, his masterful control, and, above all, the suave dishonesty of his frank avowals to Roderigo, to whom he represents himself as a plainspeaking, disenchanted, resentful, satirical bloviator —a "me-firster" who "tells it as it is." But can this be any more honest as a confession of knavery than his pledge of friendship to Roderigo? The supervisors are encouraged to giggle along with Iago at everyone's stupid persistence in enlisting him as a trusty mediator and pinning medals of honesty on his chest.

Such moves make you wonder whether his self-disclosure to the supervisors is any more reliable, genuine, or disinterested than his self-disclosure to Roderigo. Suppose it is just another conspicuously dishonest pretense of honesty, which he puts on to remind them that they're dealing with a consummate actor and villain, who is not what he is. For how could he earn the respect denied him in Venice, the respect owed the genuinely dishonest Iago, if he addressed the supervisors wearing his villainous heart on his sleeve? Thus as the soliloquy unfolds and the speaker gives them a brief but puzzling taste of his famed propensity for motive hunting, his motivation becomes

7. Nuttall, *A New Mimesis*, 143.

opaque. This opacity retrospectively touches his earlier explanations to Roderigo with like suspicion, and it is sustained throughout
the play.

To be thought of as honest in Venice serves his purposes, but it may
also be a tad humiliating. He wants more respect, more appreciation,
for the rogue he knows himself to be. Perhaps he seeks an audience he
can shock and awe in frontal assault—an audience of superior wit and
judgment capable of rewarding him with the applause and execration
he deserves. He seems intent on periodically raising the supervisors'
spirits with some vanity of the villain's art: it is his promise, and they
expect it from him.

What they expect—what he openhandedly improvises for their
listening pleasure—is dramatized and mocked in the motivational
fantasia of the second major soliloquy. This occurs in Act 2 Scene 1,
some one hundred lines after Iago got excited as he watched Cassio
and Desdemona paddling palms:

> That Cassio loves her, I do well believe it,
> That she loves him, 'tis apt and of great credit.
> The Moor, howbeit that I endure him not,
> Is of a constant, loving, noble nature,
> And I dare think he'll prove to Desdemona
> A most dear husband. Now I do love her too,
> Not out of absolute lust—though peradventure
> I stand accountant for as great a sin—
> But partly led to diet my revenge,
> For that I do suspect the lusty Moor
> Hath leaped into my seat, the thought whereof
> Doth like a poisonous mineral gnaw my inwards . . .
> And nothing can or shall content my soul
> Till I am evened with him, wife for wife . . .
> Or, failing so, yet that I put the Moor
> At least into a jealousy so strong
> That judgment cannot cure; which thing to do,
> If this poor trash of Venice, whom I trash
> For his quick hunting, stand the putting on,
> I'll have our Michael Cassio on the hip,
> Abuse him to the Moor in the rank garb—

For I fear Cassio with my night-cap too—
Make the Moor thank me, love me, and reward me
For making him egregiously an ass,
And practising upon his peace and quiet
Even to madness. 'Tis here, but yet confused:
Knavery's plain face is never seen, till used.

(2.1.284–310)

Suppose we interpret the first two lines as an expression of *Iago's* belief, the shrewd appraisal of an inside dopester who knows the human heart. We'll then be disappointed in him because events will prove him wrong. Yet nothing he later does or says supports the idea that he believes Cassio and Desdemona are mutually attracted to each other. Therefore he seems more likely to be mimicking or trying out a narrative that would meet Venetian expectations and would prevail with Othello.

The voicing of this pair of opinions is by no means straightforward, and it is with relief that the supervisors greet the sardonic ingenuity of the next three and a half lines, in which the virtues he grudgingly concedes Othello are nicely turned to potential weaknesses.

The Moor, howbeit that I endure him not,
Is of a constant, loving, noble nature,
And I dare think he'll prove to Desdemona
A most dear husband.

"I dare think," indeed. This is vintage Iago, showing the supervisors how bad he is, whetting their curiosity and desire for the villainies to come.

Yet what follows is also vintage Iago: a stark and unexpected declaration of his love for Desdemona fogged up by three disjunctive modifiers, the first two of which leave auditors mystified as they cope with the wonderfully ridiculous effect of "peradventure":

Now I do love her too,
Not out of absolute lust—though peradventure
I stand accountant for as great a sin—
But partly led to diet my revenge,
For that I do suspect the lusty Moor
Hath leaped into my seat, the thought whereof

Doth like a poisonous mineral gnaw my inwards . . .
And nothing can or shall content my soul
Till I am evened with him, wife for wife . . .

The third modifier ("But partly led to diet my revenge") returns to the suspicion announced in the first soliloquy, the "mere suspicion" that, he had said there (1.3.388–89), he will arbitrarily act on as if it were true. The echo of that coolly perverse decision combines with the heated rhetoric of jealousy to stage a preview of how Othello will feel.

In spite of Iago's rhetorical fuss and bluster, the topic of his diseased "inwards" and his determination to get even with Othello, "wife, for wife," never comes up again. It begins to look like another ad hoc improvisation, another vanity of the villain's art. This suspicion increases when Iago parenthetically throws in Cassio for good measure. The temptation for the reader is to find an explanation that supplies the motive behind such moves. But that is the very temptation the moves interrogate. Let me invent another soliloquy for Iago:

Why do I toss off these explanations of my villainy—resentment, professional disappointment, jealousy, revenge—in a manner that seems calculated to arouse skepticism? It's because my fans expect it of me. I'm satisfying and jabbing at *their* propensity for motive-hunting, not mine. They want to understand me better than I understand myself. Their problem is that in England, "where indeed they are most potent in potting" (2.3.71–72), they are also potent in bad theater and addicted to a taste for the cheap melodramatic thrills of the victim/revenger's discourse.

Some of my fans no doubt want me to claim that I've been more sinned against than sinning, so that they can justify my otherwise gratuitous indulgence in pure pleasurable sinning. I will, from time to time, give them what they want, but only as if I were an actor reflecting back to them their own flabby desire from the mirror of my performance. And if I *were* an actor, if Iago actually were to play another Iago on a stage, no thoughts and desires of the actor that weren't invested in performing the character would be any concern of this actor's audience. The dishonest Iago who confesses to the supervisors that he hates the Moor and suffers from a sense of injured merit and sexual betrayal: this is no less a part played by Iago the actor than is the honest Iago who bamboozles his fellow Venetians.

One possible exception to this portrayal is Iago's third soliloquy, uttered in 2.3, just after he has persuaded a reluctant Cassio to drink more wine. He's eager to share this news with the supervisors, whom he gratifies with a jolly report of his latest accomplishments and plans. His bluster, sparkling with figures of disdain, bubbles over into effervescent alliteration:

> If I can fasten but one cup upon him,
> With that which he hath drunk tonight already
> He'll be as full of quarrel and offence
> As my young mistress' dog. Now my sick fool, Roderigo,
> Whom love hath turned almost the wrong side out,
> To Desdemona hath tonight caroused
> Potations pottle-deep, and he's to watch.
> Three else of Cyprus, noble swelling spirits
> That hold their honours in a wary distance,
> The very elements of this warlike isle,
> Have I tonight flustered with flowing cups,
> And the watch too. Now 'mongst this flock of drunkards
> Am I to put our Cassio in some action
> That may offend the isle.
> > *Enter* CASSIO, MONTANO *and* Gentlemen.
> > But here they come.
> If consequence do but approve my dream
> My boat sails freely, both with wind and stream.
>
> > > (2.3.45–60)

In the fourth soliloquy, Iago can barely contain himself. He has just counseled the disgraced Cassio to enlist Desdemona's aid as mediator, and now, with Cassio's "Good-night, honest Iago" in their ears, the supervisors are treated to fourteen lines (331–45) in which he mockingly performs everyone else's honest Iago in scare quotes:

> And what's he then that says I play the villain?
> When this advice is free I give and honest,
> Probal to thinking and indeed, the course
> To win the Moor again? For 'tis most easy
> Th'inclining Desdemona to subdue
> In any honest suit. She's framed as fruitful

As the free elements: and then for her
To win the Moor, were't to renounce his baptism,
All seals and symbols of redeemed sin,
His soul is so enfettered to her love
That she may make, unmake, do what she list,
Even as her appetite shall play the god
With his weak function. How am I then a villain
To counsel Cassio to this parallel course
Directly to his good?   (2.3.331–45)

In short, "All I'm doing, folks, is trying to push the right buttons and do my level best to help Cassio get back into Othello's good graces." And then, with a scarifying shift of tone at line 345, he makes sure the supervisors appreciate what he has just really done: "Divinity of hell!/When devils will the blackest sins put on/They do suggest at first with heavenly shows/As I do now."[8]

As he continues to unfold his devilish plot, exhilaration and self-delight spill out in a three-line rush:

So will I turn her virtue into pitch
And out of her own goodness make the net
That shall enmesh them all.   (2.3.355–57)

At this point, Roderigo has the bad taste to interrupt his iambic villainizing with a prosy peeve (358–64). Iago impatiently counsels patience and hustles him off stage, so that he can go on briefing the supervisors.

Two things are to be done:
My wife must move for Cassio to her mistress,
I'll set her on.
Myself the while to draw the Moor apart
And bring him jump when he may Cassio find
Soliciting his wife: ay, that's the way!
Dull not device by coldness and delay!

(2.3.377–83)

---

8. "As I do now" is Just Too Much, a self-delighting metatheatrical twinkle best uttered in a tone that makes it a deictic comment on the high-toned spookery it follows.

The excitement pulsing through the nervous rhythm—the short line, the runover lines terminated by a stagy "Eureka!" and followed by a burst of alliteration that adds zing to an already peppery couplet—is *performed* for the supervisors' pleasure.

To borrow a figure from another arena, he tries "to get the crowd into the game" by dramatizing the process of villainous *inventio* and stumbling on the solution before their very eyes and ears. What he fails to consider in this euphoric moment is the boomerang lurking in his triumphant vaunt, "out of her own goodness make the net/That shall enmesh them all": he fails to consider his victims' ability—painfully on offer in the very next scene—to beat him to the punch.

Emilia's protracted silence, her protracted lie, is the power behind Iago's throne from 3.3 to the play's last scene. This thought throws a strange backlight on the diabolical chortles of the soliloquy he delivers after she gives him the handkerchief and he dismisses her. The dismissal is curt: "Be not acknown on't,/I have use for it. Go, leave me." He wants to be alone with his supervisors so that he can inform, instruct, and entertain them:

> I will in Cassio's lodging lose this napkin
> *And let him find it*. Trifles light as air
> Are to the jealous confirmations strong
> As proofs of holy writ. This may do something.
> *The Moor already changes with my poison*:
> Dangerous conceits are in their natures poisons
> Which at the first are scarce found to distaste
> But with a little art upon the blood
> Burn like the mines of sulphur.
>   *Enter* OTHELLO.
>   I did say so:
> Look where he comes. Not poppy nor mandragora
> Nor all the drowsy syrups of the world
> Shall ever medicine thee to that sweet sleep
> Which thou owedst yesterday.
>   (3.3.324–36, my italics)

This is Iago at his most pompous. Each of the two italicized statements—one voicing an intention and the other an observation—is followed by a pedantic little gloss instructing the supervisors in the fine points of the psychology of jealousy.

When the already devastated victim rages into view, the villain commends his own insight ("I did say so"). He points to the evidence of his art ("Look where he comes"). Then, melodramatically turning from the supervisors to Othello, he shows them the proper way for villains to spook their victims.

Although it has the self-satisfied ring of the master villain, this little performance feels gratuitous, feels like overkill, for two reasons. The first is that he depends, and will continue to depend, more on Emilia's complicity than he knows. The second is the shadow cast on Iago's platea strut by the belated discovery of Cassio's role.

We now know that, of the four major characters, Iago is the only one who was out of the loop up to the moment of discovery, and that, during the time he was out of the loop, he was playing the villain in the most outrageous and engaging manner.[9] The soliloquies delivered before the discovery are both more sustained and more conclusive. Three of them end scenes, four terminate in couplets, and all have more rhetorical juice and spirit in them than the last five. The latter are shorter and seem more hurried, partly because Iago is trying hard to keep up with the different plots he has going, and partly because he gets interrupted by other characters—Othello in the one just discussed and Cassio in the next three.

The same combination of spookery and sententiousness animates the sixth soliloquy, which is uttered in grotesque circumstances. After Iago has mercilessly trashed Othello and all but reduced him to the horned blabberer and goatish monster he most fears to be, Othello falls into a trance. Iago seizes this opportunity to favor the supervisors with a brief sample of Doctor Evil 's mumbo jumbo, followed by another of the cynical bromides he periodically recycles for their edification:

> Work on,
> My medicine, work! Thus credulous fools are caught,
> And many worthy and chaste dames even thus,
> All guiltless, meet reproach. —What ho! My lord!

9. Was Emilia in on this secret? If so, she apparently didn't tell Iago. But since the text gives no indication whether or not she knew of Cassio's role, and nothing rides on this question, there is no point in speculating about it.

My lord, I say! Othello![10]

Enter CASSIO.

How now, Cassio?

(4.1.44–48)

This hand-rubbing assertion of malignant agency is a bid for the kind of approval poor Othello in fact bestows on him several lines later. After Iago belabors him with such morale-building recommendations as "Would you would bear your fortune like a man!" and "Good sir, be a man" (4.1.61, 65),[11] he congratulates him for having escaped (thanks to Iago's vigilance) the plight of the millions of cuckolds who are unaware their wives are cheating on them (4.1.65–72). To this Othello gratefully replies, "O, thou art wise, 'tis certain" (4.1.74).

The only thing more embarrassing than Othello's abjectness is Iago's obvious relish in laying it on well beyond necessity. Othello has been undoing himself since early in Act 3. Even the Folio stage direction, "Falls in a traunce," suggests the transitivity of a self-induced breakdown. It is a parody, a hyperbole, of the process he has been using Iago to facilitate.

The seventh soliloquy is especially interesting in dramatic terms because of the way it is contextualized. Preparing to set Othello up with his Cassio-Bianca charade, Iago instructs him to assume the supervisors' position as an eavesdropper:

> Do but encave yourself
> And mark the fleers, the gibes and notable scorns
> That dwell in every region of his face;
> For I will make him tell the tale anew.
>
> (4.1.82–85)[12]

---

10. This is Honigmann's variant of the Folio version, which begins, "Worke on,/. My Medicine workes." The difference between the two versions is that between incantation and exultation. Honigmann borrows the variant from the Quarto, which prints the passage in prose.

11. See also 4.1.78 ("A passion most unsuiting such a man") and 4.1.89–90 ("all in all in spleen/. And nothing of a man").

12. For an interesting analysis of the way this scene generates multiple levels of discrepant awareness, see Jeremy Lopez, *Theatrical Convention and Audience Response in Early Modern Drama* (Cambridge: Cambridge University Press, 2003), 72–75.

Once again, he concludes by inviting his interlocutor to leave, "Will you withdraw?" He then turns so eagerly to the real supervisors that the invitation to withdraw seems motivated primarily by impatience to get back to his fans. He wants to impress them not only with his latest brainstorm but also with his deep insight into the folly of strumpets:

> Now will I question Cassio of Bianca,
> A housewife that by selling her desires
> Buys herself bread and clothes: it is a creature
> That dotes on Cassio—as 'tis the strumpet's plague
> To beguile many and be beguiled by one.
> He, when he hears of her, cannot refrain
> From the excess of laughter. Here he comes.
>   *Enter* CASSIO
> As he shall smile, Othello shall go mad.
> And his unbookish jealousy must construe
> Poor Cassio's smiles, gestures and light behaviour
> Quite in the wrong. How do you now, lieutenant?
>   (4.1.94–104)

The supervisors must enjoy his calling Cassio "lieutenant" as much as Cassio hates it ("the addition/Whose want even kills me" 105–6). For Iago the crowning moment of this interlude occurs when Othello, hearing Bianca mention the handkerchief, believes he has all but seen the "ocular proof" (147–56).[13] But because Cassio independently re-

---

13. Both the Quarto and the Folio assignment of speech prefixes at Bianca's entrance must be wrong. "Before me! look where she comes" is assigned to Iago, but while the Quarto leaves the next utterance unmarked, as if Iago speaks it, the Folio assigns it to Cassio: "'Tis such another fitchew; marry, a perfumed one. What do you mean by this haunting of me?" (4.1.144–46). On the one hand, why would Cassio, who has already been talking about Bianca, refer to her as *another* fitchew when he sees her? Ridley's claim, accepted by Honigmann, that "such another" carries derisive rather than deictic force ("like all the rest of them") ignores the dramatic context. That context makes it more appropriate to assign the line to Iago, who has been pretending to talk about Desdemona and wants to make sure the eavesdropping Othello doesn't get undeceived. On the other hand, although "Before me! look where she comes" may be Iago's surprised warning to Cassio—and if so, it is not meant for Othello's ears—it could as easily be uttered by Cassio, who is discomfited because he has just said "I must leave her company." But "'Tis such another fitchew; marry, a perfumed one" only makes sense as Iago's correction for Othello's benefit. That it sounds like a response to "look where she comes" is another

peats the idiom Emilia introduced, "take out the work," and Bianca angrily echoes it, we're freshly reminded at this crucial moment that the silent Emilia retains the power behind the villain's throne, the power she gained access to when Othello and Desdemona "lost" the handkerchief and themselves with it.

Iago's penultimate soliloquy differs from those it follows because the circumstances of its delivery are barely under his control, and even the directions for staging it are underindicated. In addition, he has to share the platea with, of all people, Roderigo, who dares to soliloquize for three lines before the villain reclaims his rightful place and tells the supervisors Roderigo must die. Act 5 Scene 1 begins with Iago positioning a reluctant Roderigo for the attack on Cassio.

RODERIGO

> I have no great devotion to the deed
> And yet he hath given me satisfying reasons:
> 'Tis but a man gone. Forth, my sword: he dies.

IAGO

> I have rubbed this young quat almost to the sense
> And he grows angry. Now, whether he kill Cassio
> Or Cassio him, or each do kill the other,
> Every way makes my gain. Live Roderigo,
> He calls me to a restitution large
> Of gold and jewels that I bobbed from him
> As gifts to Desdemona:
> It must not be. If Cassio do remain
> He hath a daily beauty in his life
> That makes me ugly; and besides, the Moor
> May unfold me to him—there stand I in much peril.
> No, he must die. Be't so! I hear him coming.

> *Enter* CASSIO.

> (5.1.8–22)

Since no exits are marked in the text of either the Quarto or the Folio, each of the successive soliloquies is apparently delivered with the other speaker present (at a distance) but not listening. This setup

---

reason for reassigning the latter utterance to Cassio. Finally, since "What do you mean by this haunting of me?" can only be Cassio's line; it should be separated from Iago's "'Tis such another fitchew."

conveys an impression of permeable and therefore insecure boundaries that affects the tone and development of Iago's speech. The speech itself seems less like a bravura performance than its predecessors and more like a harried series of rapid-fire assessments and decisions.

He begins by expressing a concern about Roderigo, which he then shrugs off, but the mood quickly darkens with a pair of conditional utterances ("if either of them lives I stand to lose") that lead to the obvious conclusion, "both must die." This soliloquy lacks the performative high spirits that marked Iago's previous addresses to the supervisors. He speaks as if he has painted himself into a corner. And he strikes a new note with the first of the two reasons he gives the supervisors for deciding to kill Cassio: "He hath a daily beauty in his life / That makes me ugly." Why at this juncture does he so oddly identify himself with his victim and appropriate Othello's deepest feeling as his own?

In the hugger-mugger that follows, he seems on the verge of losing control of the situation. Roderigo botches his assignment and gets wounded by Cassio, whom Iago then stabs but fails to kill. With the arrival of Lodovico and Gratiano, he regains his form, suavely orchestrates the death of Roderigo and rescue of Cassio, and is joined by Emilia for a brief moment of bonding (their last) at Bianca's expense. But the scene ends in a rush, with Iago sending his companions off in different directions:

> Kind gentlemen, let's go see poor Cassio dressed.
> Come, mistress, you must tell's another tale.
> Emilia, run you to the citadel
> And tell my lord and lady what hath happed.
> —Will you go on afore? (5.1.124–27)

"Will you go on afore" (or the Quarto variant, "Will you go on, I pray?") expresses polite impatience—compare the use of the hortatory idiom, "Please," to usher others out. He hurries them off so that he can squeeze in a quick communiqué to the supervisors, and he then utters his ninth, last, and shortest soliloquy: "This is the night / That either makes me or fordoes me quite" (128–29).[14] Anticipation or deflation, the matter is out of his hands; he can do no more.

---

14. Honigmann's Folio reading of the last two lines; the Quarto differs: "Will you go on, I pray? This is the night /. That either marks me, or fordoes me quite."

As if to celebrate the success that induced this failure, Othello at this moment all but shoulders Iago aside as he thunders on stage with his second and most resonant soliloquy, "It is the cause, it is the cause, my soul!" (5.2.1–22). Compare the mad and unwaveringly murderous force of "Yet she must die, else she'll betray more men" (5.2.6) with the plaintive and calculating tone of

> If Cassio do remain
> He hath a daily beauty in his life
> That makes me ugly; and besides, the Moor
> May unfold me to him—there stand I in much peril.
> No, he must die. (5.1.18–22)

Iago has lost the supervisors, the power of soliloquy has shifted to Othello, and by the end of the play, the villain is reduced to the figure of castration he had initially mocked. Because he can't get Emilia to keep silent, he threatens her with his sword. And if we follow the Quarto stage direction a few lines later—*The Moore runnes at* Iago. Iago *kils his wife*—the prescribed action is fuzzy enough to make Honigmann think Iago stabs Emilia while trying to avoid Othello.[15]

However you visualize or stage it, it's a copycat crime, and it signifies the disempowerment already demonstrated by Othello's killing Desdemona. Iago's subsequent "I bleed, sir, but not killed" (5.2.285) is taunting but tinny, pert but puerile—in a word, embarrassing. He sticks out his tongue ("you missed"). Yet rustling within that retort is the shade of the wounded Cassio, the shade of Desdemona's desire to bleed and live.

Iago declines into the position of the morality Vice, but with a difference. The Vice is not merely a maverick individual but the embodiment of cultural norms of evil. The wickedness this figure represents is not his own but everyone else's. Shakespeare inserts the villain into this position in such a way as to set up an ironic structure of agency. He transforms the idea that the Vice *represents* everyone else's evil desires and purposes into the idea that the villain *is empowered* by them, but empowered in a such a way as to be disempowered.

According to the principle of redistributed complicities, the self-proclaimed villain is being run, or manipulated, by his victims more

---

15. See 5.2.223–32 and Honigmann's notes.

than he knows or would like—and more than they know or would like. If there is something they deeply and darkly desire but would never acknowledge (especially not to themselves), something they would never lift a finger to bring about, they get their villain to do it for them. Nothing could humiliate Iago more than to have his special audience of supervisors watch him being reduced to the tool of his victims. He has had to huff and puff in order to keep up with them. The rapidity and ease with which his victims destroyed their relationship makes him all but dispensable relatively early in the play.

The villain's claim to autonomy is thus compromised by the efficiency with which his victims use him to undo themselves. And even Iago's last defiant stand undoes itself: "Demand me nothing. What you know, you know./From this time forth I never will speak word." Mum's the model housewife's word.

But there is nothing to demand. Victims and survivors, the dead and the quick, know everything he knows. And yet . . . it was all so easy. There must be so much more to know than he knows. Surely Othello and Desdemona, and maybe Emilia, know things he doesn't know. He must have done something not only *to* them but also *for* them, something they got him to do to and for them.

They must have had a use for him . . .

They must have used him.

How embarrassing.

31. OTHELLO'S INFIDELITY

In his powerful study of seventeenth-century attitudes toward adultery and adulteration, Michael Neill mentions:

> a widely circulated explanation for the existence of black peoples (available in both Leo Africanus and Hakluyt), blackness was originally visited upon the offspring of Noah's son Cham (Ham) as a punishment for adulterous disobedience of his father.
>
> In such a context the elopement of Othello and Desdemona, in defiance of her father's wishes, might resemble a repetition of the ancestral crime, confirmation of the adulterous history written upon the Moor's face.

Thus, Neill continues, "if he sees Desdemona as the fair page defaced by the adulterate slander of whoredom, Othello feels this defacement, at a deeper and more painful level, to be a taint contracted from him: 'Her name that was as fresh / As Dian's visage is now begrimed and black / As mine own face.'"[1]

Neill's reading gives precedence to the Second Quarto's "her name" over the Folio's "my name." This decision keeps in play the "deeper and more painful level" of Othello's performance as he watches himself urge Iago to help him do to Desdemona what he tries to believe she is doing to herself and him. But as Janet Adelman observes, whichever variant we select, "the lines point toward the mutuality of contamination: Othello sees his begrimed face as it is reflected in the blackening of Desdemona's chaste purity by his own desire."[2]

This textual indeterminacy is functional. Each variant solicits the other. The interaction between them sustains the conflict in Othello's language as it oscillates vertiginously between the terror of imminent self-contempt—"what would it mean for me to want her to be a whore if it turns out she isn't?"—and the victim/revenger's fury.

Othello can neither deal with nor ignore that question. He can't bring himself to utter the outright lie "she is the cause" or to acknowledge the extent to which he is the cause. He can only say, "it is the cause." So he continues in bad faith to punish himself by punishing Desdemona and by shifting at the end from one to another conspicuously hollow rationalization. "Speak of me as I am. Nothing extenuate, / Nor set down aught in malice" (5.2.340–41). But extenuation is the name of Othello's endgame. Iago is a devil who "ensnared my soul and body," Othello his hapless victim who did "nought . . . in hate, but all in honor," these were merely "unlucky deeds," the work of a fool, indeed a double fool, "one that loved not wisely, but too well." If it is to be reported truly, not set down in malice, what happened is not that Desdemona lost her life but that he lost his pearl, through his own stupidity. "Nothing extenuate."[3] Yet since he speaks and represents himself to himself as well as to his auditors, this endgame is executed with self-demeaning bitterness.

---

1. Michael Neill, *Putting History to the Question: Power, Politics, and Society in English Renaissance Drama* (New York: Columbia University Press, 2000), 265.

2. Adelman, *Suffocating Mothers*, 275. Adelman cites (with characteristic generosity) the prior discussions by Snow in "Sexual Anxiety and the Male Order of Things in *Othello*," 401–2, and by Cavell in *Disowning Knowledge*, 130, 136.

3. 5.2.298–99, 292, 349, 342, 340.

Kenneth Muir finds it odd that anyone (i.e., T. S. Eliot) should think "Othello is 'cheering himself up,' or that he refuses to recognize his own guilt." Othello, he insists, "does not disclaim his responsibility for his actions." On the contrary, "he looks forward to an eternity of torture for his crime."[4]

"Looks forward to" has just the right edge. He solicits damnation. He speaks and acts in a manner that will guarantee it. After trying on a pair of melodramatic oriental self-depictions—the base Judean or Indian, the weeping Arabian tree—Othello offers a glimpse of his monstrous deed under the too diaphanous veil of "a malignant and a turbanned Turk" who "Beat a Venetian."[5] Thus falsely, knowingly, with savage satisfaction, he proves his malignancy to himself by proclaiming himself the avenger of the Venetian he murdered and, in a final mockery, preempting the justice of the state by meting out his own punishment.

My reading therefore agrees with Muir's. But it would be a mistake to accept Muir's reading on its own terms. For those are the terms of a positive moral judgment made by the critic defending the protagonist from the adverse judgments of other critics. Since Othello acknowledges his guilt, Muir judges him eligible for parole, or perhaps entitled to remission. Yet the interesting and important question is not what Muir and others think of Othello but what Othello thinks of himself.

At the end, does he castigate himself for having cast away a pearl, a jewel, a "perfect chrysolite," a snowy statuette, or for having tried to reduce her to such precious possessibles? His final utterance recalls the kisses bestowed on the sleeping Desdemona just before plucking the rose (5.2.13):

> Be thus, when thou art dead, and I will kill thee
> And love thee after.   (5.2.18–19)

> I kissed thee ere I killed thee: no way but this,
> Killing myself, to die upon a kiss.
>
> (5.2.356–57)

---

4. Muir, the New Penguin *Othello*, 31–32.

5. On the Indian/Judean crux, see the interesting comments by Snow in "Sexual Anxiety and the Male Order of Things in *Othello*," 412.

The kiss he dies on is the kiss bestowed by the lover who would reverse the fate of Pygmalion's statue, the lover whose desire is to transform Desdemona's "whiter skin . . . than snow" to "monumental alabaster" (5.2.4–5).

That is as decisive an answer as the play gives to the question asked above: he prefers a Desdemona reduced to the status of an object of (his) desire. But prefers that to what? To the perception — justified by Desdemona's behavior throughout the play — that she is very much the autonomous subject of her own desire. She has not only the power but also the will to achieve her desire even if that means opposing her father for Othello's sake and opposing her husband for Cassio's sake. That power and will are vested primarily in her sexuality.

If Othello is afraid of what he has aroused in her, and she in him, it makes things worse — not better — that he is the sole object of her desire. This is Cavell's thesis, and it is expressed with great clarity and economy by Susan Snyder: "In the last scene, commanded to remember her sins, Desdemona replies, 'They are loves I bear to you' (5.2.40). 'Ay, and for that thou diest,' responds Othello, seeming to find that loving desire for her own husband as sinful as that he imagines she has for Cassio."[6]

Desdemona's "erotic submission, conjoined with Iago's murderous cunning," writes Greenblatt, "effectively, if unintentionally, subverts her husband's carefully fashioned identity."[7] This is meant as a synoptic description, but the danger of subversion is already imagined in Othello's language in 1.3. His problem is exacerbated by the fact that the danger is actualized in Desdemona's language.

She makes it clear that she was and still is half the wooer.[8] In her first speech she articulates her "divided duty" (1.3.181) with the same

6. Snyder, "Othello," 298.

7. Greenblatt, *Renaissance Self-Fashioning*, 244.

8. This is why Calderwood's use of the verb "to bed" is as inaccurate as it is objectionable: "has the Moor actually bedded his wife?" It seems "plausible that Desdemona remains unbedded or incompletely bedded"; "no time for Cassio to bed Desdemona" (*Properties of* Othello, 124, 25). It is clear from Desdemona's language that — if the locution has to be used — she and Othello bed each other.

forcefulness Cordelia displays in defying Lear (*King Lear* 1.1.95–105).
To the Duke she insists on accompanying Othello to Cyprus because
she "did love the Moor to live with him," and if she is left behind
when he goes to war "The rites for which I love him are bereft me"
(1.3.249, 258).

Her sensitivity to Othello's problem is nevertheless registered by
the care with which she addresses the Duke and phrases her decision.
First,

> Most gracious duke,
> To my unfolding lend your *prosperous ear*
> And let me find a charter in your voice
> T'assist my simpleness.
>
> (1.3.244–47, my italics)

Then:

> I saw Othello's visage in his mind,
> And to his honours and his valiant parts
> Did I my soul and fortunes consecrate,
> So that, dear lords, if I be left behind,
> A moth of peace, and he go to the war,
> The rites for which I love him are bereft me,
> And I a heavy interim shall support
> By his dear absence. Let me go with him.
>
> (1.3.253–60)

Because "prosperous ear" recalls "greedy ear" (uttered before Desdemona's entrance), it reminds us of something she has to defend against.
This makes us appreciate the tact with which she showcases her "sim-
pleness" and the care with which she states her priorities. "Mind,"
"honors," and "soul" temporarily contain the sense of "valiant parts"
before letting it slide down toward "The rites for which I love him."

In spite of her circumspection, then, the utterance betrays her desire
for the black visage and body by trying so conspicuously to exclude or
refine it. Although he immediately seconds her request—"Let her have
your voice," (261; even stronger in the Quarto: "let her will / Have a free
way")—he is at pains to emphasize that the sexual "will" motivating
the request is not his. The pains are evident in his tortured syntax:

> I therefore beg it not
> To please the palate of my appetite,
> *Nor to comply with heat, the young affects*
> *In me defunct, and proper satisfaction,*
> But to be free and bounteous to her mind.
> And heaven defend your good souls that you think
> I will your serious and great business scant
> When she is with me. No, when light-winged toys
> Of feathered Cupid seel with wanton dullness
> My speculative and officed instrument,
> That my disports corrupt and taint my business,
> Let housewives make a skillet of my helm
> And all indign and base adversities
> Make head against my estimation.
>
> (1.3.262–75, my italics)

For me, the chief problem with this request is that I find it too easy to hear him shifting the burden of appetite from himself to Desdemona: "I beg it to please not my appetite but hers and to comply not with my heat but with hers."

The lines set off in italics identify a crux that appears in both the Folio and 1622 Quarto editions and that makes this utterance appear broken if not incoherent.[9] Most editors and some critics understandably emend the passage in the interest of clarity. But in what I think

---

9. The Folio reading:

Let her have your voice.
Vouch with me Heaven, I therefore beg it not
To please the pallate of my Appetite:
Nor to comply with heat the young affects
In my defunct, and proper satisfaction.

The 1622 Quarto:

Your voices, lords: beseech you let her will
Have a free way; I therefore beg it not
To please the pallate of my appetite,
Nor to comply with heat, the young affects
In my defunct, and proper satisfaction.

(modernized version by Scott McMillin, *The First Quarto of Othello* (Cambridge: Cambridge University Press, 2001), 70).

is the most thought-provoking account of the passage, A. D. Nuttall treats Othello's incoherence as expressive of his surprised and defensive response to Desdemona's forthright assertion of her desire:

> Othello seems to be saying, "Do not think I am asking for this out of lust, for I am past all that, rather I am interested in Desdemona's mind." . . . His speech is a stumbling, eager attempt to quash the implication of lasciviousness and to recover balance by catching at Desdemona's initial emphasis on mental affinity. The two speeches, Desdemona's and Othello's, are chiastically arranged: ABBA, mind, desire, desire, mind, but Othello's answering version is strangled and broken. . . . Othello was perplexed in the extreme before Iago went to work on him. Marriage itself disoriented him.[10]

Her "emphasis on mental affinity" is expressed in her claim that she saw his visage in his mind.

This could be part of what troubles him. In a brilliant set of reflections, Dorothea Kehler interprets "I saw Othello's visage in his mind" as "an implied, unconscious rejection of the face behind which his mind dwells." She reads the statement as an indication that Desdemona "appears uneasy with Othello's blackness and with the physicality of marriage." Kehler goes on to note that "on the two occasions when Othello invites her to make love [2.3.8–10 and 2.3.252–58], the first shortly before Iago gets Cassio drunk, the second after Cassio's demotion, Desdemona conspicuously offers no reply."[11]

Of the temporal statement beginning at line 269 ("No, when light-winged toys"), Catherine Belsey remarks that, although Othello's "when" has counterfactual force ("if ever"), the proleptic sense "momentarily permits us to glimpse the distraction as a real possibility."[12] Is this possibility "glimpsed" in—by—Othello's language? If we construe "light-winged toys/ And feathered Cupid" as a displacement for

10. Nuttall, *A New Mimesis*, 138–39.

11. Kehler, "'I Saw Othello's Visage in His Mind,'" 63–71. See also http://weber studies.weber.edu/archive/archive%20A%20%20Vol.%20110.3/Vol.%205.2/5.2%20 Kehler_s.htm

12. Catherine Belsey, "Desire's Excess and the English Renaissance Theatre: *Edward II, Troilus and Cressida, Othello,*" in *Erotic Politics: Desire on the Renaissance Stage*, ed. Susan Zimmerman (New York: Routledge, 1992), 97. A kind of inverted skimmington is suggested by the reference to housewives and skillets.

Desdemona, we get a paraphrase that reinforces Nuttall's: "If ever I allow myself to be distracted by Desdemona, let me be shamed by other housewives as I will have been by this one." He has already positioned himself as the potential victim and Desdemona as the potential threat to his manly business and reputation. Even though she is only half the wooer, his "bad blame" is poised to "light on" her.

If Othello appears to protest too much in this speech, it is partly because his assurance that he won't confuse business with pleasure is instrumental to his request that they be conjoined—for Desdemona's sake, of course. But in part the stridency of tone is outlined by the Duke's terse response:

> Be it as you shall privately determine,
> Either for her stay or going: th'affair cries haste,
> And speed must answer it. (1.3.276–78)

"Settle your private affairs in private, and be quick about it; time's a-wasting." This impatient rejoinder highlights and embarrasses Othello's self-representation, making it appear more defensive and extravagant. And Othello gets the message: his only reply is, "With all my heart" (279).

In the light of these exchanges, his subsequent statement of travel arrangements reflects a more prudent and tactful concern for appearances. Desdemona will sail in another ship, escorted by honest Iago and attended by his wife (not, it should be noted, by the bachelor Cassio, who was onstage at the time and available for the assignment). Until then, Othello prudently and tactfully allows himself to spend "but an hour/Of love, of worldly matter and direction" with Desdemona (299–300).

This is one of the statements that has left critics wondering whether or not Desdemona and Othello had sex ("an hour/Of love"?), and if so, when. But that is a different issue from what having (or not having) sex means to the partners—an issue different from whether the trust between them was consummated or remained unconsummated.[13] *Othello* is not about adultery; it is about the meaning and effects of fear of adultery.

---

13. Commentary on the issue has been thoroughly canvassed, and critically but generously assessed, by Adelman in *Suffocating Mothers*, 271–73.

My reaction to the 1983 Nelson-Haines essay that seems to have become the landmark study of "empirical" research on the did-they-or-didn't-they question is that, in addition to being sexist, it is both pompous and silly.[14] Whether or not the question is decidable, *Othello* centers attention elsewhere: on the anxieties of self-representation produced by a structure of fantasy, desire, and trust or distrust, a structure that functions as a cause rather than as the effect of the quality of the sexual relation. The sexual relation may be the signifier of the structure, but it is not necessarily its objective.

I conclude from this that the question "Did they or didn't they?" may be beside the point. But if I were to attach the importance to it others do, I would be most persuaded by Graham Bradshaw's strong argument for nonconsummation.[15] Finding it "inconceivable that . . . Shakespeare never considered whether this marriage was consummated," he concludes that Othello's "'Yet Ile not shed her blood. . . . yet she must die' . . . shows how his latest resolution is insanely ensnarled with his obsessive sense of what he has never done and thinks he can never do. . . . The murder is indeed this marriage's only consummation."[16]

I have been trying to show how Othello's problem of self-representation—a problem of self-esteem and self-justification—is inscribed in his and Desdemona's language from the beginning. It is inseparable from conflicting interpretations of blackness. This conflict complicates the interlocutory negotiations that register strains both in their courtship and in Othello's account of it.

The possibility of minimizing the conflict and inhibiting the strains depends in turn on the particular set of social conditions, structural distinctions, and cultural understandings that the play depicts as its civic ideology. It has often been shown that, for Othello to defend against the negative meaning of blackness and ensconce himself in its positive meaning, there must already be a distinction—and a tension—between his conduct of the warrior's discourse and his con-

14. T. G. A. Nelson and Charles Haines, "Othello's Unconsummated Marriage," *Essays in Criticism* 33 (1983): 1–18.

15. Bradshaw, *Misrepresentations*, 163–68.

16. Ibid., 166–67.

duct of the lover's discourse; between his civic function and his social status; between his commitment to preserve public safety and his desire to "steal" Brabantio's private property; between the claims of public service to the state and those of private service to his wife.

The nub of these distinctions has been described mythologically as a distinction, and tension, between the domains of Mars and Venus. Othello's ability to control self-representation depends not only on the existence of this polarity but also on its normative asymmetry: in each of the above pairs of distinctions, the first term always takes precedence over the second. This precondition is shown to be precarious. The only thing that saves Othello from Brabantio's attempt at legal action is the attendance of "messengers . . . here about my side/Upon some present business of the state" (1.2.89–90). Thus the degree to which he controls self-representation is directly proportional to the seriousness of the Turkish threat. All the otherwise strange and diversionary business concerning the Turks is explicable in these terms.[17] So also are the shift of scene to Cyprus and the effects of the storm.

During one of his indispensable studies of the play, Michael Neill comments on the discordant dramatic energy released by the storm:

> Retrospectively we may see the storm as prefiguring the emotional turbulence of the later acts; but in its immediate context it has the effect of a welcome release to the pent-up emotional energies of act 1. . . . It is as though the air were suddenly cleared of that murk of slander and intrigue that fouled the atmosphere of Venice; and the marvelous gaiety of the Venetians' arrival helps to confirm the impression that they have indeed been translated to the traditional domain of love.

Neill views this as the positive if superficial effect of the storm. But, he continues, this is in fact "an island prepared not for love but for war; and these voyagers have come to the shut-in society of a garrison town, the sort of place that feeds on rumor and festers with suspicion." In this "conspicuously masculine realm," Desdemona is "as isolated and potentially vulnerable as Othello in the subtle world of Venice," while

---

17. "The early part of this scene (1.3), concerned with the Turkish danger, is a means of building up Othello's reputation as a soldier" (Muir, the New Penguin *Othello*, 186).

"the martial Othello" has returned "to the military environment he knows best," so that

> husband and wife may seem at first to have changed places. But . . . this impression is short-lived. . . . The siege that seems to be lifted at the opening of act 2 has, in reality, only just begun. . . . Indeed the whole action of the play might be read in terms of sinister distortions and displacements of the old metaphor of erotic siege.[18]

I cite Neill's account at length because it supplies the basic elements of a somewhat different interpretation that may be educed from his with minimal coaxing. The difference centers on the idea that for Othello to maintain control of self-representation—uphold the positive against the negative interpretation of blackness—he must be able to give his martial occupation priority over his venerean occupation of Desdemona. The destruction of the Turkish fleet makes this impossible. If the air is cleared of Venetian murk, it is also cleared of war danger.

Though Cyprus may be "an island prepared not for love but for war," this isn't the problem. The problem is that since war has failed to materialize "Othello's occupation's gone" well before the debacle begins in 3.3. The erotic siege can begin only because the martial siege was averted. One result is that, if husband and wife seem to have changed places, it is because Othello has become more vulnerable and Desdemona more assertive—an impression that is not short-lived.[19]

The storm's failure to cause the travelers from Venice more trouble than it does sets the scene for the "monstrous birth" Iago claimed to have "engendered" at the end of 1.3 (402–3). By serving as a rhetorical anticipation of the actual storm that follows, his language invests it with proleptic symbolism. Although the storm is an obvious target of theatrical and rhetorical opportunity—it cries out for special effects and inspires ultramontane hyperboles—this only renders the irrelevance of its furious spectacle more conspicuous. It simultaneously glances at the ominous separations to come and diverts attention from them to the more manageable calamities of war and weather.

---

18. Neill, *Putting History to the Question*, 211–13.

19. On Desdemona's assertiveness, especially in Act 3, see Bradshaw's stimulating comments in *Misrepresentations*, 174–77.

The tempest and its results thus stage a reductive displacement of the events they foreshadow.[20]

32. THE FURY IN THEIR WORDS

At the beginning of this study I referred to *The Merchant of Venice* and *Othello* as, respectively, a comedy and a tragedy of embarrassment. In associating our word *embarrassment* with the French verb *embarrasser* ("to obstruct or block or hamper; to clutter up or weigh down"), I added that "to embarrass" is literally "to embar": to put up a barrier or deny access. People get embarrassed when they feel or perceive that they're denied access to things, persons, and states of being they desire or feel entitled to.

I've said very little about jealousy in the preceding chapters. This is because I think the jealousy attributed to Othello can better be understood as an intense form of the affective discourse of embarrassment on which those chapters center. And though it goes without saying that Desdemona doesn't share Othello's jealousy, her response to it is itself marked by a deep current of embarrassment that surfaces in such comments as "I understand a fury in your words / But not the words" (4.2.32–33). What doesn't she understand about the words? Othello had begun to abuse her in 3.4. He struck her in 4.1 and continues to bewhore her in 4.2. Does she refuse to acknowledge these moments? Does she choose not to know what he means?

And what about Emilia? Act 4 Scene 2 opens with an exchange in which Othello closely questions her about Desdemona and Cassio. She defends Desdemona. She knows what is at stake. Why, then, doesn't she mention Iago and the handkerchief? With one disclosure she could have resolved all problems and disabused Othello.[1] Why does she reject this opportunity?

---

20. "This tempest will not give me leave to ponder / On things would hurt me more" (*King Lear* 3.4.24–25): in an odd way Lear's words are applicable to the diversionary character of the *Othello* storm.

1. See the related discussion in Chapter 28, above.

After Othello orders her to fetch her mistress, he contrasts her simplicity to Desdemona's duplicity:

> She says enough; yet she's a simple bawd
> That cannot say as much. This is a subtle whore,
> A closet, lock and key, of villainous secrets;
> And yet she'll kneel and pray, I have seen her do't.
>
> (4.2.19–23)

He doesn't realize that Emilia is not so simple, that she *could* say more, that she is the closet, lock and key, of Iago's villainous secrets. Unhappily, Emilia does realize this, and this is one of the saddest aspects of a sad situation.

Having been summoned by Othello and ushered in by Emilia, Desdemona shifts quickly from curiosity to uneasiness:

DESDEMONA
    My lord, what is your will?
OTHELLO   Pray, chuck, come hither.
DESDEMONA
    What is your pleasure?
OTHELLO   Let me see your eyes.
    Look in my face.
DESDEMONA   What horrible fancy's this?
OTHELLO   [*To Emilia*]
    Some of your function, mistress,
    Leave procreants alone and shut the door;
    Cough, or cry hem, if anybody come.
    Your mystery, your mystery: nay, dispatch! *Exit Emilia.*
DESDEMONA
    Upon my knees, what doth your speech import?
    I understand a fury in your words
    But not the words.
OTHELLO
    Why, what art thou?
DESDEMONA
    Your wife, my lord: your true and loyal wife.

(4.2.24–35)

"A fury in your words": his sarcasm surprises and upsets her. She understands the "fury" in his brothel talk to Emilia well enough to bat away "Why, what art thou?": "I am not what it sounds or feels like you're insinuating: not untrue, not disloyal."

In the interchange that follows, he stops insinuating and shoots his venom:

OTHELLO

    Come, swear it, damn thyself,
    Lest, being like one of heaven, the devils themselves
    Should fear to seize thee: therefore be double-damned,
    Swear thou art honest!

The trouble with "honest" is that by this time in the play it has become Iago's sobriquet.

DESDEMONA

                          Heaven doth truly know it.

OTHELLO

    Heaven truly knows that thou art false as hell.

DESDEMONA

    To whom, my lord? with whom? how am I false?

                                (36–41)

"To whom" and "with whom" veer toward the status of rhetorical questions: "You can't seriously believe . . . ?" But can't she imagine that he might?

OTHELLO

    Ah, Desdemon,[2] away, away, away!

DESDEMONA

    Alas the heavy day, why do you weep?
    Am I the motive of these tears, my lord?
    If haply you my father do suspect
    An instrument of this your calling back,

---

2. The familiar "Desdemon" appears six times in the play. Cassio uses it first at 3.1.55, when he asks Emilia to arrange an audience with her. All the subsequent occurrences are assigned to Othello, who uses it in every case not as a term of endearment or affection but in contexts of annoyance, complaint, or threat. Here it is a heartbroken last grasp at the intimacy he is pouring into hell.

Lay not your blame on me: if you have lost him
Why, I have lost him too.   (42–48)

"To whom, my lord? with whom? how am I false?" The series
crests at "with whom." If she imagines that whatever he accuses her of
involves being false not only *to someone* but also *with someone else*, then
she obviously knows the answer to "how?"

She understands the fury in his words, and she begins to share
it. Her questions are disingenuous. False to whom? To whom else?
Emilia? Iago? Cassio? Brabantio? Lodovico? Gratiano? False with
whom? With Iago? With Roderigo? With Montano? She is not merely
embarrassed or perplexed. She is offended.

Does Desdemona express her outrage by playing dumb? This possibility makes me sympathize with Othello's distraught repetitions of "away,"
especially after she stubbornly diverts the issue toward the entirely unrelated topic of her father's role in Othello's recall to Venice. "Don't blame
your recall on me. I share your disappointment in Brabantio."

I, in turn, briefly share Othello's impatience with her refusal to
engage—but only briefly, because he so enjoys basting the victim's
discourse with the savage ardors of reproach:

> Had it pleased heaven
> To try me with affliction, had they rained
> All kinds of sores and shames on my bare head,
> Steeped me in poverty to the very lips,
> Given to captivity me and my utmost hopes,
> I should have found in some place of my soul
> A drop of patience; but, alas, to make me
> The fixed figure for the time of scorn
> To point his slow and moving finger at!
> Yet could I bear that too, well, very well:
> But there where I have garnered up my heart,
> Where either I must live or bear no life,
> The fountain from the which my current runs
> Or else dries up—to be discarded thence!
> (48–61)

Othello all but drowns himself in a rising tide of wrath and rhetoric. She
has embarrassed him. He will register this effect in self-embarrassing

figures. He could better tolerate being a leper or a beggar or a captive than an object of scorn? Really?

It may be difficult for a generically tragic figure to avoid embarrassing himself by making himself look ridiculous. Is this difficulty something that sneaks into Othello's language? Doesn't his fear of looking ridiculous intensify his warfare against Desdemona?

As the reckless storm of self-pity floods "the fountain" of his speech, he can't forego the chance to drench her with another downpour that turns her into "a cistern for foul toads / To knot and gender in!" (62–63). Desdemona is forced not only to hear but also to respond to this nonsense. "I hope my noble lord esteems me honest" (65). Her accent falls on "hope" since he has just made it clear that he "esteems" no such thing. But she sounds *wilfully* perplexed. If she understands the fury in his words she is nevertheless offended enough to provoke him by continuing to play dumb.

> OTHELLO
> O, ay, as summer flies are in the shambles,
> That quicken even with blowing. O thou weed
> Who art so lovely fair and smell'st so sweet
> That the sense aches at thee, would thou hadst ne'er
> been born!
>
> DESDEMONA
> Alas, what ignorant sin have I committed?
>
> (67–71)

She insists she doesn't know what he's talking about well beyond the moment in which she seems to have caught his drift.

The Arden[2] editor notes that "committed" feeds Othello's fury because this "unhappily chosen word depends on its Elizabethan use absolutely as = 'commit adultery.'"[3] Wouldn't a good "Elizabethan" like Desdemona know this? "What adultery have I unknowingly (inadvertently? unwittingly?) committed?" This question betrays more than incredulity. It sparks with anger.

Othello jumps on "committed" with another barrage (4.2.72–82). Its unfairness, its nastiness, finally moves her to protest: "By heaven,

---

3. Ridley, Arden[2] *Othello*, 154.

you do me wrong" (82). The fury of his words suggests that he still needs to persuade himself, needs to stoke up his anger and fight off her continuing attractiveness. But he also needs to fight off the suspicion he has too easily and willingly turned against her. Thus he takes the cheap and easy way out.

His mastery of the art of self-embarrassment is on display when he begins to stage their encounter as a brothel scene.

OTHELLO

    Are not you a strumpet?

DESDEMONA

    No, as I am a Christian.
    If to preserve this vessel for my lord
    From any hated foul unlawful touch
    Be not to be a strumpet, I am none.

OTHELLO

    What, not a whore?

DESDEMONA   No, as I shall be saved.

OTHELLO

    Is't possible?

DESDEMONA

    O heaven, forgive us!

She can't believe this is happening. At once incredulous and disheartened, she rephrases "Is't possible?" in her own key ("O heaven, forgive us!"), but he is too deeply, and too pleasurably, entrained in the victim's discourse to let up:

OTHELLO

              I cry you mercy, then,
    I took you for that cunning whore of Venice
    That married with Othello. You! mistress!
          Enter EMILIA.
    That have the office opposite to Saint Peter
    And keep the gates of hell—you, you, ay you!
    We have done our course, there's money for your pains,
    I pray you turn the key and keep our counsel.   *Exit*.
               (4.2.82–96)

Like Desdemona, but more self-protectively, Emilia tergiversates:

EMILIA

> Alas, what does this gentleman conceive?
>
> How do you, madam? how do you, my good lady?

DESDEMONA

> Faith, half asleep.

EMILIA

> Good madam, what's the matter with my lord?

DESDEMONA

> With whom?

EMILIA

> Why, with my lord, madam.

DESDEMONA

> Who is thy lord?

EMILIA   He that is yours, sweet lady.

DESDEMONA

> I have none. Do not talk to me, Emilia;
>
> I cannot weep, nor answers have I none
>
> But what should go by water. Prithee, tonight
>
> Lay on my bed my wedding sheets; remember,
>
> And call thy husband hither.

EMILIA   Here's a change indeed! *Exit.*

> (4.2.83–108)

Desdemona seems dazed and bewildered but "With whom?" and "Who is thy lord?" are reasonable questions, because she might well wonder whether Emilia is asking about Othello or about Iago. But why are Emilia's responses so studiedly obtuse? Since Othello began the scene by aggressively questioning her about Desdemona and Cassio (4.2.1–19), she knows very well "what's the matter with my lord."

If she isn't innocently asking for information, Emilia must be continuing what I described earlier as her "voyeuristic exercise of the power of nondisclosure."[4] She wants to hear from Desdemona herself how she has been affected, and her parting aside is puzzling: "Here's a change indeed!" What leads her to exclaim about a change the reason

---

4. See Chapter 29, above.

for which she fully understands? "Here's a change indeed!" may convey her surprise. But it may also carry an undertone of satisfaction.

After she leaves, Desdemona utters her only soliloquy in the play:

> 'Tis meet I should be used so, very meet.
> How have I been behaved that he might stick
> The small'st opinion on my greatest misuse?
>   (4.2.109–11)

For "small'st" read "lowest": "I must have done something wrong but since I know myself innocent the worst thing I could have done can't be bad enough to merit this kind of treatment." Why, then, does she think it "meet" that he should so abuse her?

This strange and bitter—and perplexed—self-recrimination gets echoed later, at the end of her Barbary song, "Let nobody blame him, his scorn I approve" (4.3.51). But the most embarrassing stretch of dialogue in 4.2 occurs immediately after her soliloquy. Iago returns and humors her with a series of terse, blank-eyed questions he clearly enjoys asking, because he knows the answers (4.2.112, 116, 120, 124). Desdemona responds by representing herself as a child who has been scolded and should have been more gently treated (4.2.113–16). Then she asks, "Am I that name, Iago?," and he encourages her to say it ("What name, fair lady?").

She can't bring herself to say it. But she can't resist dancing around it: "Such as she says my lord did say I was" (4.2.121). This draws an impatient correction from Emilia: "He called her whore" (122). Things only get more embarrassing when Desdemona unburdens herself to her "good friend" and begs him to intercede:

> O God, Iago,
> What shall I do to win my lord again?
> Good friend, go to him, for, by this light of heaven,
> I know not how I lost him. Here I kneel:
> If e'er my will did trespass 'gainst his love
> Either in discourse of thought or actual deed,
> Or that mine eyes, mine ears or any sense
> Delighted them in any other form,
> Or that I do not yet, and ever did,

And ever will—though he do shake me off
To beggarly divorcement—love him dearly,
Comfort forswear me! Unkindness may do much,
And his unkindness may defeat my life
But never taint my love. I cannot say whore:
It does abhor me now I speak the word;
To do the act that might the addition earn
Not the world's mass of vanity could make me.

(4.2.150–66)

Desdemona is too frequently written off as a Sweet Little Thing. But however troubled she is, she makes the most of the rhetorical situation. Othello is unreasonable, she is forbearing, her love is steadfast, and she not only *says* the word she cannot say; she puns on it.

"Here I kneel." According to Andrew Moore, her "kneeling to pray, her reluctance even to repeat Othello's obscene language, contrasts graphically with the kneeling of Othello and Iago in 3.3."[5] True, but it also recalls those acts (3.3.454, 465). It joins them in gestural connubiality.

Iago predictably enjoys her distress. But since he is impatient to forge ahead, he hurries her off to dinner, only to be accosted by a rankled Roderigo.[6] Roderigo's opening splutter could well be aimed at the author who has kept him offstage for some 1200 lines. But it's a warmup for his finest moment:

RODERIGO I do not find that thou deal'st justly with me.

IAGO What in the contrary?

RODERIGO Every day thou doff'st me with some device, Iago, and rather, as it seems to me now, keep'st from me all conveniency than suppliest me with the least advantage of hope. I will indeed no longer endure it; nor am I yet persuaded to put up in peace what already I have foolishly suffered.

IAGO Will you hear me, Roderigo?

RODERIGO Faith, I have heard too much; and your words and performances are no kin together.

5. Andrew Moore, *Othello, the Moor of Venice—study guide*: http://www.teachit.co.uk/armoore/shakespeare/othello.htm. This is an excellent interpretive resource.

6. The following comments on Roderigo and Iago are heavily indebted to an outstanding student essay written several years ago by Alan Coyne in my undergraduate Shakespeare course.

IAGO   You charge me most unjustly.

RODERIGO   With nought but truth. I have wasted myself out of my
means. The jewels you have had from me to deliver to Desdemona would half have corrupted a votarist. You have told me she
hath received them, and returned me expectations and comforts
of sudden respect and acquittance, but I find none.

IAGO   Well, go to; very well.

RODERIGO   'Very well,' 'go to'! I cannot go to, man, nor 'tis not very
well. By this hand, I think it is scurvy, and begin to find myself
fopped in it.

IAGO   Very well.

RODERIGO   I tell you, 'tis not very well! I will make myself known
to Desdemona: if she will return me my jewels I will give over
my suit and repent my unlawful solicitation; if not, assure yourself I will seek satisfaction of you.   (4.2.175–202)

In this exchange Roderigo doesn't let Iago interrupt him. He puts
him on the defensive, mimics him, threatens him, and remains skep-
tical to the end of the scene—"I will hear further reason for this"
(4.2.245). When he next appears, on the cusp of his Great Action, Iago
must have satisfied his desire, but the "further reason" hasn't noticeably
increased his enthusiasm. Roderigo's gesture of bravado is brittle:

I have no great devotion to the deed
And yet he hath given me satisfying reasons:
'Tis but a man gone. Forth, my sword: he dies.

(5.1.8–10)

The violence that has built up during the preceding scenes explodes
in Act 5 Scene 1 in a parodic discharge of negative energy. The scene
begins with Iago positioning Roderigo for his attack on Cassio and soon
erupts in a riot of swordplay. In rapid succession Roderigo thrusts at
Cassio, Cassio stabs Roderigo, and Iago wounds Cassio (5.1.23, 26, 27).

No sooner does Iago scurry offstage than Othello enters to celebrate the results of Iago's stab work and shake his verbal fist at
Desdemona:

'Tis he. O brave Iago, honest and just,
That hast such noble sense of thy friend's wrong!
Thou teachest me. Minion, your dear lies dead,

And your unblest fate hies; strumpet, I come.
Forth of my heart those charms, thine eyes, are blotted,
Thy bed, lust-stained, shall with lust's blood be spotted.

(5.1.31–36)

When Iago returns and Cassio identifies Roderigo as his assailant, the villain melodramatically—but coolly—dispatches the poor "snipe" (5.1.61). He then caters to Cassio and gleefully dominates the remainder of the scene with histrionic attentiveness to everyone's needs. But the scene ends with his final and shortest soliloquy, a couplet haunted by the onset of a new and more uncertain tone: "This is the night / That either makes me or fordoes me quite" (5.1.128–29).

On that note Iago and the others exit, and Othello thundering onstage replaces Iago as soliloquist. In this, the second of his three soliloquies, he overgoes Iago because he shows the supervisors how to hitch the victim-revenger's discourse to the dark star of the villain's project:

OTHELLO

It is the cause, it is the cause, my soul!
Let me not name it to you, you chaste stars,
It is the cause. Yet I'll not shed her blood
Nor scar that whiter skin of hers than snow
And smooth as monumental alabaster:
Yet she must die, else she'll betray more men.
Put out the light, and then put out the light!
If I quench thee, thou flaming minister,
I can again thy former light restore
Should I repent me. But once put out thy light,
Thou cunning'st pattern of excelling nature,
I know not where is that Promethean heat
That can thy light relume: when I have plucked the rose
I cannot give it vital growth again.
It must needs wither. I'll smell thee on the tree;
O balmy breath, that dost almost persuade
Justice to break her sword! Once more, once more:
Be thus when thou art dead and I will kill thee
And love thee after. Once more, and that's the last.
So sweet was ne'er so fatal. I must weep,

> But they are cruel tears. This sorrow's heavenly,
> It strikes where it doth love. She wakes.
>
> (5.2.1–22)

According to one commentary, Othello "has a hard time trying to talk himself into killing" Desdemona.[7] On the contrary, he has too easy a time. At first he muffles his sentiment by displacing "the cause" from "she" to "it." Then he regales the supervisors with a short lecture on the aesthetics of murder. He represents himself as a connoisseur not only of his prey but also of his act and of his words about the act. But his language and sentiments betray embarrassment. And they are themselves embarrassing.

After he turns Desdemona's white skin into snow and statuary, he compares uxoricide to dousing a light and plucking a rose. He stays with the rose because it yields a better analogy: once killed, it can't be brought back to life. This is truer to what he wants, and it gives him pause: "When I pluck the rose, that's it. It will wither. So before doing that I'll first smell it while it's still alive and fresh. And Desdemona smells so good I'm almost tempted to practice injustice by letting her live. But that's her fault, not mine. She is the cause. Smelling like a rose is her way of betraying men. It's part of her 'cunning'—her artful and crafty sexual practice. She has to go. I must take God's part and punish where I love."

This performance is scary because Othello's pleasure is not merely murderous. It is erotic and rhetorical. He savors the act of murder by working out his figures of speech and reducing the act to a verbal flourish that expresses his rage at having been unmanned and victimized. Is this the rage, is this the pleasure, he's been bringing on since the handkerchief exchange?

Othello had already registered his suspicion in 4.2, and Desdemona had angrily protested. She repeats her protest now, but it is too late:

> I never did
> Offend you in my life, never loved Cassio
> But with such general warranty of heaven
> As I might love: I never gave him token.
>
> (5.2.58–61)

7. http://www.shakespeare-navigators.com/othello/index.html.

Had she not herself been so offended in 4.2, she might then have been more emphatic on this point. But now it is too late. And yet when he brings up the handkerchief, she answers in a volley of short phrases that express impatience rather than fear: "He found it then,/I never gave it him. Send for him hither,/Let him confess the truth" (5.2.66–68). Othello responds to her demand for the truth by slipping into a stream of lies (5.2.68–70).

When Desdemona learns that Cassio is dead, she reacts less like someone overwhelmed by the news than like someone threatened by it: "Alas, he is betrayed, and I undone" (5.2.75)—undone because Cassio won't be able to verify her story. This is an appropriately self-interested response, but it is also innocently self-incriminating: it links her together with Cassio. At the same time, her words are telling in their own right, because grief for Cassio is supplanted by fear for herself, a sentiment that indicates the limits of her feeling for Cassio.

Desdemona's penultimate utterances are self-justifying: "O falsely, falsely murdered!"; "A guiltless death I die" (5.2.115, 121). But they point a finger at Othello. As if she recognizes this, when Emilia's "who hath done/This deed?" gives her a second chance, she spends her final words clearing him: "Nobody. I myself. Farewell./Commend me to my kind lord."

The sudden shift from self-justification to self-incrimination is patently unconvincing. And it is too much for Othello. He doesn't know what to do. His first impulse is to feign ignorance:

OTHELLO
     Why, how should she be murdered?

EMILIA
                           Alas, who knows?

OTHELLO
     You heard her say herself it was not I.

EMILIA
     She said so; I must needs report the truth.

But after her cautiously equivocal response, his own mendacious question, reinforced by Desdemona's lie, infuriates him:

OTHELLO
     She's like a liar, gone to burning hell:
     'Twas I that killed her.

EMILIA   O, the more angel she,
And you the blacker devil!
        (5.2.124–29)

It would be shameful for Othello to let Desdemona redeem herself by absolving him. For this, she must be dishonored:

OTHELLO
She turned to folly, and she was a whore.
EMILIA
Thou dost belie her, and thou art a devil.
OTHELLO
She was false as water.
EMILIA   Thou art rash as fire, to say
That she was false. O, she was heavenly true!
OTHELLO
Cassio did top her; ask thy husband else.
O, I were damned beneath all depth in hell
But that I did proceed upon just grounds
To this extremity. Thy husband knew it all.
        (5.2.130–37)

After fighting off Othello with anaphoristic energy, Emilia hears for the first time that honest Iago was the source of these lies. It is only after several repetitions of "my husband?" that she begins to shake off her incredulity.[8]

When Othello threatens her she challenges him to do his worst: "Thou hast not half that power to do me harm / As I have to be hurt" (5.2.158–59). Changing a single word of this reply brings out its dark thematic underside: "Thou hast not half that power to do me harm / As I have to *get* hurt." During the ensuing dialogue with Gratiano, Montano, and Iago, she redistributes complicity from herself to her husband: "your reports," she accuses him, "have set the murder on" (5.2.183). Othello temporarily seeks refuge in this evasion: "Nay, stare not, masters, it is true indeed" (5.2.184). But it is not true. What "set the murder on" was Emilia's failure to divulge the information she possessed.

---

8. See Honigmann's excellent note on this repeated phrase, *Othello*, 316.

Even as she challenges Othello, she continues to equivocate about the handkerchief: "O thou dull Moor, that handkerchief thou speak'st of / I found by fortune and did give my husband" (5.2.223–24; repeated at 5.2.228–29). She did not find it "by fortune." She didn't "find" it at all. When she saw it drop she picked it up and gave it to Iago, who had "begged of me to steal't" (5.2.224, 227).

At this point the pressure of complicity that assails not only Emilia and Othello but also Iago erupts in lethal swordplay. According to the Quarto stage direction, "The Moore runnes at Iago. Iago kils his wife." Honigmann's gloss suggests that Iago's act is an accidental consequence of Othello's charge: "Othello attacks, Iago dodges away and, in doing so, stabs Emilia."

This is a possible reading of the stage direction. But it ignores not only the previous flourish implied by Gratiano's "Fie! Your sword upon a woman?" It also ignores the signs of growing anger displayed in Iago's "Villainous whore!" and "Filth, thou liest" (5.2.228, 230). Emilia's response to his accusation doesn't help her. She directs an epithet toward Othello that Iago could easily construe as aimed at himself:

> By heaven I do not, I do not, gentlemen!
> O murderous coxcomb, what should such a fool
> Do with so good a wife? (5.2.230–32)

A few lines later, in one of the harshest moments of a harsh play, while Emilia dies onstage Othello ignores her and whines about having been disarmed by Montano ("every puny whipster gets my sword"). Finding another sword, he challenges Gratiano: "Behold, I have a weapon, / A better never did itself sustain / Upon a soldier's thigh." But after driving this sentiment through three lines, he checks himself, changes tack, and veers toward the "journey's end" he now tries to control with an attempt at preemptive obituary or, as I've called it elsewhere, *autothanatography*:[9]

> I have seen the day
> That with this little arm and this good sword
> I have made my way through more impediments

9. See Berger, *Imaginary Audition: Shakespeare on Stage and Page* (Berkeley: University of California Press, 1989), 119.

Than twenty times your stop: but, O vain boast,
Who can control his fate? 'Tis not so now.
Be not afraid, though you do see me weaponed:
Here is my journey's end, here is my butt
And very sea-mark of my utmost sail.
Do you go back dismayed? 'tis a lost fear:
Man but a rush against Othello's breast
And he retires. Where should Othello go?

He knows where he shouldn't go, and goes there immediately:

Now: how dost thou look now? O ill-starred wench,
Pale as thy smock. When we shall meet at compt
This look of thine will hurl my soul from heaven
And fiends will snatch at it. Cold, cold, my girl,
Even like thy chastity. O cursed, cursed slave!
Whip me, ye devils,
From the possession of this heavenly sight!
Blow me about in winds, roast me in sulphur,
Wash me in steep-down gulfs of liquid fire!
O Desdemon! dead, Desdemon. Dead! O, O!
                                        (5.2.257–79)

At this point the captured Iago and injured Cassio return to the stage, and after Othello wounds Iago he persists in his autothanatographical mode. "What shall be said to thee?," asks Ludovico. Othello's reply is embarrassing (unless it's intentionally provocative): "Why anything;/An honourable murderer, if you will,/For nought I did in hate, but all in honour." When Cassio remonstrates ("I never gave you cause"), Othello fully demonizes Iago and continues to exculpate himself by hiding behind the victim's discourse: "I do believe it, and I ask your pardon./Will you, I pray, demand that demi-devil/Why he hath thus ensnared my soul and body?" (5.2.289–99).

Iago's reply vibrates with dismissive contempt: "Demand me nothing. What you know, you know./From this time forth I never will speak word." "What," Ludovico ludicrously asks, "not to pray?" "Torments," Gratiano threatens, "will ope your lips." "Well," Othello interjects, "thou dost best," a rejoinder that seems baffling until we recall how much additional damage he could suffer from further disclosures by Iago. In the ensuing discussion, Othello exclaims at the recital of Iago's misdeeds, and when Cassio tells him about the handkerchief, he cries out, "O fool, fool, fool!" (5.2.321). Like Lear, he was only a fool, a victim, a man more sinned against than sinning.

After Lodovico announces that Cassio will be invested with Othello's "power and command," he orders Othello to be imprisoned and questioned. Othello has other plans:

> Soft you, a word or two before you go.
> I have done the state some service, and they know't:
> No more of that. I pray you, in your letters,
> When you shall these unlucky deeds relate,
> Speak of me as I am. Nothing extenuate,
> Nor set down aught in malice. Then must you speak
> Of one that loved not wisely, but too well;
> Of one not easily jealous, but, being wrought,
> Perplexed in the extreme; of one whose hand,
> Like the base Indian, threw a pearl away
> Richer than all his tribe; of one whose subdued eyes,
> Albeit unused to the melting mood,
> Drops tears as fast as the Arabian trees
> Their medicinable gum. Set you down this,
> And say besides that in Aleppo once,
> Where a malignant and a turbanned Turk
> Beat a Venetian and traduced the state,
> I took by th' throat the circumcised dog
> And smote him—thus!
>
> (5.2.336–54)

"Some service" already sounds the note of conspicuous understatement. "No more of that." Let's not talk now about how much I've done for you and how much you owe me. Spare me that embarrassment. Let's talk about how you can pay me back—what I'd like you to say when you get around to telling my story.

Don't try either to justify me or to speak maliciously about me, but speak of me as I am. Then you'll have to acknowledge that I had some bad luck. (Why are his deeds "unlucky"? Because he got caught?) I loved "not wisely but too well." Since "too well" can mean "too much," the adversative construction slides into "unwisely." It's not my fault. I made a mistake. I was "perplexed" because I was "wrought": not only "wrought up" but also "wrought upon." My hand, as if acting on its own, threw away the pearl. Ridley reads "perplexed" as "distracted" but Honigmann introduces a qualification: "*We* know that the stronger 'distracted' is applicable, yet *he* may mean bewildered by misleading evidence."

That may be what Othello wants to mean, but it isn't what he says when he haplessly converts his suicide to an orgasmic act of love. Troping, alliterating, and rhyming, he goes out in a burst of rhetorical fire:

> I kissed thee ere I killed thee: no way but this,
> Killing myself, to die upon a kiss.
>
> (5.2.356–57)

The insane chiasmic justice of this *osculum mortis* splits him in two. Then a single blow finishes off both the Venetian general and the malignant Turk. No way but this? He killed her after he kissed her. He understands the fury in his deeds but not the deeds.